MW00785962

The U.S.-Mexico Border

Recent Titles in the
CONTEMPORARY WORLD ISSUES
Series

Books in the **Contemporary World Issues** series address vital issues in today's society such as genetic engineering, pollution, and biodiversity. Written by professional writers, scholars, and nonacademic experts, these books are authoritative, clearly written, up-to-date, and objective. They provide a good starting point for research by high school and college students, scholars, and general readers as well as by legislators, businesspeople, activists, and others.

Each book, carefully organized and easy to use, contains an overview of the subject, a detailed chronology, biographical sketches, facts and data and/or documents and other primary source material, a forum of authoritative perspective essays, annotated lists of print and nonprint resources, and an index.

Readers of books in the Contemporary World Issues series will find the information they need in order to have a better understanding of the social, political, environmental, and economic issues facing the world today.

The U.S.-Mexico Border

A REFERENCE HANDBOOK

Michael C. LeMay

An Imprint of ABC-CLIO, LLC

Santa Barbara, California • Denver, Colorado

Library of Congress Cataloging-in-Publication Data

Names: LeMay, Michael C., 1941– author.

Title: The U.S.-Mexico border : a reference handbook / Michael C. LeMay.

Other titles: United States-Mexico border

Description: Santa Barbara : ABC-CLIO, [2022] | Series: Contemporary world issues | Includes bibliographical references and index.

Identifiers: LCCN 2021029626 (print) | LCCN 2021029627 (ebook) | ISBN 9781440874796 (hardcover) | ISBN 9781440874802 (ebook)

Subjects: LCSH: Mexican-American Border Region—History. | Mexican-American Border Region—Social conditions. | Mexican-American Border Region—Emigration and immigration. | Border security—United States. | Immigration enforcement—Mexican-American Border Region. | United States—Foreign relations—Mexico. | Mexico—Foreign relations—United States.

Classification: LCC F787 .L46 2022 (print) | LCC F787 (ebook) | DDC 972/.1—dc23

LC record available at https://lccn.loc.gov/2021029626

LC ebook record available at https://lccn.loc.gov/2021029627

ISBN: 978-1-4408-7479-6 (print)
978-1-4408-7480-2 (ebook)

26 25 24 23 22   1 2 3 4 5

This book is also available as an eBook.

ABC-CLIO
An Imprint of ABC-CLIO, LLC

ABC-CLIO, LLC
147 Castilian Drive
Santa Barbara, California 93117
www.abc-clio.com

This book is printed on acid-free paper ∞

Manufactured in the United States of America

Contents

Preface

This book examines the U.S.-Mexico border region, which is an apt subject given the greatly increased political concern over this border since 2000. The COVID-19 pandemic has sharply raised the level of concern about contagious diseases entering the country through the millions of people crossing this border. The threat of international terrorism, also subject to a heightened level of concern since the attacks of September 11, 2001, adds to the political controversies surrounding the U.S.-Mexico border. There remains a persistent wariness in American politics, at both the state and the national levels, that the United States has "lost control" over the border.

The U.S.-Mexican border is one of the busiest in the world. An estimated 5 million cars and trucks cross the border daily. An estimated one-half million undocumented immigrants cross the border annually. Apprehensions of persons attempting to cross the border range between 500,000 and 700,000 annually. Approximately 80 percent of the goods made in Mexico are shipped across the border to the United States, and 65 percent of those goods are produced on the Mexican side of the border, in the border region, by maquiladoras (factories in Mexico, explained further in chapter 2).

This book aims at helping the reader to better understand the U.S.-Mexico border region. It is a highly complex region in terms of its demographics, its economy, its environment, its culture, and its politics. It is a region experiencing considerable social change. The process of incorporating its diverse population into American society is complex and presents some profound problems; American government and society must face up to these problems, cope with them, and hopefully develop some solutions for them.

This book focuses on how the U.S.-Mexico border region has changed and evolved since 1848, when the border line was basically settled by the Treaty of Guadalupe Hidalgo. The flow across the border of people, goods, and, with them, ideas and customs is a subject worthy of a focused examination. It is the aim of this volume to present critically important information about this unique region in a way that is unbiased, thoughtful, and accessible and in a way that hopefully inspires the reader toward further research and exploration of the subject.

Like all volumes in the Contemporary World Issues series, this too is aimed at the college, public, and university library and at the general public that is simply interested in the region. As with all the volumes in the series, this book too follows a pre-scribed format. Chapter 1 discusses the historical background of the border region, how and why it came to be as it is today. It examines the cultural, economic, political, and social aspects that make the region unique. It distinguishes seven periods in the region's historical development and describes critical events in each period. In doing so, it synthesizes a considerable body of academic literature on the region in a manner that hopefully makes it accessible to the reader.

Chapter 2 discusses a dozen vexing problems of perennial concern to the region. They illustrate to the reader the complexity of the border region. The chapter discusses proposed solutions to these problems, but in a manner that enables the reader to make their own assessment of the solutions. It analyzes the problems and controversies but does not advocate for possible solutions to them. It then describes how proposed solutions come to be placed on the agendas of governments (at international, national, and state levels) and also describes some of the persons and groups that are involved as stakehold-ers in the public policymaking debates over how best to cope with the problems of the region.

Chapter 3 is composed of essays by scholars and activists who are involved in the region and who have the expertise to discuss the topic of their essay from a perspective that is different from and that adds to the perspective that this author brings to the discussion about the region. The essays are a collection of voices from diverse disciplinary backgrounds and represent various positions on all sides of the political debates arising from the problems facing the border region.

Chapter 4 offers profiles of and discusses key organizations and people who have impacted or continue to impact the border region. Many dozens of organizations and people associated with those organizations are worthy of being profiled here, but space constraint has limited the number of those included. The chapter profiles 20 organizations. Organizations not profiled here are referred to and discussed in the prior chapters. In selecting the organizations to be profiled in the chapter, the author was careful to include those acting across a span of time and those that used a variety of approaches toward the region and its problems. The author has purposely ensured that the organizations are demographically diverse and representative of other organizations active in the border region. The organizations have been selected to exemplify government policy-making agencies, nongovernment advocacy organizations, and "think-tank" organizations that provide important research and analysis of the border region. Likewise, the 20 people profiled in the chapter are representative of persons involved in the region across a span of time; they are also representative of the four approaches to incorporation that are discussed in chapter 2. Moreover, the persons profiled have been selected to provide some analysis of the region and its complex culture, economy, politics, and social relations. They represent government actors and nongovernment activists who advocate for or against proposed solutions to the problems facing the region.

Chapter 5 presents data and documents gathered from the governmental or scholarly discourse on the border region. Examination of these key data (presented in the form of three maps, three figures, and seven tables) and of 15 primary source documents excerpted in the chapter will enable the reader to assess for themselves why the problems of the region are so complex and so difficult to resolve.

Chapter 6 contains a variety of resources. It presents an annotated bibliography of 102 academic books on the region or scholarship that is helpful to better understand the region. More than 40 scholarly journals that publish original research relevant to the border region are listed and described. Finally, to bring a degree of "life" to the data, about two dozen feature-length films are listed and annotated.

A chronology of key moments in the history of the U.S.-Mexico border region is then presented. Finally, in the back matter of the book, a glossary of key terms and concepts used in the previous chapters is included for easy reference. The book closes with a comprehensive subject-matter index.

The U.S.-Mexico Border

1 Background and History

Introduction

The U.S.-Mexico borderlands region refers to an area of about 62 miles (or 100 kilometers) north and south of the international boundary line. For some important aspects, the region is considered as 100 miles on either side of the border line. The border line demarcates the boundary between the two nations that was basically set, with some subsequent modifications, by the Treaty of Guadalupe Hidalgo in 1848 (Davenport 2004; Mora 2011; St. John 2012). It contains six states on the Mexican side of the line: Baja California, Sonora, Chihuahua, Coahuila, Nuevo Leon, and Tamaulipas. It comprises four states on the U.S. side: California, Arizona, New Mexico, and Texas. There are 15 pairs of sister cities in the region. On the Mexican side, there are 80 municipalities (many of which are small pueblos), and on the U.S. side, there are 44 counties. On the U.S. side, the border region is located within 10 congressional districts:

- California's 51st Congressional District, which includes San Diego
- Arizona's 2nd and 3rd Congressional Districts, each of which contains parts of the Tucson metropolitan area

---

Inspecting a freight train from Mexico for smuggled immigrants, El Paso, Texas, 1938. El Paso was an important border crossing point, and smugglers often used trains in attempts to cross there. (Library of Congress)

- New Mexico's 1st, 2nd, and 3rd Congressional Districts, in which Albuquerque, Las Cruces, and Santa Fe are the major cities respectively
- Texas's 23rd Congressional District, with parts of San Antonio and El Paso; its 15th, embracing Guadalupe Hidalgo; its 28th, within which is located the fast-growing Laredo; and its 34th, which includes Brownsville Texas and the easternmost and southernmost parts of the region

Thus, the region extends coast-to-coast, from the Pacific Ocean to the Gulf of Mexico.

The four largest binational metropolitan areas in the region are San Diego/Tijuana; El Paso, Las Cruces, and Ciudad Juarez; McAllen-Reynoso; and Laredo-Nuevo Laredo (Ganster and Lorey 2008; Vila 2000, 2003).

San Diego, with an estimated population of just over 1.5 million, is the eighth largest city in the United States and the second largest in California. Its sister city is Tijuana, Mexico. The two together form the San Diego-Tijuana metropolitan area, which has a population of nearly 5 million. San Diego is the economic center of the metropolitan area, driven by the military/defense industry, tourism, international trade, and manufacturing.

El Paso, Texas, is the county seat of El Paso County, located in the far western part of Texas. It has a population of just over 680,000, making it the twenty-second most populous city in the United States. It is located across the border from Ciudad Juarez, which has a population of just over 215,000. The population of the El Paso metropolitan area, which is part of the larger El Paso-Las Cruces metropolitan area, is about 1.1 million. The international metropolitan region (i.e., of El Paso, Las Cruces, and Ciudad Juarez) has a population of about 2.5 million. It has the largest bilingual and binational workforce in the Western Hemisphere (Davenport 2004).

At about 150,000 in population, McAllen, Texas, is the largest city in Hidalgo County, Texas, and the 22nd most populous city in the state. It is situated in the southernmost tip of the Rio Grande Valley, across the border from the Mexican city of Reynosa. McAllen is the fifth most populous metropolitan area in Texas, and the binational Reynosa-McAllen metropolitan area has a population of more than 1.5 million. The area's growth has been especially rapid since the introduction of the maquiladora economy resulting from the NAFTA-induced cross-border trade (Bacon 2004).

Laredo is situated on the north bank of the river Rio Grande in South Texas, across from Nuevo Laredo, Tamaulipas, Mexico. In 2010, its population of 236,000 made it the tenth most populous city in Texas and the third most populous in the U.S.-Mexico border region (after San Diego, California, and El Paso, Texas). Its cross-border metropolitan population is about 640,000.

One major geographic feature demarcating the international line is the river Rio Grande (known in Mexico as Río Bravo or Río Bravo del Norte). This river often meanders, however, and by treaty provisions new cutoffs and islands are transferred from one nation to the other as necessary as a result of the river changing its course. In 1970, a Boundary Treaty settled all outstanding boundary disputes related to the Rio Grande border.

The international line spans 1,954 miles—from California to the southern tip of Texas—and the population within the entire border region is approximately 15 million. The region is so fast growing, however, that the U.S. Census Bureau estimates that its population will rise to 30 million by 2025. According to the 2010 U.S. Census, the combined population of the four U.S. states comprising the region is just over 70 million. On the Mexican side, the six border states have a combined population estimated to be 20 million. The region has two of the fastest-growing metropolitan areas in the United States: Laredo and McAllen. Demographically, the region is occupied by Anglos and Hispanics but is also home to about 90,000 Native Americans, who belong to 154 tribes and 25 Native American nations (Ebright and Hendricks 2019; Office of Global Affairs 2020).

The borderlands region is very dynamic but underserved medically, with pressing health and social conditions, higher uninsured rates, high migration rates, highly inequitable health conditions, and a high rate of poverty. On the Mexican side, it is experiencing rapid industrialization spurred by the maquiladora assembly plants and the accompanying rapid urbanization. The entire region exhibits an economy in transition. As an international border line, it marks the area where adjacent jurisdictions meet, wherein the conjunction and separation of national laws and customs blend into a zone in which the movement of people and goods are highly regulated, examined, discussed, and often hidden. Historically, the region has been shaped by fences and barriers, river engineering projects, and surveillance infrastructures that have redesigned its natural landscape (Alvarez 2019; Anderson and Gerber 2009).

As is typical of all borderlands, or "frontera" regions, commerce is particularly important here. So too are concerns about identities as well as a blending of identities (cultural, ethnic, political, racial, and social). The smuggling of people and goods accentuates concerns with trade in and across the region. Companies use national differences in labor and environmental laws and regulations to enhance their profits; often, the effect of this is great social injustice (Cadaval 2020; Donnan and Wilson 1999; Lusk, Staudt, and Moya 2012).

Geographically, the region is characterized by two deserts (the Sonora and the Chihuahua), rugged hills, abundant sunshine, and two major rivers (the Colorado and the Rio Grande). Texas has the longest stretch of border with Mexico, and California has the shortest stretch. On the Mexican side, Chihuahua has the longest border with the United States, while Nuevo Leon has the shortest.

Economically and culturally, the international border line conjoins the United States, considered a first-world economy, with Mexico, often characterized as "third world" or "developing." The rapid growth of a capitalist economy within the Mexican side of the borderlands region has influenced the development of a U.S.-Mexico border culture as well as other cultural processes, such as acculturation, creolization, and cultural diaspora. It is a region exhibiting stark cultural differences, social inequity, and governmental power to regulate individual opportunity by ascribing national identity (Lorey 1999; Lusk, Staudt, and Moya 2012; Meeks 2008).

The Border before 1848

Before the Guadalupe Hidalgo Treaty of 1848, the boundary was quite different from the international line it is today. The region was sparsely populated during the mid-16th century, when the discovery of silver drew settlers from Spain particularly but also colonizers from different backgrounds. The area became part of what was then known as New Spain, but it did not belong to any country and was basically the territorial homeland of hundreds of native tribes. That changed when the United States, via the Louisiana Purchase in 1803, bought land from France and began its steady march westward in largely military moves to pursue what it called its "Manifest Destiny."

The border between the United States' western territories and New Spain was poorly defined, and no border as such was established until the Adams-Onis Treaty (Grandin 2019; Henderson 2011). The Adams-Onis Treaty of 1819 (8 Stat. 252) was negotiated between John Quincy Adams, U.S. secretary of state under President James Monroe, and Luis de Onis, the Spanish minister. It ceded Florida to the United States and defined the boundary between the United States and New Spain. It only lasted until 1921, when Spain acknowledged the independence of Mexico, but the Treaty of Limits (1828) signed between the United States and Mexico recognized the border as defined by the Adams-Onis Treaty.

The government of Mexico attempted to create a buffer area between the United States and its mainly settled lands by encouraging thousands of settlers to relocate to what is now the State of Texas. The Mexican government even offered inexpensive land to Anglo settlers to help develop the land and to pacify Native American tribes (particularly the Apache and

Comanche). That ploy, however, did not work out well for Mexico. In 1835 Texas declared its independence from Mexico and established the Republic of Texas, which lasted until 1845, the year it was annexed by the United States. Frequent conflicts over Texas between Mexico and the United States led to the Mexican American War (1846–1848). Mexico lost the war, which was officially ended by the Treaty of Guadalupe Hidalgo in 1848. The treaty resulted in Mexico having to cede most of its northern territory to the United States. The treaty also established the boundary line basically as it is today. Mexico lost all of what is today California, Arizona, New Mexico, Utah, and Nevada and parts of Colorado, Wyoming, Kansas, and Oklahoma. The treaty ended all disputes over Texas and its boundary with Mexico. Further definitions of the U.S.-Mexico border line were completed by the Gadsden Purchase (1853–1854).

The purchase, by the Treaty of Mesilla, signed June 8, 1854, was concerned with a 30,000-square-mile area of southern Arizona and southwestern New Mexico that the United States acquired from Mexico. It provided the land necessary for completion of a southern transcontinental railroad and resolved lingering conflicts left over from the Treaty of Guadalupe Hidalgo. The United States agreed to protect Mexico from Native American attacks and to compensate Mexico for damages from incursions by U.S. citizens into the area. U.S. president Franklin Pierce sent James Gadsden, the U.S. minister to Mexico, to negotiate with Mexican president Antonio Lopez de Santa Anna (Office of the Historian 2020). The purchase left several thousands of people living in the disputed lands, many of whom were Mexican nationals. Several border towns sprang up along this boundary, and many Mexican citizens were given free land in the northern regions of Mexico in exchange for returning and repopulating the area (Byrd and Mississippi 1996).

The people most commonly residing in the area acquired through the Gadsden Purchase included many Native American societies, Spaniards whose lands were granted by the Spanish crown, Mestizos (people of mixed Native American and Hispanic heritage), and English-speaking Anglo settlers from the United States. But the area also had Jewish families from central Mexico seeking respite from religious persecution. Because of its concern regarding American expansionism (Manifest Destiny), the Mexican government granted land to groups as diverse as the Chinese, the Mennonites, the Molokan Russians, the Black Seminoles, and the Kickapoo Indians, who were all allowed to settle with the stipulation that they defend the territory against Apache and Comanche raids (Cadaval 2020).

Another development in the United States had important consequences for the border region—the Compromises of 1820 and 1850 over the slave-state/free-state controversy. By 1820, growing sectional tensions over the issue of slavery led to enactment of the Missouri Compromise of 1820. Missouri had sought statehood in 1818, which would make it the first state west of the Mississippi River. The issue of Missouri statehood spurred deep and bitter debate in a Congress that was divided into pro- and anti-slavery factions. The issue was at a stalemate until late 1819, when Speaker of the House Henry Clay proposed admitting Missouri as a slave state and Maine, spun off from part of Massachusetts, as a free state. The law also banned slavery from the remaining Louisiana Purchase lands located north of the 36"30' parallel. The compromise was essentially repealed by the Kansas-Nebraska Act of 1854, and in 1857, the Supreme Court ruled the compromise unconstitutional by the *Dred Scott* decision.

The Missouri Compromise helped keep the peace. In the decades between 1820 and 1850, westward expansion continued, and more Louisiana Purchase lands were organized as territories. As a result, the issue of slavery continued to divide the nation. In 1845, by annexation, Texas joined the union as a slave state. The Compromise of 1850 admitted California as a free state but required the state to send one pro-slavery senator to maintain the balance of power in the Senate. In 1854,

Kansas and Nebraska territories were organized and sought statehood. The Kansas-Nebraska Act stated a doctrine of popular sovereignty, that the settlers of each territory should decide the issue of slavery for themselves.

In *Dred Scott v. Sandford* (60 U.S. 393, 1857), the Supreme Court ruled that the Missouri Compromise was unconstitutional. The majority opinion was written by Chief Justice Roger Taney. Seven justices comprised the majority and ruled that Congress had no power to prohibit slavery in the territories, since the Fifth Amendment guaranteed slave owners could not be deprived of their property—which slaves were legally considered to be—without due process of law. The Dred Scott decision and the Kansas-Nebraska Act set the stage for the outbreak of the Civil War.

1848–1865: The Mexican-American War, the Treaty of Guadalupe Hidalgo, and the Consolidation of the Border Line

As previously stated, in the 1820s and 1830s, Mexico had encouraged various people and groups, including Anglos from the United States, to settle in what it called El Paso del Norte (Passage to the North). The area would later become the Republic of Texas. By inviting these settlers, the Mexican government thought they were establishing a buffer zone with the United States. They also viewed the increase in European-derived population as a desirable development to better control conflicts with hostile Native American tribes, like the Comanche and Apache. During this colonial period, the area was a frontier (*frontera* in Spanish) that attracted the most adventurous explorers and missionaries.

Instead of getting their desired buffer zone, however, the Mexican government seeded the very conditions that led to the Mexican American War. The eastern region along the Rio Bravo (later called the Rio Grande in the United States) was a hospitable one and became the locus of regional towns like

Laredo and El Paso del Norte. El Paso became the first and largest town built on the river. Rio Bravo came to be viewed as the "symbol of separation" in Texas and made up roughly half the length of the border (Cadaval 2020; Mora 2011; Mora-Torres 2001).

When the Republic of Texas gained independence from Mexico in 1836, the U.S. government decided against the annexation of Texas as a new state. It did so in large measure because, as noted earlier, northern political interests in a bitter and evenly divided U.S. Congress did not want Texas added as a new slave state. Also contributing to rising tensions, the Mexican government encouraged border raids and warned that the annexation of Texas would lead to war.

In the presidential election of 1844, the "dark horse" candidate, James K. Polk, won the office. Polk became the 11th president of the United States (POTUS), serving from 1845 to 1849. He had been speaker of the House of Representatives (1835–1839) and then governor of Tennessee. Polk was a protégé of President Andrew Jackson, a member of the Democratic Party, and a staunch advocate of Jacksonian democracy. Polk was a firm adherent of the doctrine of Manifest Destiny, which held that it was the destiny of the United States to spread across the continent to the Pacific Ocean (Boneman 2008; Leonard 2000; Woodworth 2010). During the 1844 election, Polk had campaigned on annexing Texas and sought to purchase California and Oregon from Mexico. Polk coveted New Mexico and the Southwest portion of what was then northern Mexico. When President Polk's offer to purchase these lands was rejected by the Mexican government, Polk instigated a fight by moving troops into the disputed lands between the river Rio Grande and the river Nueces, part of the Mexican state of Coahuila.

In April 1846, Mexican cavalry attacked U.S. troops in the disputed zone. They were under the command of General Zachary Taylor. The Mexican cavalry laid siege to an American fort along the Rio Grande. General Taylor brought in reinforcements and with superior fire power (the U.S. Army had much better rifles and artillery) he defeated the Mexican forces at the battles of Palo Alto and Resaca de la Palms. Having gotten the outbreak of hostilities he desired, President Polk pressed the U.S. Congress to declare war on Mexico, which it did on May 13.

The Mexican American War (1846–1848) was the first armed conflict in which the United States engaged that was fought for the most part on foreign soil. Although both countries participated in border skirmishes and rhetorical conflict ("saber rattling"), the United States was the more aggressive one. Mexico was politically divided and militarily ill prepared for the conflict (it never did declare war on the United States). After a series of skirmishes along the Rio Grande, the war began in earnest. In 1846 there were only about 75,000 Mexican citizens living north of the Rio Grande. U.S. forces led by Colonel Stephen Kearny and Commodore Robert Stockton conquered the disputed lands with minimal resistance. General Taylor led the "Army of Occupation"—comprised of United States Regulars, Volunteers, and Texas Rangers—against Mexican general Pedro Ampudia and captured Monterrey, Mexico, in September, 1846.

After suffering a series of losses, Mexico turned to an exiled strongman, General Antonio Lopez de Santa Anna, the Mexican general who had lost the war of independence that had established the Republic of Texas. General Santa Anna had convinced President Polk that if allowed to return to Mexico from Cuba, he would end the war on terms favorable to the United States. When Santa Anna arrived in Mexico, however, he double-crossed Polk and took control of the Mexican army, leading it into battle. In February 1847, at the Battle of Buena Vista, the Mexican army suffered heavy losses and was forced to withdraw. Santa Anna assumed the Mexican presidency, by force, in March 1847. United States troops led by General Winfield Scott landed at Veracruz and marched toward Mexico City. General Scott successfully laid siege to Mexico City. Skirmishes continued for some months, but essentially the war was over. Santa Anna resigned from the presidency, and the United States negotiated a treaty with a newly established Mexican government to formally end the war.

The Treaty of Guadalupe Hidalgo was signed on February 2, 1848. Article 8 of the treaty allowed granting U.S. citizenship to those Mexicans who remained in the ceded territories and did not declare their wish to remain citizens of Mexico (LeMay and Barkan 1999, 25–26). The treaty ceded about a third of Mexico's land to the United States and established the Rio Grande (rather than the Nueces River) as the U.S.-Mexico border. Moreover, under the terms of the treaty, Mexico recognized the annexation of Texas by the United States and agreed to sell California and the remainder of its territory north of the Rio Grande for $15 million, plus the U.S. assumption of certain damage claims (Cadaval 2020; Mora 2011; Mora-Torres 2001; St. John 2012).

Within months after the signing of the Treaty of Guadalupe Hidalgo, gold was discovered in California, and the Gold Rush began. It brought huge numbers of people to California from other parts of the United States as well as from Europe, Russia, and China. The Californian economy expanded, and the so-called robber barons led a boom in railroad construction and related industrialization. "Robber baron" was the term used for powerful industrialists who, during the Gilded Age, used questionable practices to amass their great fortunes. In California, the "Big Four" robber barons were Collis Huntington, Leland Stanford, Mark Hopkins, and Charles Crocker. They were industrialists who invested in western railroads, most notably in building the Central Pacific Railroad. Railroad financing provided for a dramatic expansion of the private financial system. Railroad construction was more expensive than construction of factories and required developments in the private financial system. Between 1860 and 1900, investment in railroads grew to billions of dollars. New York became the dominant financial market, and the British invested heavily in railroads all around the world (particularly so in the United States).

The first continental railroad was a combination of the Union Pacific from Omaha to Utah and the Central Pacific from Utah to California. It opened the Far West to development in mining and ranching. The Homestead Act of May 20, 1862, provided free land to individual citizen homesteaders and to the railroads. In turn, the railroads sold cheap land to European farmers (LeMay and Barkan 1999, 27–28). By 1890, the settlement of the Great Plains led to the "end of the frontier," as articulated in the thesis by historian Frederick Jackson Turner (Ambrose 2000; Brown 2009; Sandler 2015).

The Southern Pacific Railroad linked New Orleans to Los Angeles and ran across the territories of Texas, Arizona, and New Mexico. It brought an influx of homesteaders, ranchers, and miners who swelled the population of the Southwest and the borderlands.

Los Angeles and San Diego experienced rapid development, and San Diego soon became one of the dominant economic anchors of the border region. Between the end of the Civil War in 1864 and 1900, California became integrated into the expanding United States. With the completion of the transcontinental railroad in 1869, the pace of urbanization, industrialization, and agriculture development increased rapidly. California's population rose from 380,000 in 1860 to 1,213,398 by 1890. The substantial spike in population was due to immigration from other parts of the United States as well as from Latin America, Asia, and Europe. Los Angeles, incorporated as a city in 1850, grew from 1,610 to more than 50,000 by the 1890 census. The discovery of gold in 1848 brought Chinese immigrants, who were soon forced out of the gold fields. They took on the backbreaking and dangerous work of building the Central Pacific Railroad. They comprised about two-thirds of its workforce of some 10,000 (Ambrose 2000; LeMay 2009; Sandler 2015). By the 1870s, anti-Chinese xenophobia had spiked, and this led to violence and an all-out assault on them in San Francisco's Chinatown in 1877.

California's booming agricultural economy created an insatiable need for farm labor, and migrant workers from Mexico came in great numbers. A succession of ethnic groups performed farm labor: Native Americans in the 1850s and 1860s followed by the Chinese, Japanese, Filipinos, and Mexicans. During this period, California's Native American population was decimated. It reached its nadir of an estimated 20,000 in 1900. That demographic decline was attributed to disease, malnourishment, and outright violence. In California, less than half of the Native American population lived on reservations; most of them worked in California's cities or as migrant farm laborers.

Between 1865 and 1900, California's booming international population was rapidly industrializing and urbanizing. Economic inequality became rampant as the economic divide between the rich and poor became, figuratively, a chasm as wide and as deep as the Grand Canyon. Racial discrimination and segregation were widespread and directed at Indians, Mexicans, and Asians (Chinese, Japanese, and Filipinos) who lived in segregated neighborhoods, worshipped in segregated churches, and were legally forced to attend segregated schools (Crouch 2007; LeMay 2009; Paddison 2005).

Mexico's loss in the Mexican American War and the concessions it was forced to accept by the Treaty of Guadalupe Hidalgo and the subsequent modifications by the Gadsden Purchase in 1854 all played a role in establishing the current border. Mexico lost what is today the territory north of the Rio Grande. While Texas was never governed as a territory but was annexed as a state in 1845, the following states were governed as territories until they were formally admitted into the Union in the following years: California, 1850; Arizona, 1912; New Mexico, 1912; Utah, 1896; Nevada, 1864; Colorado, 1876; Wyoming, 1890; Kansas, 1861; and Oklahoma, 1907.

In the decade after the Mexican American War, U.S. cattle barons and agricultural interests from the East and Midwest invested substantial capital and forged mercantile connections.

They dominated U.S.-Mexico trade across the Texas river border. They would go on to assert dominion over the earlier Spanish and Mexican settlers. They created an environment of cultural and economic conflict that characterizes the U.S.-Mexico borderlands region to the present day. The New Mexico Territory was particularly desired, as part of the Gadsden Purchase agreement, to provide a more easily constructed route for a future southern transcontinental railroad for what became the Southern Pacific Railroad (constructed in 1881–1883).

The territory of New Mexico was organized in 1850 and lasted until New Mexico was admitted into the Union in 1912. It contained most of the present-day state of New Mexico, more than half of the present state of Arizona, and portions of the present-day states of Colorado and Nevada. The land area purchased by the Gadsden Purchase agreement that was designated as New Mexico Territory was about 30,000 square miles, and proposals to divide it into a separate Territory of Arizona were advocated in 1856, when concerns rose about the ability of the territorial government in Santa Fe to administer the southern portions of the territory. Population in what is now Arizona expanded from less than 10,000 in 1870 to more than 88,000 by 1890. In 1860, a convention met in Tucson calling for an Arizona provisional government. With the outbreak of the American Civil War, many in the territory were in favor of the Confederacy and a secession convention met in Mesilla and Tucson in 1861. It adopted an ordinance of secession and petitioned the Confederate Congress for admission. Confederate forces took Fort Fillmore at Mesilla, and Confederate lieutenant colonel John Baylor took possession of the territory for the Confederacy, with Mesilla as the capital and himself as governor. In January 1862, the Confederate Territory of Arizona was officially created by proclamation of President Jefferson Davis.

The Confederate Territory of Arizona, however, was short lived. The Battle of Glorieta Pass, in May 1862, forced the Confederate forces back south to El Paso, Texas. In 1862, the

U.S. House of Representatives, controlled by Republicans, created the U.S. Arizona Territory with Tucson as its capital. President Abraham Lincoln signed a law on February 24, 1863, officially organizing the U.S. Arizona Territory by enactment of the Arizona Organic Act, also known as the Arizona Territory Act. The Arizona Territory Act abolished slavery. It split off the western portion of the New Mexico Territory and made it part of the Arizona Territory, which later became the southernmost portion of the newly admitted (to the Union) State of Nevada. The Territory of Arizona was admitted to statehood on January 6, 1912.

The New Mexico Territory was organized in 1850, with Santa Fe as its capital. From 1851 to 1852, its territorial governor was James S. Calhoun. It was officially established in February 1851. Its population was then slightly more than 61,000. It grew to just over 160,000 by 1890.

The town of Las Cruces was built north of the border line by Mexicans who took their chances in the United States. The town of La Mesilla was built just south of the border by men and women who chose not to live in a country that had waged war against the Mexican Republic. Yet La Mesilla was incorporated into the United States when the border was redrawn in 1854 (in part because of changes in the flow of the Rio Grande). The two towns, less than five miles apart, were deeply divided by conflicting ideas about race and nation and what it meant to be a "Mexican" in the United States (Mora 2011).

The period between 1848 and the Mexican Revolution in 1910 was a critical period in Mexican history. It was a period of state-building, of emergent capitalism, and of growing linkages to the economically dominant United States to the north that shaped class formation and struggles (e.g., between the industrial Monterrey and the deteriorating countryside). By 1910, states on both sides of the divide assumed much of their modern character and developed a labor market that was dependent on massive migration from central Mexico to the borderlands region (Mora-Torres 2001).

Being a slave state, Texas had joined the Confederacy in the Civil War. When the Confederacy was defeated, U.S. Army soldiers arrived in Texas in June 1865 to take possession of the state, restore order, and enforce the emancipation. In 1866, like many of the former Confederate states, Texas instituted the Texas Black code. Under President Andrew Johnson's administration, the readmitted states determined their system of laws. Black codes were enacted in Florida, Louisiana, Mississippi, and South Carolina. Texas convened a constitutional convention in 1866, and it failed to ratify the Thirteenth Amendment although it did grant Blacks the right to personal property, the right to enter contracts, and the right to sue and be sued. Most federal troops in Texas were posted along the coastal corridor. In the central portions of the state freed slaves were still subject to abuse, beatings, and shootings, and in parts of East Texas, still held in bondage. President Johnson appointed Union General Andrew Hamilton as provisional governor, and Hamilton granted amnesty to ex-Confederate officers. Returning veterans seized state property and a period of extensive violence and disorder took place, led by veterans who became outlaws and established their bases in the Indian Territory. They plundered and murdered with little distinction of party. Congress officially readmitted Texas in March 1870.

1865–1890: Post–Civil War Migration and Development

The Rio Grande shifted south between 1852 and 1868, and by 1873 the moving river-center cut off portions of Mexican territory. A treaty in 1889 established an International Boundary and Water Commission (IBWC) to maintain the border, allocate river waters between Mexico and the United States, and provide for flood control and river water sanitation. Jurisdictional issues over water rights in the Rio Grande River Valley continued to cause tensions between farmers along the border (Caffey 2004; Ebright 1994; Ebright and Hendricks 2019).

During the post–Civil War years and the Reconstruction, the U.S.-Mexico border region was impacted by what has been termed by many historians as "the Gilded Age." With some variations depending on the historian, the age runs from around 1865 to around 1900 (Calhoun 2007; Crouch 2007; Edwards 2005; White 2017). In the borderland region, the Gilded Age marks a period of railroad construction and major growth in industry, mining, farming, and ranching. In New Mexico, the territory's development was impacted by the notorious Santa Fe Ring, in which Thomas Benton Catron and Stephen Benton Elkins were involved as major power influencers. It was a loose consortium of political and economic leaders whose activities included a legacy of dirty deals and self-serving political favoritism, and what their critics describe as the great land grab (Caffey 2004; Ebright 1994).

The "ring" was a label applied to many of the political machines in a host of cities during the Gilded Age. It is aptly applied to that found in Tucson (Sheridan 1995). The establishment of huge ranches by cattle barons and the region's general agricultural opportunities drew investors from the East and Midwest with substantial capital and extensive mercantile connections. They soon dominated U.S.-Mexico trade across the Texas river border. They acquired extensive tracts of land in Texas and asserted dominion over the earlier Spanish and Mexican settlers, creating an environment of cultural and economic conflict that characterized the border region. The Santa Fe Ring, for example, during its most active stage from 1872 to 1884, was attracted to land, government contracts, mining claims, timber, railroads, and cattle and sheep ranches (Caffey 2004).

The 1880s witnessed older, established communities populating a string of small coal-mining towns on both sides of the Rio Grande River Valley, from Laredo/Nuevo Laredo to Eagle Pass/Piedras Negras and Del Rio/Ciudad Acuna. In Del Rio, the San Felipe spring fed a network of canals that created a lushness not otherwise seen in South Texas. It attracted the establishment of Italian vineyards. In New Mexico, the Santa Fe Ring took part in land-grant adjudication chicanery. To their critics, they were nothing less than land-grabbing thieves, but they also served as the vanguard working to bring railroads to the territory, supported schools and churches, organized a historical society, and sustained benevolent and fraternal organizations. Ebright and Hendricks (2019) note that their impact is felt to this day because they were so involved in land issues and water rights—issues that have still not been resolved and continue to be the stuff of perennial contention. They regularly battled Indian Pueblos and Hispano land-grant and water rights holders. This was because there was a clash of ideas between the Anglo culture's sense of individual-ownership and legally protected land and water rights and the more communal cultural perceptions of land and water rights characteristic of the Native American and Hispano communities. At one time, Catron was the single largest landowner in the state of New Mexico (Ebright and Hendricks 2019).

Within Mexico, between 1876 and 1900, the border region depended on its proximity to the United States, and border communities boomed, aided by the Mexican government's support for investment from the United States. Railroads were built to connect the northern Mexican states even more to the United States, and the population on the Mexican side of the border grew greatly, spurred by the mining industry. Mining was dominated by U.S. investors who controlled more than 80 percent of the mining industry (Anderson and Gerber 2009; Ganster and Lorey 2008; Lorey 1999; St. John 2012).

In the 1870s and 1880s, railroads advertised widely in Europe to attract immigrants to the territories and the American West. "American fever" spread through Europe like an epidemic. The railroads were eager to sell the 181 million acres of land granted to them by the national government to help them finance construction costs. Union Pacific alone spent an estimated $815 million to attract settlers and get them settled, often on Homestead Act (1862) lands. Burlington, Santa Fe, Northern Pacific, and Kansas Pacific were equally openhanded and involved. The Kansas Pacific and the Santa Fe railroads recruited some 2,000 Mennonite immigrants who came as entire communities from Russia's Crimea region (today's Ukraine). The Mennonites settled in Kansas and Texas. They brought with them Turkey Red, a hardy winter wheat that could survive the harsh weather of the Plains because of its deep root system. They purchased some 100,000 acres with help from the railroads (Bernard 1987, 317; LeMay 2013, vol. 2: 10; LeMay 2009, 193–200).

Although San Antonio, Texas, technically lies beyond the border region, it grew substantially and its growth was clearly linked to railroad developments in the border region. It grew from having less than 3,500 inhabitants in 1850 to become the seventh most populous city in the United States today. In 1860 its population was 8,235 and German was the predominate language spoken. Immigrants from Germany had to travel via Galveston to reach San Antonio. San Antonio experienced new economic growth sparked by its railroad—the Galveston and San Antonio Railway. By 1881, there was a second railroad to serve the city—the International Great Northern, from Laredo to San Antonio. The city's population had reached 20,550 by 1880 and grew to 37,673 by 1890. By 1900 five railroads passed through San Antonio, spurring its economic and population growth even further. In 1900 its population was 53,321; by 1910 it had reached 96,614, and by 1920, the number was at 161,379. San Antonio served as an important military center during the Spanish-American War.

Several other border cities in Texas grew markedly during this period. The population of Laredo, Texas, for example, grew from 1,256 in 1860 to 11,319 by 1890—an increase of about 220 percent. The population of El Paso, Texas, grew from 428 in 1860 to 10,338 by 1890, an increase of about 1,300 percent. Hidalgo's population was at 1,182 in 1860, and by the 1890 census, its population had topped 6,500. The population of Brownsville, Texas, grew from 2,734 in 1860 to 6,134 in 1890.

1890–1930: The Border Boom

The 1890s ushered in the Progressive Era of American politics (Zentner and LeMay 2020). It was notably a "reform" era in American politics, but it was also a period in which American nationalism and expansionism influenced much of U.S. foreign policy and colonialization prevailed at the southern border (Anderson and Gerber 2009; Grandin 2019).

The Immigration Act of March 3, 1891 (29 Stat. 1084; LeMay and Barkan 1999, 69–70) authorized the implementation of immigration inspection stations at all ports of entry along the Mexican (and Canadian) borders. The border cities mentioned in the earlier section were locations for inspection apart from being border crossing sites. The population of Laredo grew from 11,319 in the 1890 census to over 36,600 by the 1930 census. El Paso experienced the highest growth in population among the border cities in Texas—from 10,338 in 1890 to 102,421 in 1930. Hidalgo increased its population from 6,500 in 1890 to just over 77,000 in 1930. The population of Brownsville, on the easternmost tip of Texas and the borderland region, grew from just over 6,100 in 1890 to just over 22,000 in 1930. Growth was less spectacular but still significant on the western part of the border. The population of Las Cruces, New Mexico, nearly doubled in a span of 20 years, growing from 3,836 in 1910 to 5,811 in 1930. The population of Nogales, Arizona, was at 1,194 in 1890 and grew to just over 6,000 in 1930. Calexico was a tiny burg of 797 inhabitants in 1910 but grew to 6,299 inhabitants in 1930. San Diego had the greatest population growth compared to any other city on the U.S.-Mexico border. Its population grew from 16,159 in 1890 to 147,995 in 1930. A significant portion of that population growth came from "Mexicanos" (Gonzales 2009; Montejano 1987).

Designed to administer U.S. immigration and control the borders, the Immigration and Naturalization Service (INS) was established by Congress with the Act of June 29, 1906 (34 Stat. 596; LeMay and Barkan 1999, 93–97). Before 1910, Mexican immigrants traveled frequently between Mexico and the United States, often crossing to seek work; they were able to go back and forth because of the lax enforcement at the borders. During this period, U.S. immigration laws were tighter and more strictly enforced against Asians and Europeans. Until the 1920s, transnational movement back and forth was largely unhindered and often virtually unregulated. In part, this was because U.S. farmers had a requirement for Mexican field workers. By 1920, an estimated 40 percent of the total U.S. fruit and vegetable output was produced by Mexican farm laborers. U.S. agriculture, especially in the border region, depended on inexpensive Mexican labor. Mexicanos also played prominent roles in the rail and mining industries. By 1920, they made up nearly 45 percent of the workforce in Arizona's copper mines and nearly 85 percent of the railroad workers in the Southwest region (Gonzales 2009, 122–123).

The Mexican Revolution, beginning in 1910, was instrumental in causing the significant increase in border population, as many people moved to or across the border seeking refuge. Between 1910 and 1930 migration patterns were established from states in Mexico to particular regions or towns or cities on the border. Refugees from central Mexico settled in the Texas valley and were later joined by immigrants from their hometowns. Migrants from the northwestern Mexican states of Zacatecas, Durango, and Sinaloa went to Ciudad Juarez or El Paso, Texas (Cadaval 2020; Gonzales 2009; Montejano 1987). During this period, ethno-racial categories and identities among Native Americans, Mexicanos, and Anglos crystallized in the borderlands (Meeks 2008).

Mexican immigrants dominated agricultural labor in California after 1900, taking on the brutal work because it was often the only job available to them. The dislocations and the disrupted economy that resulted from the Mexican Revolution provided the economic motivation that propelled many Mexicans northward. Once in California, however, they experienced rampant discrimination. Even middle-class Mexican men and women could only find work as day laborers, farm workers, and maids. "Greaser" films in the early 1900s depicted Mexicans as dirty, gap-toothed, treacherous, and soulless, attributing to them every vice that could be depicted on the silver screen (Bender 2012, 11–30). They tended to live in segregated Mexican enclaves (barrios), and constant in-migration invigorated Mexican culture, traditions, and language in both urban barrios and rural colonias. They blended old and new practices—much like they used both Spanish and English—to forge new identities as Mexican Americans (Gonzales 2009; Paddison 2005; Sanchez 1993).

The Santa Fe Ring diminished in power and number in the 1890s, but Catron and Elkins continued their political careers into 1910. Reformers, however, began to turn the tide against rampant corruption (Caffey 2004). Organized labor in the United States objected to the use of cheap Mexican labor, which they maintained drove down wages and working conditions. In the 1920s, organized labor unions formed informal agreements to exclude Mexicans from membership and lobbied the U.S. Congress to regulate Mexican immigration. The American Federation of Labor (AFL) was particularly active and sought to limit Mexican emigration through relationships with Mexico's major labor organizations and the Mexican government. Immigration restriction gained momentum in the 1920s, as labor organizations on both sides of the border indicated that Mexican immigrants would not seek naturalization (Sanchez 1993, 96). The degree of success they had in increasing regulation along the border is indicated by the establishment, in 1925, of the U.S. Border Patrol (Act of February 27, 1925, 43 Stat. 104-1050; Hernandez 2010; Kang 2017; LeMay 2006, 127; LeMay and Barkan 1999, 152).

World War I (1917–1918) had a significant impact on certain population groups in the borderlands. After the war, and in recognition of their outstanding contributions and services during the war, the U.S. Congress passed the Act of November 6, 1919, "Granting Citizenship to Certain Honorably Discharged Indians Who Served during the World War" (41 Stat. 350). It granted citizenship to honorably discharged Indians who had served during World War I but had not been considered citizens when they left the reservations (LeMay and Barkan 1999, 121–122).

Another border group affected by World War I was Hispanics, mostly Mexican Americans, who had served in the war. They were already native-born citizens, so it was not a question of citizenship. Returning Hispanic veterans, however, were emboldened by the experience of their service in the war to organize to fight the rampant discrimination against them so widely evident in Texas and California. They became involved in the establishment of several organizations: the League of United Latin American Citizens (LULAC, founded in 1921 in Corpus Christi, Texas), the G.I. Forum (founded in 1948 in Corpus Christi, Texas), the Order of the Sons of America (La Orden de los Hijos de America, founded in 1921 in San Antonio, Texas), and the Community Service Organization (CSO, founded in 1947 in Los Angeles, California) (LeMay 2009, 299–302; Ramos 1998). The two organizations most relevant to the borderlands area during this time period were LULAC and the Order of the Sons of America.

LULAC is the largest and oldest Hispanic organization in the United States. As mentioned earlier, it was begun by a group of Hispanic veterans seeking to end ethnic discrimination against Latinos. It embraced an assimilationist ideology or a political accommodation strategy (LeMay 2009, 299–300). It admitted only U.S. citizens as its members. Newer immigrants from Mexico resisted its assimilationist strategy because of their strong ties to Mexican culture, limited English proficiency, and willingness to work for low wages. LULAC emphasized a role for women and established a national office for women in 1938. It worked in particular against segregated schools. It is often compared to and viewed as the Hispanic equivalent of the National Association for the Advancement of Colored People (NAACP), an organization related to the Black civil rights movement (Burt 2007; Marquez 1993; Kaplowitz 2005; Orozco 2009; Strum 2010).

The Order of the Sons of America (OSA) was formed by Mexican American citizens in San Antonio, Texas, in October 1921, and it soon established chapters throughout Texas. It countered discrimination against Mexican Americans and limited their membership to native-born or naturalized citizens; its leadership was typically comprised of Spanish-speaking Mexican Americans belonging to the middle and upper classes; many of them were attorneys, teachers, and business entrepreneurs. In 1929 the Order of the Sons of America merged with the League of Latino American Citizens to form the LULAC (Burt 2007).

1930–1942: The Interwar Years

The economy of the borderland region—and for that matter, the economy of all of the United States—went from the "boom" of the 1890–1930 period to the "bust" of the 1930–40 decade (Ganster 2015; Henderson 2011; Kang 2017; Lorey 1999). Indeed, so profound was the bust that the entire decade has been called the "Great Depression." It was the most severe and long-lasting downturn of the economy in the history of the United States. This was also a decade that saw a great economic depression affecting much of the Western world. At its nadir, unemployment in the United States reached an estimated 25 percent of the workforce. In 1932 the Great Depression ushered the election of Franklin Delano Roosevelt and his New Deal Administration (LeMay 2009, 132–135; Zentner and LeMay 2020, 169–179).

The decade of the Great Depression exhibited a pronounced decline in immigration to the United States that impacted the entire nation, including the border region. Annual legal immigration to the United States declined from 241,700 immigrants in 1930 to 70,756 in 1940. During the depth of the Depression years (1932–1936), annual legal immigration ranged between a low of 29,470 immigrants in 1934 to 36,329 in 1936 (LeMay 2013, vol. 2: 3–4). The Great Depression substantially reduced overall immigration to the United States for three decades (LeMay 2009, 355).

At the start of the Depression, between 1929 and 1931, President Herbert Hoover deported hundreds of thousands of people, mostly Mexican immigrants. During the lifetime of the repatriation programs, from 1929 to 1939, Mexicans were encouraged or forced to repatriate. During the period 1929–1931, many Mexican immigrants who resided in the United States and the border region returned to Mexico more or less voluntarily. Estimates as to how many were "forcefully repatriated" during the Great Depression decade range from about 400,000 to 2 million (Balderrama and Rodriquez 2006; Hoffman 1974). Among the many persons deported to Mexico, it is likely that 50–60 percent were citizens illegally deported and denied their due process rights, with immigration inspectors acting as interpreter, accuser, judge, and jury (Balderrama and Rodriquez 2006).

Federal, state, and local programs rounded up and shipped about 1 million persons to Mexico. The raids were significant in scope, essentially full-scale paramilitary operations. They typically raided public places and herded those swept up on to trains and buses. Part of the issue was that immigration from Mexico was not formally regulated until the Act of February 5, 1917 (39 Stat. 874; LeMay and Barkan 1999, 109–112). The 1917 law, known as the "Regulating the Immigration of Aliens to and Residence of Aliens in the United States," was passed over the veto of President Woodrow Wilson. Historian Roger Daniels calls it the first significant general restriction of immigration ever passed (Daniels 1990, 278–279). Many Mexican immigrants had entered prior to 1917, when record keeping and paperwork were lax. As a result, they often lacked papers to prove their legal status when swept up and deported. The sweeps and summary deportation of so many meant that hundreds of thousands lost goods and property they had held in the United States, for which they were never compensated. The sweeps and deportations of many violated due process, equal protection, and Fourth Amendment rights. On departure, many of their cards were stamped that they had been "county charities," which meant they would likely be denied readmission on the grounds of being liable to become a public charge.

Several border cities were particularly affected by the Depression. El Paso, Texas, for example, saw a reduction in its population from 102,485 in the 1930 census to 96,810 by the 1940 census, a decline of 5.5 percent. The population of Brownsville, Texas, essentially stayed the same (it had 22,021 inhabitants in 1930 and 22,083 inhabitants in 1940), which meant that outmigration had offset the growth due to natural births and internal migration by non-Hispanic whites. The population of Calexico, California, declined from 6,299 in 1930 to 5,415 in 1940. The population of Nogales, Arizona declined by 14.5 percent, from 6,006 in 1930 to 5,135 in 1940.

However, San Diego, California faced the Great Depression challenge better than most other parts of the United States, largely because of its defense industry. San Diego's population actually grew by 38 percent during the Great Depression decade, from 148,000 in 1930 to 203,000 in 1940, a percentage rate better than that of the state of California as a whole. The state used New Deal Public Works Administration (PWA) relief money to build and open San Diego State College (now San Diego State University). The U.S. Navy expanded the Pacific Fleet, assembling more than 48 warships and 400 naval aircraft and increasing the naval forces by 55,000 sailors and 3,000 officers. San Diego's assembly plant built the Navy's flying boats, and the Ryan Aeronautical Company built the famous *Spirit of St. Louis*. The city hosted the California-Pacific International Exposition in 1935–1936. The exposition drew an estimated 7.2 million visitors, contributing to the city's prosperity by boosting its tourism industry (San Diego History Center 2020).

On January 5, 1940, President Franklin Roosevelt issued Executive Order 8430. It required unauthorized immigrants to register with the INS. The executive order transferred the INS from the Department of Labor to the Department of Justice (LeMay and Barkan 1999, 175–177). Congress also passed the Act of October 14, 1940 (54 Stat. 1137; LeMay and Barkan 1999, 180–183). It codified all previous naturalization laws, including denial of naturalization to Chinese, Japanese, and Korean immigrants. The most significant impact of that executive order and the Act of October 14, 1940, on the borderland region was felt in the San Diego area, which had a higher Asian immigrant and Asian American population, including numerous Filipinos.

1942–1964: The Bracero Program

The Bracero Program set in place many patterns and aspects of both legal and undocumented immigration to the United States that persist to this day. The name Bracero Program comes from the Spanish term *bracero*, meaning strong-arm. In English, it could mean a manual or unskilled laborer. The Bracero Program refers to a series of laws and agreements between Mexico and the United States for the legal importation of temporary contract laborers. It began in August 1942 as a wartime measure to provide much-needed labor to the U.S. economy and in response to lobbying by U.S. growers over wartime labor shortages. It was subsequently enacted by Congress and ran until 1964 (Andreas 2000; Calavita 1992; Chomsky 2014; Cohen 2011; Craig 1971; Kang 2017; Kirstein 1977; LeMay 1994, 2009, 2013; Navarro 2005; Snodgrass 2011).

During its 22 years of operation, the Bracero Program had a profound and lasting impact. Approximately 4,500,000 temporary crossings took place (many Bracero workers came year after year, so the total population was, of course, far fewer than 4 million persons). It began small, with just over 4,000 workers in 1942. It grew to an allotted 75,000 agricultural workers in 1945, and to nearly 450,000 in its peak year of 1956. One of its provisions was especially important to city development in the southwestern part of the United States. Its railroad component supplied unskilled and skilled labor to lay and maintain railroad tracks. During its time, the railroad linkage was critical for a city's economic and population growth. The railroad portion of the Bracero Program had a quota of 50,000 workers over and above the 75,000 agricultural workers allotted to it (Calavita 1992; Kirstein 1977).

The program began with an agreement between U.S. president Franklin Roosevelt and Mexican president Manuel Avila Comacho. They signed the agreement as an emergency wartime measure to supply labor to fill the void in the U.S. agricultural sector when millions left the farms for high-wage wartime production jobs in America's explosively expanding metropolitan areas, or to replace citizens drafted into the war (LeMay 2013, 144; Snodgrass 2011, 79). The Bracero Program filled a mutual need—the United States needed workers, and Mexican farmers and other unskilled workers needed jobs. The program controlled the entry of temporary workers in a legally recognized way. When it ended, it was essentially replaced by the post-1965 uncontrolled flow of unauthorized immigrants from Mexico. In 1964, migrants using the Bracero Program numbered some 350,000. The 1965 Immigration Act limited legal immigration from Mexico to 20,000. As a result, hundreds of thousands simply came illegally—as undocumented immigrants. The Bracero Program set in motion chain-migration patterns that have persisted for decades, with immigrants coming from specific locations in Mexico to particular locations—and often employers—in the United States (Andreas 2000; Calavita 1992; Cohen 2011).

Ironically, the program filled a labor void that had been created by the Mexican Repatriation Program of the mid-1930s, when more than a million Mexican immigrants and perhaps as many as 60,000 Mexican American citizens were deported or pressured to leave in response to the Great Depression. As the U.S. economy began to gear up for the war effort, the United States experienced a labor shortage (Chavez 1984; Cohen 2011; Griswold del Castillo 2008; Navarro 2005). By 1943, the number of temporary workers (they came for up to nine months in a year) had increased to 44,000, and by 1944 it was 62,100, which is when Congress enacted legislation for the program that previously relied on an executive order, known as the "Supply and Distribution of Farm Labor Act of February 14, 1944" (58 Stat. 11; LeMay and Barkan 1999, 197–198; LeMay 2009, 108–109).

Funds authorized by the Supply and Distribution of Farm Labor Act were used for recruiting, placing, and training Bracero Program workers; for their transportation, supervision, subsistence, protection, health, and medical and burial services; and for providing temporary shelter to these workers and their families. After 1944, funds were appropriated to the Office of Emergency Management established by President Roosevelt to enable the War Management Commission to provide for the temporary migration of workers to industries and services deemed essential to the war effort, including the timber and lumber industries. It was authorized to be used for their transportation from Mexico to points of entry and dispersion in the United States, and also to return to their place of origin in Mexico (LeMay and Barkan 1999, 197–198).

The program initially drew laborers from the west-central states of Mexico, such as Coahuila, Comarca, Lagunera, Jalisco, Guanajuato, Michoacan, and Zacetecas. The failure of the post–Mexican Revolution agricultural reforms caused many to seek work "del norte," and the Bracero Program became especially popular among those workers for whom seasonal work in the United States seemed to be a good opportunity despite the poor conditions in the fields and in the temporary housing provided in U.S. labor camps (Cohen 2011; Navarro 2005).

In the post–Korean War period, opposition to the influx of so many Mexicans led to a brief pushback. In 1954 the United States had a mass deportation of undocumented workers, which was known as Operation Wetback (Garcia 1980; Kang 2017). It deported many, amid politics similar to the deportation efforts launched during the administration of President Donald Trump (Gutierrez 1995).

The Bracero Program had significant impact on the economy of border cities in Mexico like Ciudad Juarez, Chihuahua, and on border towns in the United States like El Paso, Texas. El Paso became a historic recruiting site and gathering point for the bracero workers and continued to be so for undocumented migrants after the Bracero Program ended in 1964. The population of El Paso grew from 96,810 in the 1940 census to 339,615 by the 1970 census, and to 649,121 by the 2010 census. Less spectacularly, but significantly, the population of Hidalgo, Texas grew from 106,000 in 1940 to 181,535 by 1970. The population of Brownsville, Texas, grew from 22,000 in 1940 to more than 52,500 by 1970, and the population of Las Cruces, New Mexico, grew from just over 8,000 in 1940 to slightly less than 38,000 by 1970. The population of Laredo grew from 39,000 in 1940 to almost 70,000 in 1970. Not all such growth was due to Mexicanos, of course, but a significant portion of it can be attributed to their migration combined with their high birthrates, which far exceeded the birthrates of other groups, particularly those of non-Hispanic white women (LeMay 2013, Vol 3: 146).

The Bracero Program's cessation in 1964 followed an agreement that President Lyndon Johnson supported to enable enactment of the Immigration Act of October 3, 1965 (79 Stat. 911; LeMay and Barkan 1999, 257–261). The impact of the end of the Bracero Program contributed to political pressure to reinstitute some sort of a guest-worker program since passage of the Immigration Reform and Control Act of November 6, 1986 (IRCA) (100 Stat. 3360; LeMay and Barkan 1999, 282–288). The taint of the Bracero Program's exploitive nature and notoriety for human rights abuses, however, serves as a deterrent to efforts to reinstitute an expanded guest-worker program (LeMay 2006, 266; Wilkens-Robertson 2004). Perhaps the program's greatest significance is that it forged the chain-migration links that persisted from 1964 to 1986, and indeed, have persisted up to the present time (Andreas 2000; Bustamente 1981; Calavita 1992; Gutierrez 1995; LeMay 2015; Snodgrass 2011).

1965–2000: Trends in Migration

In the early 1960s, the socioeconomic status of Mexican Americans in the borderland region was lower than that of African Americans in terms of housing, income, and formal educational status. The brown-power and Chicano movement of migrant workers in California and the land-grant struggle in New Mexico evidenced a revolt among young Chicanos. Brown-power advocates learned lessons for strategy and tactics from the Black civil rights movement, including the use of boycotts, marches, church-based organizing of protests, and the taking over of buildings in protest of discrimination. They provided new leadership and formed new Hispanic movement organizations that worked among and created affective bonds within social and political networks that spanned everything from the grassroots to the transnational (Hennessy 2013; LeMay 2009, 199–309; Griswold del Castilo 2008). The Chicano movement began using the term "Chicano" as a matter of self-pride. It became a mass membership movement evident in the borderlands in both rural areas (colonias) and urban barrios. It gave rise to leaders like Cesar Chavez and Dolores Huerta of the United Farm Workers (UFW) and Reies Lopez Tijerina of the Alianza Federal de Mercedes. The number of organized protests rose from zero in 1960 to 35 in 1965 to 90 in 1970 to 110 in 1973 (LeMay 2009, 299).

The movement begun by Cesar Chavez and Dolores Huerta, often referred to as "La Causa," began in 1965 in Delano,

California, with a strike by Filipino and Hispanic workers harvesting grapes. La Huelga—the strike—used strikes and boycotts against grape and lettuce growers. The movement involved liberal clergy, radical union organizers, and student groups. Striking migrant workers faced violence and yet remained committed to nonviolence.

There soon developed militant Chicano student groups like the Brown Berets (styled after the Black Panthers) and United Mexican American Students (UMAS) in California and the National Organization of Mexican American Students (NOMAS, meaning "no more" in Spanish) in Texas. A similar sense of militancy characterized the land-grant movement of Reies Tijerina, known as "El Tigre"—the tiger. Tijerina began the Alianza Federal de Mercedes in February 1962. He first tried to work through the courts, asserting claims to land taken illegally from Mexicans living in Texas and New Mexico after the Treaty of Guadalupe Hidalgo. Tijerina argued that those treaty right lands—totaling millions of acres and ranging across Texas, New Mexico, Arizona, California, Nevada, Utah, Colorado, and into Wyoming—were stolen in land grabs after the Mexican-American War. The land grab is perhaps best exemplified by Thomas Catron, the erstwhile "King" of the Santa Fe Ring. In launching the land-grant movement, Tijerina argued that Chicanos had to demand their rights and fight for them. Chicano men had to be macho men (Steiner 1969, 195).

Inspired by Tijerina, Hispano farmers in Tierra Amarilla (a small town in New Mexico with a population of 700 in the 2000 census) set up a farmer's cooperative that posted on its door, "Che is alive and farming in Tierra Amarillo" (Steiner 1969, 41). When court action failed to restore lands, Tijerina adopted the tactic of civil disobedience. In October 1966, he led a group that occupied the Echo Amphitheater at Kit Carson National Forest. When protestors burned down a guard post, Tijerina was arrested and convicted of assaulting two forest rangers. While out on bail, in June 1967, he led the takeover of the county courthouse in Tierra Amarilla. He also participated in the Poor People's March on Washington in 1968. In 1969, he was sent to federal prison for two years for the Kit Carson National Forest incident. While in prison, his health declined. He was released early only after promising not to hold any office in the Alianza movement. Members of the Minutemen, a paramilitary white-extremist organization, attacked Alianza's offices and set fire to its health clinic; they also threatened Tijerina's family. Alianza declined after Tijerina left its leadership (LeMay 2009, 305).

Another militant Chicano leader of the 1960s was Rodolfo "Corky" Gonzales, who founded the Crusade for Justice in Denver in 1965. Corky Gonzales also helped organize Chicano participation in the Poor People's March. The Crusade for Justice had its own "defense" security force and it organized barrio youth. It claimed a membership of 1,800 in 1967. Gonzales adopted the trope *Aztlan* at a Chicano conference in Denver in 1969, and he helped organize the Movimiento Estudiantil Chicano de Aztlan (MECHA). Gonzales inspired groups like the UMAS, the Mexican American Youth Organization (MAYO), and the Brown Berets (Chavez 1984; Massey et al. 1990; McClain and Steward 1995, 50–51, 203–205; Navarro 2005). Corky Gonzales also helped Jose Angel Gutierrez organize the La Raza Unida Conference in 1967 in El Paso, Texas. La Raza Unida formed La Raza Unida Partido (the People's Party) that led the Chicano voter revolt in 1970 in Crystal City, Texas, a small town in the borderland region that, in the 1970 census, had a population of just over 8,000. It was 80 percent Mexican American but had a town government that was 100 percent Anglo. Gutierrez and La Raza Unida Partido ran candidates for office, organized community cooperatives, supported Chicano businesses and, in the early 1970s, won numerous city offices, essentially capturing the government of Crystal City (LeMay 2009, 306).

In Los Angeles, barrio youth organized by the Brown Berets struggled with the police. They claimed, "More Chicanos are killed by cops on the streets of the Southwest than any other minority group in the population," and in a barrio newspaper they called it "Chicano birth control." Such activities and slogans are echoed today by the Black Lives Matter movement (LeMay 2009, 308).

In the 1980s, the more radical groups gave way to a host of mostly Hispanic student organizations that used the political accommodation approach to coping with discrimination. These included, for example, the Political Association of Spanish Speaking Organizations (PASSO), the Mexican American Political Association (MAPA), the Mexican American Student Association (MASA), the MAYO, the MECHA, the UMAS, and the NOMAS. They all used standard electoral politics, stressing Chicano pride more than radical reform. The Mexican American Legal Defense and Education Fund (MALDEF), founded in 1967, used a strategy based on court cases and voter drives, like the NAACP (LeMay 2009, 309; McClain and Steward 1995, 204–205).

The Chicano movement's switch in strategy and tactics brought measurable results. Between 1970 and 1988, Hispanic elected officials increased from under 800 to more than 3,400. Hispanics served prominently in the Bill Clinton administration; for instance, Henry Cisneros served as secretary of housing (U.S. Department of Housing and Urban Development [HUD]), Frederico Pena served as White House chief of staff, and Antonia Novella served as U.S. surgeon general. Hispanics elected to the U.S. Congress formed the Hispanic Congressional Caucus, which has grown and developed into one of the most notable caucuses in the U.S. House of Representatives (Hagedorn and LeMay 2019, 174, 202).

Other political developments further impacted the demographics of the border region. On November 6, 1968, President Lyndon Johnson issued the Proclamation on the Multilateral Protocol and Convention Relating to the Status of Refugees (LeMay and Barkan 1999, 267–269). The proclamation adopted the United Nation's definition of refugee that significantly affected the migration of Central American refugees to the borderland region. Congress passed the Act of October 20, 1976, "To Amend the Immigration and Nationality Act of 1965," that extended the preference system to Western Hemisphere nations and was intended to ease the backlog of Mexicans applying for legal immigration to the United States. For a short while, it cut the waiting period for immigrants from Mexico by about half (LeMay and Barkan 1999, 270–272).

A few years later, Congress passed the Act of March 17, 1980 (94 Stat. 102; LeMay and Barkan 1999, 272–275), known as the Refugee Act. It increased the number of refugees allowed annually to 50,000 and authorized the president to notify Congress if he determined that events warranted an increase in that number. In 1984 72,000 persons were authorized to enter, and 67,750 actually arrived. In addition, another 11,600 persons who resided in the borderland region, many from Central America, were granted asylum.

As mentioned earlier, the cessation of the Bracero Program led to a huge spike in the number of undocumented immigrants coming from Mexico. Most of them settled in the Southwest region. Nationally, it led to a prevailing sense that the United States had lost control of the border. In 1977 the Jimmy Carter administration and Congress established the Select Commission on Immigration and Refugee Policy (SCIRP). It recommended extensive policy reforms, notably including "closing the back door" to illegal immigration and advocating measures to "demagnify" the draw of the U.S. economy through a device known as "employer sanctions" (LeMay 1994, 35–36). The employer sanctions approach was used in the Immigration Reform and Control Act (IRCA) of November 6, 1986 (100 Stat. 3360; LeMay and Barkan 1999, 282–288).

In addition to its provisions for sanctions, IRCA enacted an amnesty program that allowed an estimated 3 million unauthorized immigrants, the majority of them Mexicans and Central Americans, to legalize their status and eventually even become naturalized citizens. The legalization program had a huge impact on the southwestern states and especially

the borderland region. Well over 3 million previously undocumented immigrants were able to legalize their status. Mexicans especially benefited from the program. While Mexicans
made up 55 percent of the estimated undocumented population resident in the United States in the 1980 census, they
comprised 75 percent of the legalization application pool
(LeMay 1994, 125–127). Undocumented immigrants from
other countries in the pool were notably from El Salvador
(5.5 percent), Guatemala (2.3 percent), Haiti (2.0 percent,
and located mostly in Florida), Colombia (1.1 percent), and
Philippines (1.0 percent). Applicants for legalization using the
program came from 20 other countries that each comprised
less than 1 percent of the total legalization pool: Dominican
Republic, Pakistan, India, Peru, Jamaica, Honduras, Nicaragua, Ecuador, Poland, Nigeria, Iran, Canada, Korea, China,
Bangladesh, United Kingdom, Brazil, Ghana, Belize, and
Argentina (LeMay 1994, 127). Many of those from countries
not relevant to the borderland region were in undocumented
status because they were "visa overstayers." But those from
nations in Central America and South America were most
often located in Southwest United States, and many were in
the borderland region.

The several major cities in the borderlands grew steadily,
and often significantly, between 1965 and 2000. Brownsville,
Texas, for example, rose in population from 52,522 in 1970
to 139,722 in 2000. The population of Hidalgo, Texas, grew
from 181,535 in 1970 to 569,463 in 2000. The population
of El Paso nearly doubled, growing from 339,615 in 1970 to
563,662 in 2000. The population of Las Cruces, New Mexico,
jumped from 37,857 in 1970 to 74,267 in 2000. The population of Nogales, Arizona, rose from 8,946 in 1970 to 20,878
in 2000. Even Calexico, California, always a small city, grew in
population from 10,625 in 1970 to 27,109 in 2000. The most
spectacular growth, however, was that of San Diego, California. It had a population of 696,769 in 1970 but rose to just
over 1,228,000 by the 2000 census.

When Congress saw that IRCA failed to slow the undocumented flow for more than a mere two years, it passed the Act of November 29, 1990 (104 Stat. 4981; LeMay and Barkan 1999, 288–295). The Immigration Act of 1990 (IMMACT), as it was known, attempted to address legal immigration and clarify some of the provisions of IRCA. IMMACT provided for a temporary stay in the deportation for certain unauthorized immigrants to support family unity or immigrants who had temporary protected status. Many of them were from Mexico and Central America and resided in the border region (LeMay 2006, 190–192).

Canada, Mexico, and the United States entered into a trade agreement on January 1, 1994, known as the North American Free Trade Agreement (NAFTA) (Bacon 2004). It was designed to remove trade barriers between the three countries. It was highly successful in doing so, and it was especially relevant to the borderlands area as it greatly spurred development of the factory (maquiladoras) complex on the Mexican side of the border. The maquiladoras, in turn, spurred rapid urbanization of Mexico's northern cities and the development of a "border culture" and its transnational social spaces. Critics of NAFTA decry that it also spurred repression, exploitation of child labor, deplorable housing conditions in cities like Ciudad Juarez and Tijuana, and corporate retaliation against union organizers (Ashbee, Clausen, and Pedersen 2007; Bacon 2004; Danelo 2008; Ganster 2015; Lorey 1999; Martinez 2006; Staudt, Payan, and Kruszewski 2009).

Frustrated with the failure of the Congress to get control of the undocumented flow, California attempted to reduce that flow by passing the "Save Our State" initiative, known as Proposition 187. It denied a host of welfare benefits to undocumented immigrants on the theory that undocumented immigrants were being drawn by California's welfare programs (LeMay 2006, 193–195). Most of Proposition 187's provisions were declared unconstitutional, however, by the federal district court decision in *LULAC et al. v. Wilson et al.* (908 F. Supp. 755,

CDCal, 1995, 787–791; LeMay 2006, 193–195; LeMay and Barkan 1999, 296–299).

However, Proposition 187 did send a message to Congress about the degree of frustration caused by illegal immigration. Congress reacted by passing two laws in 1996 that essentially placed into U.S. law the Proposition 187 provisions declared unconstitutional (as state infringements of federal immigration policy). The first law was the Act of August 22, 1996 (known as the Personal Responsibility and Work Opportunity Act [PRWOA]). The second law was the Act of September 30, 1996 (known as the Illegal Immigration Reform and Immigrant Responsibility Act [IIRIRA]). Both acts were signed into law by President Bill Clinton (LeMay 2006, 195–199; LeMay and Barkan 1999, 301–310).

One provision of the IIRIRA—Section 104—had an important impact on the border region, and this was the authorization for and issuance of the border crossing card (BCC). It is an identity document and a B1/B2 visa that serves as a standalone document that allows entry into the United States for Mexican citizens to visit the border areas of the United States for less than 72 hours. It was issued by the INS to Mexican citizens residing in Mexico and to members of the U.S. diplomatic missions in Mexico. It was a machine-readable document known as a "laser visa." In 2008, a second version of this document was introduced with enhanced graphics and technology. It is issued by the Department of State. It includes a radio-frequency identification (RFID) chip. It is used extensively by Mexican citizens who cross, often daily, into the United States to work and to shop (LeMay 2006, 198; LeMay 2019; LeMay and Barkan 1999, 304–310).

The failure of IRCA in 1986 and of IMMACT in 1990 to bring the flow of undocumented immigrants under control led to increasing political pressures to militarize the border. The Department of Justice and the Immigration and Naturalization Service began to use the strategy and tactics of the Pentagon's doctrine of "low-intensity conflict" characterized by a broad range of provisions for social control over specific civilian populations (Dunn 1997; Hennessy 2013). Ironically, the "crackdown at the border" approach had unanticipated and counterproductive consequences. Many of the undocumented migrants from Mexico, who had previously crossed the border back and forth many times, were forced to remain in the United States permanently for fear of being unable to return to work. That ironically resulted in what became known among them as the "jaula de oro"—the cage of gold (Cult and Carrasco 2004; Minian 2018).

2000 to Today: Militarizing the Border after 9/11

By 2000, Mexicans accounted for 30 percent of the total foreign-born population in the United States. Their increasing share in the foreign-born population was especially pronounced in California, Arizona, New Mexico, and Texas. When international terrorists struck during the attacks of September 11, 2001, President George W. Bush issued Executive Order 13228. It established an Office of Homeland Security and a Homeland Security Council within the Executive Office of the President (LeMay 2006, 294).

Congress followed up on President Bush's executive order by passing two laws that most dramatically shifted U.S. immigration and security policy in the direction of creating "Fortress America" and a militarization of the U.S. Southern border: the USA Patriot Act and the establishment of a federal Department of Homeland Security. The USA Patriot Act removed many restrictions on law enforcement's ability to gather intelligence through physical searches, wiretaps, electronic surveillance, and increased access to criminal records (LeMay 2006, 205–208; Frey 2019; Torr 2004, 29). The establishment of the Department of Homeland Security (DHS) on November 25, 2002, created the third largest cabinet-level department in the federal government's executive branch, abolished the INS, and dramatically increased the size of the Border Patrol.

The Border Patrol grew from having 9,212 agents in 2000 to having 19,437 agents by 2017 (U.S. Customs and Border Protection 2020).

While the administration talked about balancing security and openness, the vast amount of DHS's resources and efforts went into time-consuming background checks on foreigners, new controls at the border, and aggressive enforcement against anyone caught committing even the most minor infraction of the labyrinthine immigration regulations. In the aftermath of establishing the DHS, security background checks for green cards and citizenship applications were measured in years rather than months. The "war on terrorism" was waged largely through anti-immigrant measures (Alden 2008, 9–14; Ackerman and Furman 2013; Andreas 2000). The Border Patrol redefined its mission in terms of how it protected the vast borders by increased attempts to control drug and human trafficking across the border. To do so, the Border Patrol used an array of All Terrian Vehicles (ATVs), four-wheel drive trucks, patrol cars, Black Hawk helicopters, motorcycles, piloted aircraft and unmanned surveillance drones, special response teams, and horseback surveillance by Native American trackers known as Shadow Wolves (Gaynor 2009; Krauss and Pachedco 2004; Levario 2012; Maril 2006; Payan 2006).

In 2004, Congress passed the Intelligence Reform and Terrorism Prevention Act. It established a Director of National Intelligence (DNI). It also included immigration provisions, like adding 2,000 additional Border Patrol agents each year for five years, improving screening procedures, and imposing new standards of information that must be contained on state-issued drivers' licenses. Critics of the law decried its use of the "czar" approach and its potential for and actual abuse of human rights (Frey 2019; LeMay 2006, 231; Slack, Martinez, and Whiteford 2018; Staudt, Payan, and Kruszewski 2009).

On October 26, 2006, President Bush signed the Secure Fence Act into law (120 Stat. 2636–2640; LeMay 2013, vol. 3: 68–69, 254). It appropriated $1.2 billion to construct a steel fence along the 2,000-mile southern border, at an estimated cost of $2.8 million per mile. To date, about 700 miles have actually been constructed. It authorized more vehicle barriers, check points, and lighting, all designed to prevent people from entering illegally. However, its most significant impact has been to shift the places where undocumented immigrants seek to cross, from the existing checkpoints to the desert areas of Arizona and the harsh terrains of New Mexico and Texas. A further result of the Secure Fence Act, and an unanticipated consequence, has been a sharp increase in the number of deaths in the desert, the increased use of coyotes (human smugglers), and an increase in border vigilante violence (Chacon and Davis 2006; Danelo 2008; De Leon 2015; Ellingwood 2009; Truax 2018).

Despite efforts to curtail immigration, especially undocumented migration across the southern border, the border cities continued to grow between the years 2000 and 2010. Looking at their population growth from cities east to west during the 2000–2010 decade, a pattern of substantial growth is evident in most border cities. The population of Brownsville, Texas was 175,023 in 2010, a 25 percent increase from its population in 2000. The population of Hidalgo, Texas had grown to 774,769 by 2010, a 36 percent increase over its 2000 mark. El Paso, Texas reached a population of 649,121 in 2010, just over a 15 percent increase from 2000. The population of Laredo, Texas, had grown to 236,091 by 2010, having increased by 34 percent from its 2000 population. The population of Las Cruces, New Mexico, reached 97, 618 in 2010, a 31.5 percent increase over its 2000 population. Only Nogales, Arizona, saw a decline— its population of 20,837 in 2010 was 0.2 percent lower than its population in 2000. Calexico, California, had grown to a population 38,573 by 2010, registering a healthy 42.3 percent increase compared to its population in 2000. Finally, San Diego, California, reached and exceeded the 1.3 million population mark by 2010, showing an increase of 7 percent over its population in 2000.

Failure by Congress to enact a comprehensive immigration reform bill in the early years of President Barack Obama's administration prompted him to issue two executive orders—in 2012 and 2015—that had a significant effect on Hispanics living in the border region: DACA and DAPA. DACA is an acronym for Deferred Action for Childhood Arrivals. It addressed the problem of "the Dreamers"—children who were brought to the United States as undocumented immigrants. DACA was enacted in 2012 and required the Dreamers to meet certain requirements: (1) they were brought in by their unauthorized parents before they were 16; (2) they have lived in the United States continuously since January 2, 2010; (3) they were present on June 15, 2012; (4) they graduated from a U.S. high school or obtained a General Education Degree (GED) or are currently enrolled in a post-high-school U.S. educational institution; and (5) they paid an application fee of $465. In 2015, President Obama issued DAPA, Deferred Action for Parental Accountability. DAPA affected an estimated 4.4 million persons who were parents of Dreamer children. President Obama also granted temporary protected status to 5,000 Unaccompanied Alien Children (UAC) for whom it was deemed unsafe to return to their country of origin (they were mostly from El Salvador, Guatemala, Honduras, and Mexico). Between 2009 and 2014, more than 67,300 UAC arrived in the United States (LeMay 2018, 252).

In a surprising presidential election victory in 2016, Donald Trump won the election in the Electoral College despite losing the popular vote by 3 million votes. President Trump had campaigned on an "anti–illegal immigration" stance, promising to build a wall on the border and make Mexico pay for it. He rescinded President Obama's DACA and DAPA executive orders (although a federal court upheld the DACA program). On January 25, 2017, President Trump issued Executive Order 13767 titled "Border Security and Immigration Enhancement Enforcement Improvement." It ordered the building of a wall; it asked Congress to fund a wall along hundreds of miles on the southern border at an estimated $3–6 billion of U.S. tax-payer money (none from Mexico); and it used an "emergency executive order" to fund a "pilot project" to build several "pro-totype" sections of a wall (LeMay 2019, 37–38). He also issued Executive Order 13768 on January 25, 2017, which was titled "Enhancing the Public Safety in the Interior of the United States." It cut funding for what the administration labeled "sanctuary cities" and enhanced expedited removal policies— essentially taking a 180-degree shift from President Obama's immigration policies. It also created an office called the Victims of Immigration Crime Enforcement to serve the victims of crimes committed by immigrants. In January 2018, President Trump pushed the DACA/DAPA issue to a crisis level, declar-ing them unlawful without congressional legislative authoriza-tion (which he never got), and giving Congress a deadline of March 6, 2018, to enact a law on the matter. Congress failed to act, and Trump annulled them. A federal district court ordered the administration to partially reinstate DACA, allowing those in the program to apply for renewal of their protected status.

On February 22, 2017, President Trump used an executive order to cut in half the number of refugee admissions. On July 16, 2019, he issued an asylum ban that required any asylum-seeker traveling through another country (i.e., Mexico) to apply for asylum in that country first. On September 11, 2019, the Supreme Court upheld President Trump's authority to require Central American migrants to seek asylum in another country (Mexico) and be denied that asylum before they could apply for asylum in the United States.

The Trump administration used DOJ policy changes to enforce what it labeled a "zero tolerance" policy that effectively separated several thousands of children from their parents or families and held them in detention centers at the border. Sev-eral children died while in U.S. custody. Although the Trump administration's DOJ announced that it rescinded that separa-tion policy, many hundreds of young children could not be reunited with their families. In April 2019, the administration

contended that the U.S.-Mexico border had reached a breaking point after more than 76,000 migrants crossed the border
in March. However, a host of critics of the administration have
charged it with using a program of intentional cruelty in its
treatment of asylum-seekers, refuge-seekers, UAC, and undocumented immigrants as a method to "deter" their migration
across the southern border. No such treatment is used against
persons crossing the northern border without authorization
(Alvarez 2019; Bobrow-Strain 2019; Cantu 2019; Grandin
2019; Regan 2016; Slack, Martinez, and Whiteford 2018;
Truax 2018).

Conclusion

This chapter discussed eight historical periods in the development of the U.S.-Mexico border and the border region.
It described the boundary set by the Adams-Onis Treaty in
1819. It traced the building up of tensions between the two
countries—after the Republic of Texas won its independence
in 1836 and over the annexation of Texas into the United
States. The chapter described how those conflicts and tension
in the disputed Adams-Onis defined territory, and how those
tensions led to the Mexican-American War. It described the
Treaty of Guadalupe Hidalgo, signed in 1848, that set the new
boundary and the subsequent modification of that boundary
by the Gadsden Purchase in 1853–1854.

Railroad developments prior to 1865 helped spur the development and growth of several border cities on both sides of
the border line established by the 1848 treaty and the Gadsden
Purchase. These developments led to substantial growth and
increase in migration across the border during the post–Civil
War period. The chapter described how the Gilded Age affected
developments in the border region. It described the impact of
the robber barons and the land grab by the Santa Fe Ring. It
showed how that development impacted Hispano and Pueblo
communities. The chapter described the border boom period

of 1890–1930, considered as the Progressive Era and detailed the population growth in the major border towns and cities in the region.

The Great Depression followed the boom period, and the interwar years saw a decline in growth in the region. The Depression's economic pressures led to the forced repatriation of an estimated 1–2 million Mexicans and Mexican Americans in the mid-1930s. The chapter then described the enactment and impact of the Bracero Program (1942–1964) and how that program laid the foundation of the chain-migration patterns that have characterized the border region ever since.

The 1965–2000 era saw new migration, both legal and undocumented, that followed the old patterns established during the Bracero era. The chapter described the laws enacted by the United States during the era that enhanced migration from Mexico and Central America to the border region. Finally, the chapter described the post-2000 era, characterized by the attempt to build "Fortress America." It highlighted the Bush, Obama, and Trump administrations' immigration policy changes and how they have impacted the border region.

The chapter cited insights from an extensive body of literature on the border region, hopefully providing the reader with a myriad of sources for further reading on the subject. It showed the border region to be a complex one with cultural, economic, social, and political influences that have given it its distinctive character and shaped its history. That history also exhibits the conflicts and strains that have given rise to a myriad of problems and concerns that will be discussed in greater detail in the next chapter. Possible solutions to those problems and controversies will also be discussed.

References

Ackerman, Alissa, and Rich Furman. 2013. *The Criminalization of Immigration: Causes and Consequences.* Durham, NC: Carolina Academic Press.

Alden, Edward. 2008. *The Closing of the American Border*. New York: Harper Collins.

Alvarez, C. J. 2019. *Border Land, Border Water*. Austin: University of Texas Press.

Ambrose, Stephen. 2000. *Nothing Like it in the World: The Men Who Built the Transcontinental Railroad, 1863–1869*. New York: Simon and Schuster.

Anderson, Joan, and James Gerber. 2009. *Fifty Years of Change on the U.S.-Mexico Border*. Austin: University of Texas Press.

Andreas, Peter. 2000. *Border Games: Policing the U.S.-Mexico Divide*. Ithaca, NY: Cornell University Press.

Ashbee, Edward, Helene Clausen, and Carl Pedersen, eds. 2007. *The Politics, Economics, and Culture of Mexican-U.S. Migration*. New York: Palgrave/Macmillan.

Bacon, David. 2004. *The Children of NAFTA*. Berkeley: University of California Press.

Balderrama, Francisco, and Raymond Rodriquez. 2006. *Decade of Betrayal: Mexican Repatriation in the 1930s*. Albuquerque: University of New Mexico Press.

Bender, Steven. 2012. *Run for the Border*. New York: New York University Press.

Bernard, Edward. 1987. *The Story of the Great American West*. Pleasantville, NY: Readers Digest Books.

Bobrow-Strain, Aaron. 2019. *The Death and Life of Aida Hernandez: A Border Story*. New York: Farrar, Straus and Giroux/Macmillan.

Boneman, Walter. 2008. *Polk: The Man Who Transformed the Presidency and America*. New York: Random House.

Brown, David. 2009. *Beyond the Frontier*. Chicago: University of Chicago Press.

Burt, Kenneth. 2007. *The Search for a Civic Voice: California Latino Politics*. Claremont, CA: Regina Books.

Bustamente, Antonio Rios, ed. 1981. *Mexican Immigrant Workers in the United States.* Los Angeles: UCLA, Chicano Studies Research Center.

Byrd, Bobby, and Susannah Mississippi, eds. 1996. *The Late Great Border: Reports from a Disappearing Line.* El Paso: Cinco Puntos Press.

Cadaval, Olivia. 2020. "United States-Mexico Borderland/Frontera." http://festival.si.edu/past-program/1993/us-mexico-borderlands.

Caffey, David. 2004. *Chasing the Santa Fe Ring.* Albuquerque: University of New Mexico Press.

Calavita, Kitty. 1992. *Inside the State: The Bracero Program, Immigration, and the INS.* New York: Routledge Press.

Calhoun, Charles W., ed. 2007. *The Gilded Age: Perspectives on the Origins of Modern America.* Lanham, MD: Rowman and Littlefield.

Cantu, Francisco. 2019. *The Line Becomes a River.* New York: Penguin Books.

Chacon, Justin A., and Mike Davis. 2006. *No One Is Illegal.* Chicago: Haymarket Books.

Chavez, John. 1984. *The Lost Land: The Chicano Image of the Southwest.* Albuquerque: University of New Mexico Press.

Chomsky, Aviva. 2014. *Undocumented: How Immigration Became Illegal.* Boston: Beacon Press.

Cohen, Deborah. 2011. *Braceros: Migrant Citizens and Transnational Subjects in the Post-War United States and Mexico.* Chapel Hill: University of North Carolina Press.

Craig, Richard. 1971. *The Bracero Program: Interest Groups and Foreign Policy.* Austin: University of Texas Press.

Crouch, Barry, ed. 2007. *The Dance of Freedom: Texas African Americans during Reconstruction.* Austin: University of Texas Press.

Cult, Nicholas, and David Carrasco. 2004. *Alambrista and the U.S.-Mexico Border.* Albuquerque: University of New Mexico Press.

Danelo, David. 2008. *The Border: Exploring the U.S.-Mexico Divide.* Mechanicsburg, PA: Stockpile Books.

Daniels, Roger. 1990. *Coming to America.* New York: Harper.

Davenport, John. 2004. *The U.S.-Mexico Border: The Treaty of Guadalupe Hidalgo.* Philadelphia: Chelsea House.

De Leon, Jason. 2015. *The Land of Open Graves.* Berkeley: University of California Press.

Donnan, Hastings, and Thomas Wilson. 1999. *Borders: Frontiers of Identity.* London: Routledge.

Dunn, Timothy. 1997. *The Militarization of the U.S.-Mexico Border, 1978–1992.* Austin: The University of Texas Press.

Ebright, Malcolm. 1994. *Land Grants and Suites in Northern New Mexico.* Guadalupe: Center for Land Grant Studies.

Ebright, Malcolm, and Rick Hendricks. 2019. *Pueblo Sovereignty.* Norman: University of Oklahoma Press.

Edwards, Rebecca. 2005. *New Spirits: America in the Gilded Age, 1865–1905.* New York: Oxford University Press.

Ellingwood, Ken. 2009. *Hard Line: Life and Death on the U.S.-Mexico Border.* New York: Vintage Books.

Frey, Juan Carlos. 2019. *Sand and Blood.* E-book: Public Affairs Press.

Ganster, Paul. 2015. *The U.S. Border Today.* Lanham, MD: Rowman and Littlefield.

Ganster, Paul, and David Lorey. 2008. *The U.S.-Mexico Border into the Twenty-First Century.* Lanham, MD: Rowman and Littlefield.

Garcia, Juan Roman. 1980. *Operation Wetback: The Mass Deportation of Mexican Undocumented Workers in 1954.* Westport, CT: Greenwood Press.

Gaynor, Tim. 2009. *Midnight on the Line: The Secret Life of the U.S.-Mexico Border.* New York: St. Martin's Press.

Gonzales, Manuel. 2009. *Mexicanos: A History of Mexicans in the United States, 2e.* Bloomington: Indiana University Press.

Grandin, Greg. 2019. *The End of the Myth.* New York: Henry Holt.

Griswold del Castilo, Richard, ed. 2008. *World War II and Mexican American Civil Rights.* Austin: University of Texas Press.

Gutierrez, David G. 1995. *Walls and Mirrors: Mexican Americans, Mexican Immigrants, and the Politics of Ethnicity.* Berkeley: University of California Press.

Hagedorn, Sara, and Michael LeMay. 2019. *The American Congress.* Santa Barbara, CA: ABC-CLIO.

Henderson, Timothy. 2011. *Beyond Borders.* Hoboken, NJ: Wiley-Blackwell.

Hennessy, Rosemary. 2013. *Fires on the Border.* Minneapolis: University of Minnesota Press.

Hernandez, Kelly L. 2010. *Migra! A History of the U.S. Border Patrol.* Berkeley: University of California Press.

Hoffman, Abraham. 1974. *Unwanted Mexican Americans in the Great Depression: Repatriation Pressures, 1929–1939.* Tucson: University of Arizona Press.

Kang, S. Deborah. 2017. *The INS on the Line.* New York: Oxford University Press.

Kaplowitz, Craig. 2005. *LULAC, Mexican Americans and National Policy.* College Station: Texas A & M University Press.

Kirstein, Peter. 1977. *Anglo over Bracero: A History of the Mexican Worker in the United States from Roosevelt to Nixon.* San Francisco: R & E Research Associates.

Krauss, Erich, and Alex Pachedco. 2004. *On the Line: Inside the Border Patrol.* New York: Citadel/Kensington Press.

LeMay, Michael. 1994. *Anatomy of a Public Policy: The Reform of Contemporary American Immigration Law.* Westport, CT and London: Praeger Press.

LeMay, Michael. 2006. *Guarding the Gates: Immigration and National Security.* Westport, CT: Praeger Security International.

LeMay, Michael. 2009. *The Perennial Struggle, 3e.* Upper Saddle River, NJ: Prentice Hall.

LeMay, Michael. 2013. *Transforming America: Perspectives on U.S. Immigration.* Santa Barbara, CA: Praeger Press.

LeMay, Michael. 2015. *Illegal Immigration, 2e.* Santa Barbara, CA: ABC-CLIO.

LeMay, Michael. 2018. *U.S. Immigration Policy, Ethnicity, and Religion in American History.* Santa Barbara, CA: Praeger Press.

LeMay, Michael. 2019. *Immigration Reform: A Reference Handbook.* Santa Barbara, CA: ABC-CLIO.

LeMay, Michael, and Elliott Barkan. 1999. *U.S. Immigration and Naturalization Laws and Issues: A Documentary History.* Westport, CT: Greenwood Press.

Leonard, Thomas. 2000. *James K. Polk: A Clear and Unquestionable Destiny.* Wilmington, DE: Scholars Resources Inc.

Levario, Miquel Antonio. 2012. *Militarizing the Border.* College Station: Texas A & M University Press.

Lorey, David. 1999. *The U.S.-Mexican Border in the 20th Century: A History.* Lanham, MD: Rowman and Littlefield.

Lusk, Mark, Kathleen Staudt, and Eva Moya, eds. 2012. *Social Justice in the U.S.-Mexico Border Region.* New York: Springer.

Maril, Robert. 2006. *Patrolling Chaos.* Lubbock: Texas Tech University Press.

Marquez, Benjamin. 1993. *LULAC: The Evolution of a Mexican American Political Organization.* Austin: University of Texas Press.

Martinez, Oscar. 2006. *Troublesome Border, 2e.* Tucson: University of Arizona Press.

Massey, Douglas, Rafael Alarcon, Jorge Durand, and Humberto Gonzales. 1990. *Return to Aztlan: The Social Process of International Migration from Western Mexico.* Berkeley: University of California Press.

McClain, Paula, and J. Steward. 1995. *Can't We All Get Along? Racial and Ethnic Minorities in American Politics.* Boulder, CO: Westview Press.

Meeks, Eric. 2008. *Border Citizens.* University Park, TX: Southern Methodist University Press.

Minian, Ana Raquel. 2018. *Undocumented Lives.* Cambridge, MA: Harvard University Press.

Montejano, David. 1987. *Anglos and Mexicans in the Making of Texas, 1836–1986.* Austin: University of Texas Press.

Mora, Anthony. 2011. *Border Dilemmas.* Durham, NC: Duke University Press.

Mora-Torres, Juan. 2001. *The Making of the Mexican Border.* Austin: University of Texas Press.

Navarro, Armando. 2005. *Mexicano Political Experience in Occupied Aztlan: Struggles and Change.* Lanham, MD: Rowman Altamira Press.

Office of Global Affairs, Health and Human Services. 2020. "About OGA." https://www.hhs.gov/about/agencies/oga/about-oga.

Office of the Historian, Department of State. 2020. "Gadsden Purchase, 1853–1854." https://history.state.gov/milestones/1830-1860/gadsden-purchase.

Orozco, Cynthia. 2009. *No Mexicans, Women, or Dogs Allowed.* Austin: University of Texas Press.

Paddison, Joshua. 2005. "1866–1920: Rapid Growth, Large Scale Agriculture, and Integration into the United States." Calisphere. https://calisphere.org/exhibitions/essay/5 /population-growth.

Payan, Tony. 2006. *The Three U.S.-Mexico Border Wars.* Westport, CT: Praeger Security International.

Ramos, Henry. 1998. *The American G. I. Forum: In Pursuit of the Dream, 1948–1983.* Houston, TX: Arte Publico Press.

Regan, Margaret. 2016. *Detained and Deported.* Boston: Beacon Press.

Sanchez, George. 1993. *Becoming Mexican American: Ethnicity, Culture, and Identity in Chicano Los Angeles.* New York: Oxford University Press.

San Diego History Center. 2020. "Timeline of San Diego History: 1930–1959." https://sandiegohistory.org/archives /biographysubject/timeline/1930-1959.

Sandler, Martin. 2015. *Iron Rails, Iron Men and the Race to Link the Nation.* Somerville, MA: Candlewick Press.

Sheridan, Thomas. 1995. *Arizona: A History.* Tucson: University of Arizona Press.

Slack, Jeremy, Daniel Martinez, and Scott Whiteford. 2018. *The Shadow of the Wall.* Tucson: University of Arizona Press.

Snodgrass, Michael. 2011. "The Bracero Program, 1942–1964." In *Beyond the Border: The History of Mexican-U.S. Migration*, edited by Mark Overmyer-Valisquez, pp. 70–102. New York: Oxford University Press.

St. John, Rachel. 2012. *Line in the Sand.* Princeton, NJ: Princeton University Press.

Staudt, Kathleen, Tony Payan, and Anthony Kruszewski. 2009. *Human Rights Along the U.S.-Mexico Border.* Tucson: University of Arizona Press.

Steiner, Stan. 1969. *La Raza.* New York: Harper and Row.

Strum, Philippa. 2010. *Mendez v. Westminiser: School Desegregation and Mexican-American Rights.* Lawrence: University Press of Kansas.

Torr, James D., ed. 2004. *Homeland Security.* San Diego: Greenhaven Press.

Truax, Eileen. 2018. *We Built the Wall.* London and New York: Versa Books.

U.S. Customs and Border Protection. 2020. "Border Patrol Overview." https://www.cbp.gov/border-security /along-us-borders.

Vila, Pablo. 2000. *Crossing Borders.* Austin: University of Texas Press.

Vila, Pablo. 2003. *Ethnography on the Border.* Minneapolis: University of Minnesota Press.

White, Richard. 2017. *The Republic for Which It Stands: The United States during Reconstruction and the Gilded Age, 1865–1896.* New York: Oxford University Press.

Wilkens-Robertson, Michael. 2004. *The U.S.-Mexican Border Environment.* San Diego: San Diego State University Press.

Woodworth, Steven. 2010. *Manifest Destinies: America's Western Expansion and the Road to the Civil War.* New York: Knopf.

Zentner, Scot, and Michael LeMay. 2020. *Party and Nation.* Lanham, MD: Lexington Books.

2 Problems, Controversies, and Solutions

Introduction

This chapter focuses on some major problems and controversies impacting the U.S.-Mexico border region. A dozen such problems have been or currently are evident in the region, many of them interrelated. In addition to addressing the issue of how and why these problems have emerged, the chapter discusses why the problems are so persistent. Some of the problems seem to defy any solution that can be effectively implemented by the U.S. government. Problems related to refugees and asylum, for example, arise not only from controversies within U.S. policy-making and politics but also from the failures of other governments in their economies, laws, and procedures. Such failures in other nation-states propel the migration of asylum-seekers and refugees. In the case of the U.S.-Mexico border region, they come particularly from Mexico and Central America. Such issues are further complicated by international legal rights and agreements.

One of the more recent problems to arise is a result of U.S. government policy: the use of border barriers (fences, bollard-style steel fences, wall portions) and the related militarization of the border. Customs and Border Protection describe the assorted barriers as "force multipliers." Given that they are

---

U.S. Customs and Border Protection agents apprehend migrants caught crossing the U.S.-Mexico border illegally, in California. Such crossings have surged since 2000. (Gerald L. Nino/U.S. Customs & Border Protection)

authorized, built, and supervised by government policy, a solution to the problems caused by them is within the power and authority of the U.S. government. However, the politics surrounding the border fence or wall and the militarization of the border make any solution unlikely for the foreseeable future.

Several scholars have raised issues regarding the problem of "colonization"—in this context, cultural or economic colonization—in the border region. Any solution to the colonization by the government is made more difficult by the fact that much of the problem and the controversies surrounding it are the result of private actions that are not readily susceptible to government policy. Closely related to this is the problem of economic cycles of booms and busts, both of which are influenced by government policy but, again, largely determined by private actors. They, too, are subject to international pressures generated by the trend toward a global economy.

The complex natural environment of the border region raises environmental problems complicated by land and water rights controversies. The controversies are generated by conflicting interests of ranchers on both sides of the border, by corporations pursuing their own economic interests often to the detriment of the environment, and by various groups of individuals on both sides of the border over the use of water from the region's two major rivers.

Foreign policy problems and controversies are perennial, and in the case of the border region, they are complicated further by the tense relations between Mexico and the United States. Mexico is usually categorized as a third-world or developing economy. However, it shares a 2,000-mile border with the United States, a superpower with the richest economy in the world. That juxtaposition often generates conflicts. Again, closely related are the problems and controversies around the global economy issue of trade agreement. In the case of the border region, these are problems and controversies arising from the North American Free Trade Agreement (NAFTA) and its many seen and unforeseen consequences. NAFTA has recently been replaced (or more accurately, amended) by the new United States-Mexico-Canada Agreement (USMCA), the free-trade agreement signed in November 2018. It is too soon to assess whether the USMCA is a solution or whether it will simply have its own set of unforeseen consequences, which is more likely.

Illegal immigration (both from Central American countries into Mexico, and from Mexico into the United States) is a problem affecting the borderlands region, especially since 1970. Illegal immigration has defied multiple attempts to find a solution. It is a problem that is largely determined by "push" factors in countries of origin. As a result, it is a problem not easily solved or even temporarily resolved by U.S. government or state government policies, such as California's Proposition 187, that address "pull" factors.

Cross-border migration over medicine is a perplexing problem exacerbated by differences in the economies of the two nation-states. Solutions that have been tried or proposed to date seem to have had little impact on the problem. Again, an effective resolution will likely require an international agreement and changes in the practices of many private actors (pharmaceutical companies, for instance, and ordinary citizens on both sides of the border seeking cheap medicines or treatments that are available in one country but unavailable, heavily regulated, or expensive in the other).

The political incorporation of persons of minority status, particularly Mexican Americans, living in the borderland region is a persistent problem. Chicano (and Filipino) groups have long fought against devices like gerrymandering, voter dilution, and voter suppression laws and policies adopted by state and local governments in the region. Considerable strides have been made in recent decades in addressing the controversies of political (and related economic) incorporation, but a "solution" has not, to date, been reached.

Public health and health accessibility are problems endemic to the region. Some aspects of those controversies relate to the disparate economies of Mexico and the United States. Others relate to the ethnic relations between and among Anglos,

Chicanos, and Native American tribes that reside in the U.S.-Mexico border region. Resolutions, if not solutions, are sometimes reached by interlocal agreements, some formally arranged and others informal agreements and practices between communities on both sides of the border, especially communities from "twin cities" or "sister cities" on the border.

The U.S.-Mexico border is a culturally complex region due to its considerable demographic diversity. As a result, problems and controversies often arise over the process of social change. This process is inevitable in the border region, where differing cultural customs, norms, ideas, and images come into sustained contact, clash, and sometimes merge. This chapter discusses social change in the border region. In essence, "solutions" are simply a result of the natural evolution in those cross-cultural exchanges that compel social change.

The chapter discusses solutions offered by a host of practitioners and social science scholars studying the region. This is not an exhaustive discussion of past or current problems evident in the borderland region, but rather, it should be viewed as a starting place for conversation and study and, hopefully, future research by readers.

Asylum and Refugee Problems

Asylum refers to the protection granted by a nation-state to a person who has left their country of origin as a political refugee. Asylum is an ancient judicial concept under which an individual persecuted by the government of their own country, or by other more dominant ethnic groups or organizations within their country, may be protected by another sovereign authority, such as a nearby country, or by church officials who could offer sanctuary. The right to seek asylum is guaranteed under Article 14(1) of the Universal Declaration of Rights. It states, "Everyone has the right to seek and to enjoy in other countries asylum from persecution." The Universal Declaration of Human Rights was adopted by the United Nations (UN) in

1948. A 1951 convention established the definition of refugee, as well as the principle of non-refoulement (forbidding the return of asylum-seekers to a dangerous place) and the rights of those granted refugee status. In 1967, the UN adopted the Protocol Relating to the Status of Refugee as a guide to national legislation enacted by member-states concerning political asylum. Sending true victims of persecution back to their persecutors is a violation of the principle of non-refoulement, part of the customary and trucial Law of Nations (protective laws based on truces). The United States recognizes the right of asylum of individuals as specified by both international and federal law. In U.S. immigration law, an asylee is defined as a person who is unable or unwilling to return to his or her country of origin because of persecution or a well-founded fear of persecution. The asylee is eligible to become a permanent resident after one year of continuous residence in the United States (LeMay 2015, 357). A refugee in U. S. law is defined as a qualified applicant for conditional entry into the United States whose application could not be approved because of an inadequate number of preference visas as determined by the Act of November 3, 1965 (79 Stat. 911; LeMay and Barkan 1999, 257–261), and its subsequent amendments. The status of refugees in U.S. law was also affirmed by the Proclamation of President Lyndon Johnson of November 6, 1968, on the Multilateral Protocol and Convention Relating to the Status of Refugees (LeMay and Barkan 1999, 267–269), and by the Act of March 17, 1980 (94 Stat. 102; LeMay and Barkan 1999, 272–275), known as the Refugee Act. The 1980 law authorized the annual number of refugees at 50,000 and provided for an additional number of 5,000 "asylum-seekers" (LeMay 2018, 34). Between 1980 and 2000, the United States accepted more refugees than did any other nation-state.

The tradition of accepting asylum-seekers and refugees was reaffirmed by President Ronald Reagan in July 1981 (LeMay and Barkan 1999, 276–277). It was further affirmed by the U.S. Congress when it passed the Act of November 29, 1990

(104 Stat. 4981; LeMay and Barkan 1999, 288–295). The Family Unity and Temporary Protected Status title (III) of the 1990 Act, known as Immigration Act of 1990, or simply "IMMACT," empowered the attorney general to grant asylum or refugee status, and to develop administrative rules and procedures regarding them for the Department of Justice (DOJ), the Immigration and Naturalization Service (INS) (now the Department of Homeland Security [DHS]), agents of the Border Patrol (now U.S. Customs and Border Protection [CBP]), Immigration and Customs Enforcement (ICE), immigration-court judges, and related programs, such as the Office of Refugee Resettlement (ORR) within the Department of Health and Human Services (HHS).

The issue of refugee and asylum-seekers has become a particularly vexing problem in the border region since the 1990s. U.S. law specifies that the determination of asylum and refugee status is done on a case-by-case basis. A "fear hearing" is held to determine if the individual has a "well-founded fear of persecution." If the number of individuals seeking asylum or refugee status is a few thousand annually, the system is adequate to handle them. It becomes a vexing problem when the numbers seeking such status are so high as to overwhelm the capacity, at the southern border, to cope with the issue, particularly in detention centers run by the DHS or in the centers of the ORR. It became particularly controversial after 2001, and even more so after 2017 with the administration of President Donald Trump (Human Rights First 2020).

Since 2001, increased internal enforcement to detect and deport undocumented immigrants has risen sharply (Ackerman and Furman 2013; Bender 2012). Critics of the DHS and CBP charge that asylum and deportation procedures have become increasingly corrupt, often seemingly arbitrary, and have systematically forced refugees to endure heart-wrenching travails with narcotic and human traffickers who operate in Mexico with absolute impunity (Truax 2018). Authors Lawrence Taylor and Maeve Hickey have reported on how children are often forced to find shelter in the drainage tunnels between the cities of Nogales, Sonora, Mexico and Nogales, Arizona (Taylor and Hickey 2001).

Migration from Central America to the United States reached crisis levels when push factors causing hundreds of thousands of persons to flee from the Northern Triangle of Central America (NTCA). NTCA is a region composed of El Salvador, Guatemala, and Honduras. It is considered one of the most dangerous places on earth, and violence within NTCA has caused unprecedented levels of migration. The United Nations High Commission for Refugees (UNHCR) has called this violence-induced migration a humanitarian crisis (Geneva Declaration on Armed Violence and Development 2015).

The United States has seen a record number of asylum applications since 2014, but other Central American countries are also having to deal with the migration flow from NTCA within their borders: Mexico, Belize, Costa Rica, Nicaragua, and Panama have had a 432 percent increase in asylum applications. In Mexico, detentions went up 71 percent in 2014, and the country deported 150,000 Central Americans from NTCA. Mexico approved only 24.7 percent of asylum applications in 2014. But that seems generous when compared to the United States, which is much more restrictive. The United States only approved 3.7 percent of asylum applications in 2014. A major push factor in this migration flow is violence against women. It caused a 500 percent increase in women applying for asylum in the border region (Amnesty International 2016; Geneva Declaration on Armed Violence and Development 2015).

A closely related problem is that of unaccompanied alien children (UAC). In 2014, UAC from NTCA reached 68,500 at the U.S.-Mexico border. UAC are defined as children who have no lawful immigration status in the United States, are under the age of 18, and have no parent or legal guardian in the United States, or no parent or legal guardian in the United States available to provide care and physical custody (Health and Human Services 2020).

UAC are referred to the ORR within the Administration for Children and Families in the HHS by another agency, most often the DHS. They are typically apprehended by immigration authorities while trying to cross the border, although many who successfully cross the border then immediately turn themselves in to authorities and declare their intention to apply for asylum. The rise in UAC since 2003 has been substantial. Since 2003, ORR has cared for 340,000 UAC. From 2003 to 2012, fewer than 8,000 children were referred annually to ORR. Since fiscal year 2012, annual numbers have risen steadily and dramatically. A total of 13,625 were referred in 2012. In fiscal year 2013, there were 24,668 UAC referred from DHS. That number jumped to 57,496 in 2014, to 33,726 in 2015, to 59,170 in 2016, and to 40,810 in 2017, and in fiscal year 2018, 49,100 UAC were referred to ORR (Health and Human Services 2020). Their numbers have overrun the capacity of ORR to deal with them safely and humanely, and recent reports have confirmed multiple deaths of children while in U.S. custody, and evidence of unacceptable conditions (lack of beds, oral hygiene supplies, clothing; poor quality food, and so on).

In 2018, President Trump issued an executive order cutting the annual number of refugees from 50,000 to 25,000 and asylum numbers from 5,000 to 2,500. Then, in May 2020, the Trump administration used the coronavirus pandemic as the reason to virtually close the southern border to refugees and asylum-seekers and to expel asylum-seekers and children to the escalating violence on the Mexican side of the border. The acting secretary for the DHS effectively eliminated asylum and other humanitarian protections at the border and sent those already on the U.S. side of the border to the life-threatening dangers and appalling conditions faced by asylum-seekers on the Mexican side. UAC were effectively blocked by the order from seeking protection in the United States, putting their lives and safety at increased risk. A senior researcher for Human Rights First (HRF) issued a report in 2020 that found "the CBP is turning away asylum-seekers who have been kidnapped, tortured and threatened in Mexico, telling them that protection in the United States is not available due to an order of the Center for Disease Control and Prevention (CDC). The United States has the ability, if it chooses to do so, to safeguard both public health and the lives of people seeking humanitarian protection. The latter does not need to be sacrificed to protect the former" (Human Rights First 2020). Human Rights First found that many CBP officers and Border Patrol agents were failing to observe even the most basic health precautions at border posts, like wearing masks and maintaining social distancing during the coronavirus pandemic. HRF concluded that the CDC order was merely a pretext to justify the Trump administration's immigration policy goals. In Mexico, Human Rights First found that the asylum-seekers returned to the Mexican side of the border under the so-called Migrant Protection Protocols (MPP) reported 1,100 cases of kidnapping, rape, and assault. The study found that protection interviews by the CBP were cancelled because of the CDC order. HRF found an utter lack of communication about court postponements of their "credible-fear" hearings that put asylum-seekers in even greater danger in some of the most violent places in North America, like Nuevo Laredo (Human Rights First 2020). The HRF report found numerous instances of refusal of a fear screening altogether. Asylum-seekers from Cameroon, Cuba, Congo, and the east African country of Eritrea, among other countries, have been forced to wait in Mexico while seeking U.S. asylum and have been left stranded in Mexico with its increasingly dangerous and difficult conditions. HRF estimates that the CDC order has been used to expel or block at least 4,000 families, adults, and children per month from requesting refugee protection in the United States, and more than 1,000 UAC have been expelled to Mexico, El Salvador, Guatemala, and Honduras under cover of the CDC order.

As mentioned, HRF has tracked more than 1,000 cases of murder, rape, kidnapping, torture, and assault against asylum-seekers and refugees under the Migrant Protection Protocols

(MPP), including 265 kidnappings or attempted kidnappings of children returned to Mexico under MPP. Nearly 11,000 MPP hearings were cancelled by DHS without a means to inform asylum-seekers of those cancellations, nor the means to explain when new hearings would be rescheduled. HRF called on the Trump administration to rescind its March 20 CDC order and to end all policies that violate U.S. asylum and immigration law and U.S. Refugee Protocol obligations. The administration refused to end its policies. HRF then recommended its actions to Congress. As the report's author stated, "What's happening at the southern border isn't about public health—it's about using a global health crisis to scapegoat people seeking humanitarian protection and to nullify the laws and treaties created to protect them" (Human Rights First 2020).

A solution, or at least resolution, to asylum and refugee problems is within the policy authority of the government. However, the Trump administration clearly lacked the political will to find a solution. Critics contend that the cruelty of the Trump administration's policy was intentional. It was intended to deter asylum-seekers and refugees from even attempting to come to the United States to seek refuge.

Border Barriers and the Militarization of the Border

The U.S.-Mexico border has become increasingly militarized since 1978 (Dunn 1997). Border Control has used the strategy and tactics of the Department of Defence doctrine of "low-intensity conflict." This approach is aimed at specific populations and raises human rights concerns for the borderland region, affecting racial and social relations among Anglos, Mexicans, and Chicanos (Frey 2019; Gerdes 2014; Levario 2012). Measures to increasingly militarize the southern border have been escalating for three decades. Since the 1990s, expedited removal policies amounting to mass deportations have been used by the Border Patrol under the INS. Under the Trump administration's announced "zero tolerance" policy, they were used by the CBP at detention centers, not only forcing family separation but also forcing migrants back across the border exposing them to terror at the hands of drug cartels who operated with virtual impunity (LeMay 2006, 28; Payan 2006; Slack, Martinez and Whiteford 2018).

In 1986, when the Immigration Reform and Control Act (IRCA) enacted an employer sanctions approach, the Border Patrol began to raid places of suspected large-scale employment of undocumented immigrants. The Omnibus Drug Abuse Law (Pub. L. 99-570), also passed in 1986, added a new responsibility to the Border Patrol to include drug interdiction. In addition to its work guarding refugee camps located in the border region, and identifying, prosecuting, and deporting undocumented immigrants, the Border Patrol partnered with the Drug Enforcement Agency (DEA) in a program known as Operation Alliance (LeMay 2019, 15; LeMay2006, 184).

Militarization at the border increased during the administration of President Bill Clinton in 1996, with the enactment of the Illegal Immigration Reform and Immigrant Responsibility Act of September 30, 1996 (IIRIRA) (LeMay 2019, 18–19; LeMay and Barkan 1999, 304–310). IIRIRA authorized an increase in Border Patrol agents by 1,000 a year for five years, increasing the total force from 5,000 to 10,000 agents, and reallocated many agents to border control functions. It funded an additional 900 agents to investigate and prosecute cases of smuggling and harbouring. Illegal Immigration Reform and Immigrant Responsibility Act authorized the building of a border fence and funded $12 million to construct a triple fence along a 14-mile strip at the U.S.-Mexico border just south of San Diego. It required the INS to develop an alien identification card (Border Crossing Card) that included a biometric identifier (fingerprint) that was machine-readable for use at border crossing point scanners. It increased the penalty for fleeing through checkpoints and authorized expedited deportation of those convicted. It allowed the INS to enter into agreements with state and local law enforcement agencies to help in investigating, arresting, detaining, and transporting unauthorized immigrants especially at the southern border. It increased INS authority to investigate and imposed increased penalties for document fraud and for smuggling unauthorized immigrants. IIRIRA authorized undercover operations to track immigrant smuggling rings. It authorized the seizure of assets of violators of immigration statutes, including vehicles, boats, airplanes, and real estate if they were used in the commission of a crime or were the profit from the proceeds of a crime (aimed mostly at drug and human smuggling operations along the southern border) (LeMay 2015, 238–243).

The crackdown at the border against undocumented immigrants involved the use of hundreds of Border Patrol agents and the beginnings of the 14-foot steel wall or fence on the U.S. side to better control drug and human smuggling violence on both sides of the border. It increased tensions between the United States and Mexico (Davidson 2000). The Border Patrol was given funding to expand its military equipment and technology for border control, including the purchase and use of Department of Defence military surveillance helicopters, four-wheel-drive armoured trucks, motorcycles, and All Terrain Vehicles (ATVs) (Krauss and Pacheco 2004).

The tempo of increasing militarization at the border increased after the terrorist attacks of September 11, 2001. Congress responded to the attacks by enacting the USA Patriot Act of October 24, 2001, which included many sections for increased protection at the borders and enhanced immigration provisions (LeMay 2006, 205–208; LeMay 2015, 246–247; LeMay 2019, 20–24). Critics of the act decry its use. They charge that the USA Patriot Acts (I and II) have led to many human rights abuses. The alleged abuses include warrantless detention, detention for indefinite time and without due process, and denial of the right to contact a family member or lawyer to those detained (Torr 2004).

Congress further enhanced the trend toward militarization at the border when it enacted the Homeland Security Act of

November 19, 2002 (LeMay 2015, 247–250). Title IV creates within the DHS a bureau of Border and Transportation Security to secure the borders, territorial waters, ports, terminals, waterways, and air, land, and sea transportation systems, and to coordinate these functions at ports of entry encompassing air, sea, and land. It abolished the INS and established a Bureau of Border Security. It waived environmental provisions to speed up the construction of physical barriers on the border (i.e., a border fence).

In 2006, President George W. Bush signed into law the Secure Fence Act (Pub. L. 109-367). Its formal title is An Act to Establish Operational Control over the International and Maritime Borders of the United States. It approved $1.2 billion to construct a 700-mile fence on the southern border (Alden 2008, 274). No provision or even suggestion was made to construct any such physical barrier on the northern border with Canada. The Act authorized and funded 600 miles of fence construction. The Act further authorized surveillance at international land and maritime borders by the effective use of personnel and technology, including use of unmanned (drone) aerial vehicles, ground-based sensors, and satellite, radar, and camera devices. The Act authorized enhancement of physical infrastructure to prevent unlawful entry and approved the development and installation of additional checkpoints by CBP to construct all-weather access roads; it also increased the use of vehicle barriers at checkpoints. It authorized the DHS to construct additional reinforced fencing west of Tecate, California as well as in Calexico, California; Columbus, New Mexico; El Paso, Texas; Laredo, Texas; Del Rio, Texas; and Brownsville, Texas. In these priority areas, DHS was charged with installing an interlocking surveillance camera system, and to complete the fencing construction by May 30, 2008 (LeMay 2015, 265–266). By FY 2008, DHS spending on border enforcement totalled $10 billion, most of it for Border Patrol agents (Alden 2008, 301).

In 2006, Congress renewed the USA Patriot Act (LeMay 2019, 28–29). The Bush administration further militarized the southern border that year with Operation Jump Start, in which 6,000 National Guard troops were ordered to the Mexican border, serving there from 2006 to 2008, to assist the DHS and CBP in controlling the border. By 2008, the DHS had installed ten-point fingerprint readers at most border checkpoints (Alden 2008, 268; LeMay 2019, 82–93).

Barack Obama was elected president in 2008. In 2010, the administration increased expedited removals at the southern border. The Obama administration further increased militarization at the border with Operation Phalanx, a six-month operation in 2010. The operation assigned 1,210 Army National Guard troops along the 1,935-mile southwest border to support the CBP. Their tasks included ground surveillance, criminal investigation analysis, command-and-control, mobile communications, transportation, logistics, and training. Operation Phalanx used 12 national-guard helicopters as well as several fixed-wing aircraft to provide aerial operations, known as Operation River Watch II. Operation River Watch II covered 200 miles of border from Laredo, Texas, to the Gulf Coast and assisted in the apprehension of 17,900 undocumented immigrants trying to illegally cross the southern border between July 2010 and June 2011. Critics of Operation Phalanx and Operation River Watch II opposed their further militarization of the border and their hindering of negotiations for a binational agreement between Mexico and the United States to deal with immigration matters (LeMay 2019, 82–83; U.S. Customs and Border Protection 2011).

The Border Patrol increased the number of its agents steadily, almost every year from 2000 to 2017. In 2000 there were 9,212 agents. By 2014 the number of agents reached a high point of 20,863, and in 2017 there were 19,437 agents, an increase of about 300 percent from 2000. Ironically, as the number of agents increased, the number of apprehensions at the border decreased, from 1,843,679 in 2000 to 303,916 in 2017, an eight-fold decrease in apprehensions (LeMay 2019, 219).

Another unintended consequence of the increase in Border Patrol and its militarization, and of the War on Terrorism, was that enforcement was aimed increasingly at economic migrants, refugees, and families from Central America seeking jobs, safety, and freedom in the United States. Critics argue that the United States is no safer, families are being ripped apart, the undocumented living in the border region live in a state of increasing fear, and thousands have died in detention centers or while crossing the border. They argue that the border militarization policy has increased race-based violence and "border brutalism." Militarization has driven more working-class Mexican migrants to enter the United States surreptitiously, relying on coyotes. It has embedded the coyote system as a cultural practice of the region. These critics predict an unfolding apartheid in South Texas due to militarization (Frey 2019; Grandin 2019; Spener 2009). Critics, including former Border Patrol agents, contend that a consequence of militarizing the border is the demoralization of agents who are aware of its dehumanizing effect. Militarization enhances violence on both sides of the border, and results in a violently unequal America (Bobrow-Strain 2019; Cantu 2019).

The height of the militarization of the border and the use of physical border barriers was arrived at with the administration of President Donald Trump. He campaigned on building a border wall and on the premise that he would make Mexico pay for it. Immediately after taking office, President Trump made a 180-degree shift in immigration policy from that of his predecessor, Barack Obama. Ironically, President Trump, who had accused President Obama of an unconstitutional abuse of his office by what he labelled an imperial use of executive orders, advanced his own agenda by use of executive orders. Where President Obama had used executive orders 33 times a year in his eight years in office, President Trump did so 55 times in his first year as president. President Trump's first executive order concerned the pursuit of undocumented immigrants. It was issued on January 25, 2017 and was titled "Border Security and Immigration Enhancement Enforcement Improvements (Executive Order 13767)." It ordered the building of a wall on the U.S.-Mexico border. However, President Trump needed congressional action to build and fund a wall along the hundreds of miles of border, estimated to cost $3–6 billion. Since there was no funding for that within the budget that he was inheriting from the Obama administration, President Trump used an executive order to fund merely a "pilot project." He did so by shifting a few million dollars from the existing budget of the DHS to build several "prototypes" or model sections of a wall (as opposed to a fence). He also issued Executive Order 13768, "Enhancing the Public Safety in the Interior of the United States." It cut funding for what President Trump labelled broadly as "sanctuary cities." In May 2017, he used an executive order again to establish an agency called the Victims of Immigration Crime Enforcement (VOICE) (LeMay 2019, 35–37).

In January 2018, President Trump pushed the Deferred Action for Childhood Arrivals (DACA)/Deferred Action for Parental Accountability (DAPA) issue to a crisis level, declaring that they were unconstitutional without legislative action to approve them. He annulled DACA, giving Congress until March 5 to enact legislation to "fix the problem." It failed to do so. He rescinded DAPA, an action that was upheld in a federal district court. His rescinding of DACA, however, was overruled in federal court (LeMay 2019, 40–42).

The Trump administration used enhanced expedited removal to deport a record number of immigrants in 2019. Expedited removal allows immigration authorities to remove an individual without a hearing before an immigration judge. It can be used for undocumented immigrants who were caught within 100 miles of a land border and within 14 days of arrival. In June 2018, the Border Patrol arrested nearly 700,000 immigrants who had crossed the border in FY 2018–2019. The crackdown was based on the president's 2017 DHS expansion as part of the "Border Security and Immigration Enforcement Improvement Policies."

In July 2019, President Trump announced a new asylum ban—the Third Country transit asylum bar, issued July 16, 2019. It was upheld by the Supreme Court on September 11, 2019. The ban stipulated that Central Americans seeking asylum had to seek asylum in another country before applying in the United States. It effectively bans asylum for most refugees seeking protection at the U.S. southern border. It attempts to bypass Congress, and critics contend that the ban violates U.S. law and treaty obligations. It bars asylum attempts by any person who merely passes through a third country in route to the United States. The ban requires that they must first be "firmly resettled" in a transit country. The September 11 Supreme Court ruling held that the bar is in full effect, after staying a federal district court ruling in California that had enjoined the asylum ban. Litigation opposing the asylum ban has been brought by the American Civil Liberties Union, the Center for Constitutional Rights, the Southern Poverty Law Center, Human Rights First, the Capital Area Immigrant Rights Coalition, and nine asylum-seekers in a case pending in the D.C. district court (Human Rights First 2019).

Finally, in May 2020, the Trump administration waived several environmental regulations to fast-track construction of nearly 70 miles of border fence barriers and roads in Webb and Zapata counties, Texas. The waivers allowed the DHS to circumvent regulations mandated in the National Environment Policy Act, the Federal Water Pollution Control Act, and the National Historic Preservation Act. The Texas fence construction project was part of an announced goal to build 450 miles of additional barrier fencing. The 69 miles to be constructed in Zapata County, Texas, were in addition to a 52-mile project in Webb County. U.S. representative Henry Cuellar, D-Laredo, opposed the project, arguing the administration should concentrate its efforts on fighting the COVID-19 pandemic instead of on building an "expensive, ineffective border wall"

(Aguilar 2020). The new fencing barriers replaced older sections of fencing. They were steel bollard type sections filled with concrete and were supposedly very hard to scale or to penetrate. However, some protestors cut through them using only an electric saw purchased at a local hardware store for about $100.

Insofar as border barriers are problematic, they can be "solved" by a change in U.S. law and policies that authorize them. However, while legally a possible remedy, politically that solution is extremely unlikely. While undocumented immigration remains an issue, border barriers are inevitable. According to a 2019 public opinion poll, 58 percent of the American public is opposed to the construction of a "border wall" or expansion of the border fence (Gramlich 2019). The Trump administration was stymied by congressional refusal to fund construction of a wall. The use of border fences is entrenched in American politics and policy. It will remain so for the foreseeable future. Any solution to the problems associated with the use of barriers at the borders—such as deaths in the Arizona desert and undocumented immigrants held in southwestern border detention centers—will likely only come from changes in administrative rules on enforcement that have since been issued as executive orders by the Joseph Biden administration.

Colonization

Colonization can be defined as the process of settling among and then establishing control over the indigenous people of an area. For the indigenous peoples of the United States, colonization is a condition of life and a perennial problem. It is an issue that has become part of the fabric of the borderlands region. It affects both the Hispanic and Native American populations of the region (Ebright and Hendricks 2019; Hernandez 2018; Meeks 2008).

Colonization is fundamentally a concept of relative power. It underscores various other related problems evident in the region—vigilantism, urbanization in the region on both sides of the border, violence against minorities and women, economic, political, and social incorporation, exploitation and walling-off of minorities from such inclusion, and the predominance of culture along with the blending of cultures. The colonization process is complex and often ad hoc policies are used to enforce or to resist colonization (Alvarez 2019; Ebright and Hendricks 2019; Kang 2017).

In the southwestern border the colonization process and the period establishing it went through various stages: under Spanish rule, under Mexican rule, under the Republic of Texas rule, and then for the U.S.-Mexico border region, under U.S. rule in the states of Texas, New Mexico, Arizona, and California. The most pronounced and evident use of the process was in New Mexico and Texas (Casey and Watkins 2014; Ebright and Hendricks 2019; Hernandez 2018; La Vere 2013; Meeks 2008; Newcomb 1972).

The Spanish, then the Mexicans, and then the Anglo-Texans were the first to use colonization against Native American tribes. The name Texas comes from the way early Spanish settlers in the region pronounced the Caddo Indian word *taysha*, meaning "friend." Many Native American tribes are referred to as Pueblo Indians. This comes from the Spanish word *pueblo* for "town" or "village" (Native Languages of the Americas n.d.). Pueblo also refers to the adobe houses built by the Pueblo people. There are 19 recognized or designated Pueblos in New Mexico, one in Arizona (Hopi), and three in Texas. In Texas, the tribes that coped with Spanish and Mexican colonization included the Apache, Caddo, Coahuiltecan and Carrizo, Comanche, Jumano, Karankawa, Naches, and Tonkawa. After the Europeans arrived, they relocated and brought in the Kickapoo Pueblo (in Eagle Pass, Texas), the Ysleta del Sur Pueblo (El Paso, Texas), and the Alabama-Coushatta Tribe of Texas (Livingston, Texas). In New Mexico, there are four language groups of tribes that have Pueblos: the Keres speakers, the Tewa speakers, the Tiwa speakers, and the Zuni speakers. In discussing Pueblo sovereignty and resistance to encroachment of land and water rights, Malcolm Ebright and Rick Hendricks focus on the Pojoaque, Tesuque, Nambe, and Isleta Pueblos in New Mexico, and the Ysleta del Sur in Texas as prime examples of their shared experiences in colonization. They show how these Pueblos have used land and water communally, acquired land, sold land, protected their existing land bases from encroachment (by the Spanish, Mexicans, and Anglos), and used advocates like Native American agents and lawyers, federal courts, and land claims courts and boards (Ebright and Hendricks 2019).

In 1891, the United States established the Court of Private Land Claims to adjudicate land grants. The court failed to adequately protect Pueblo interests. In 1924, the U.S. federal government established the Pueblo Land Board, comprising three non-Native members, which attempted to adjudicate titles to Pueblo land. It lasted until 1930 and, during its six years of operation, awarded more than 36,000 acres of Pueblo grant land—which is most of the valuable irrigated land—to non-Natives. The Mexican government forced tribes to relocate and to live separate from Hispanics. The U.S. government, of course, forced most Indian tribes to live on reservations (Anton et al. 2013).

There are quite a few Indian reservations in the borderlands region. Going from east to west, Texas, for example, has the Alabama-Couhatta Tribe of Texas in Livingston, the Kickapoo Traditional Tribe of Texas in Eagle Pass, and the Ysleta del Sur Pueblo in El Paso, Texas. In New Mexico, there is the large Mescalero Apache Reservation and parts of the Navajo Nation (near Socorro). Arizona has the most reservations, including again parts of the Navajo Nation, the Tohono O'odam Nation, the San Carlos Apache, the Hualapai Tribe, the Gila River Indian Community, the Colorado River Indian tribes, the Havasupai Indian reservation, the Fort-Yuma-Quechan Tribe, the Ak-Chin Indian Community, the Cocopah Indian reservation, the Pascua Yaqui Tribe, and parts of the Zuni Indian reservation.

There are numerous small reservations (usually called Mission Bands) in San Diego County, California: the Barona, Campo Band of Kemeyaay Indians, Cuyapaipe Band of Mission Indians, Inaja-Cosmit Band of Indians, Jamui Indian Village, La Jolla Band of Indians, La Posta Reservation, Los Coyotes Band of Mission Indians, Manzanita Band of the Kumeyaay Nation, Pala Band of Mission Indians, Pauma/Yuima Band of Mission Indians, and the Viejas Band of Kumeyaay Indians.

One way that Native Americans on reservations have fought back against the debilitating effects of colonization has been through the establishment of Indian casinos and gaming (mostly card rooms and bingo halls). According to the National Indian Gaming Commission (NIGC) there are 460 Native gaming establishments (casinos, bingo halls, and card-game rooms) in the United States that are operated by 240 federally recognized tribes. The NIGC is an independent regulatory agency within the Department of Interior established by the Indian Gaming Regulatory Act (IGRA) of October 17, 1988 (102 Stat.2467). Against a legal challenge, the IGRA retained tribal sovereignty to create casino halls. Many such gaming establishments have been located on reservations within the U.S.-Mexico border region. In southern Texas, for example, one can find Naskila Gaming in Livingston, Texas, and Kickapoo Lucky Eagle Casino Hotel in Eagle Pass, Texas. Five casinos are located within the border region in New Mexico: Inn of the Mountain Gods in Mescalero, Sunland Park Racetrack and Casino in Mescalero, Casino Apache in Mescalero, Billy the Kid Casino in Ruidos Downs, and Zia Park Casino Hotel and Racetrack in Hobbs. There are three casinos in southwest Arizona operating in the Tucson area: Casino of the Sun (Pascua Yaqui Tribe), Casino Del Sol, and Desert Diamond Casino and Hotel. In San Diego County, California, there are 10 small tribal lands that run gaming operations: Barona Valley Ranch Resort and Casino, Bay 101, Casino Pauma, Harrah's Resort San Diego, Jamul Casino, La Jolla Slot Arcade, La Posta Casino, Pala Casino Resort and Spa, Viejas Casino, and the Village Club

Casino (500 Nations 2018). The use of casinos and gaming operations does not solve the colonization problem in that they are still on reservation lands, but the income and wealth generated by many such casinos have done much to alleviate the worst aspects of colonization. Indeed, some of the smaller bands in California now have all or most of their members in the status of millionaires. The tribes' wealth enables them to lobby Congress and influence state and local politicians and thereby "solve" most of the negative effects of colonization.

Colonization is also a problem for Hispanics in the borderlands region. The problem is exemplified by barrios and colonias. The term "barrio" refers to a district of a town in a Spanish-speaking country; in the United States, the term refers to the Spanish-speaking quarter of a town or city, particularly one with a high level of poverty. Colonias, in Mexican cities, are neighborhoods that have no jurisdictional autonomy or representation. In the United States, colonias are located along the Mexico-U.S. border and are typically viewed as "border slums." They emerged with the advent of informal housing, mostly since the 1950s and early 1960s. They are very exploitive of their residents. They began as informal housing solutions for very-low-income, Hispanic wage-earners (Vila 2000). Colonias are subdivisions of substandard housing that lack basic services such as potable water, electricity, paved roads, proper drainage, and waste management (HUD Exchange n.d.). Their iconic image is of a scattered rural homestead or inappropriately subdivided land, with housing units made of salvaged materials and having no utilities (Vila 2000).

Traditional homeownership financing is rare among colonia residents, and the areas often consist of ramshackle housing units built incrementally with found material on expanses of undeveloped land. They have a predominately Latino population; typically 85 percent are Latinos under age 18 who are U.S. citizens. The broader U.S. culture views them as places of lawlessness, poverty, backwardness, and ethnic difference (Vila 2000). They are found throughout the southern border area, one of the poorest regions in the United States. They were often formed when landowners illegally sold and subdivided rural lands to buyers who did not understand the terms under which the land was sold. Most colonias have no water infrastructure and lack wastewater or sewage services. Where sewer systems do exist, they lack treatment plants, so untreated wastewater is dumped into arroyos and creeks that flow into the Rio Grande or the Gulf of Mexico, contributing to environmental problems (Hernandez 2018).

More than 2,000 colonias have been identified in the United States, mostly in Texas, but also in New Mexico, Arizona, and California. HUD now designates 1,800 in Texas, 138 in New Mexico, 77 in Arizona, and 32 in California (HUD Exchange n.d.). Most were in existence before the enactment of the Cranston-Gonzalez National Affordable House Act of 1990 (P.L. 101-625; HUD Exchange n.d.).

Colonias grew rapidly in the 1990s due to globalization and the passage of NAFTA in 1994, which industrialized the U.S.-Mexico border. Texas has the largest number of colonia residents, with approximately 400,000 persons living in 1,800–2,000 colonias, as defined by funding sources such as HUD, the U.S. Department of Agriculture (USDA), and state and local governments. Many in Texas were settled as homesteads, the iconic colonia settlement pattern. New Mexico has the second largest concentration of colonias (about 150), many being unincorporated, long-standing communities in rural small towns designated as colonias by county resolutions because of their lack of water, sewers, or safe and sanitary housing. Arizona has 77 colonias as designated by county resolutions, like in New Mexico, due to lack of potable water, inadequate sewers, and a lack of safe and sanitary housing. California has 32 colonias, mostly in rural parts of San Diego County (HUD Exchange n.d.).

Solutions for the colonia problem involve policymakers making decisions that enhance living conditions and an incremental approach to a housing strategy allowing informal housing options to exist to create opportunity. Since the passage of the National Affordable Housing Act (NAHA), with its state community block grants, HUD regulations, Environmental Protection Agency (EPA) regulations, USDA rules, and state codes have changed or modified legal definitions of colonias. This has enabled more flexible use of block grants. Texas has developed a set of self-help centers administered by non-profit organizations to provide on-site technical assistance to residents of colonias. They have converted contracts for deed to get residents out of rent-to-own-style contracts and made legal reforms to laws governing subdivision. They have increased the requirement to provide utilities at developer's expense or to post bonds to cover the expense of sewer and water utilities. They have closed loopholes in subdivision laws to bring subdivisions up to code and passed protections for purchaser's equity. Texas has expanded colonia-related programs such as the Owner-builder Loan Program, the Colonia Initiatives Advisory Committee, and a new Colonia Model Subdivision Program. New Mexico has begun closing loopholes utilized by colonia developers. Arizona has taken similar action against what are known as "wildcat" subdivisions (HUD Exchange n.d.).

Drugs, Guns, and Human Trafficking

Certain parts of the border region are especially dangerous due to the trafficking (smuggling) of drugs and humans going one way (Mexico to the United States), and guns going the other way (United States to Mexico). Lawmakers in the United States had attempted to stop the cross-border flow through a strategy of apprehension and deterrence. The INS, and now ICE, have put in place several efforts at border control. These include Operation Gatekeeper in San Diego, California (1994), Operation Hold the Line in El Paso, Texas (1994), Operation Rio Grande in McAllen, Texas (1997), Operation Safeguard in Tucson (1999), and the Arizona Border Control Initiative (2007) along the Arizona border (Department of Homeland Security

2018; Vulliamy 2010). On the Mexican side, these areas (e.g., Tijuana, Ciudad Juarez, Reynosa) are home to criminal operators headed by drug lords and their cartels, fugitives, crooked police, and corrupt politicians (Ellingwood 2009; Kirkpatrick 2012; Vulliamy 2010). Drugs, guns, and human trafficking are a multibillion-dollar-a-year illegal enterprise dominated by drug cartels, street gangs (like the MS-13), and corrupt government officials (House of Representatives 2004; Kirkpatrick 2012). A July 2018 smuggling attempt, for example, discovered by CBP, netted $635,000 worth of narcotics. The same July, CBP arrested 18 human smugglers attempting to smuggle 117 undocumented migrants in Texas and New Mexico. Between 2014 and 2018, CBP reported 1,468 deaths on the U.S.-Mexico border. For instance, in 2016, 151 died attempting to cross the Rio Grande river in Texas, and in 2017, 191 immigrants perished attempting to cross it (Department of Homeland Security 2018).

The border barriers (fences, wall portions, and traffic barriers at the border inspection stations) do not stop the flow of drugs, guns, and humans across the border. They may depress some trafficking, but mostly they divert the flow. Cartel smugglers tunnel under fences, climb over them, or simply go around them. Narcotics trafficking is so lucrative that the cartels can readily afford to dig relatively sophisticated tunnels from under buildings on the Mexican side to houses on the U.S. side to smuggle drugs in one direction and weapons back in the other direction. In January 2020, the CBP discovered the longest smuggling tunnel ever found at the border—4,309 feet long, it had a lift, a rail track, drainage and air ventilation systems, and high voltage electrical cables that connected an industrial site in Tijuana with a site in San Diego. The area is used by Mexico's Sinaloa cartel, one of the largest drug-trafficking operations along the border. The tunnel's average depth was 70 feet below the surface; and it was 5.5 feet high and 2 feet wide. Its sophistication and length evidence the time-consuming efforts transnational criminal organizations are willing to undertake to facilitate cross-border smuggling. More than a dozen tunnels have been found in the California border with Mexico since 2016. The second-longest tunnel was just short of 3,000 feet in length. In April 2016, a tunnel found in San Diego was used to transport an unprecedented cache of cocaine and marijuana. In August 2018, a 600-foot tunnel that stretched from a former KFC in Arizona to a site in Mexico was found. In March 2020, CBP discovered a tunnel from a restaurant in Mexico to a house in California, and in August 2020, CBP discovered an unfinished tunnel with rails, lighting, and ventilation in Tijuana (BBC 2020).

The drug cartels quickly discovered the profitability (at less danger and risk) of smuggling humans. A CBP arrest in July 2018 caught smugglers who had stashed 70 unauthorized immigrants from El Salvador in a "stash house" in Texas. The smugglers' services cost more than $12,000. There have been instances where smugglers have purchased and equipped trucks, sometimes with false compartments, to smuggle people across the border. In 2018, several instances of smuggling undocumented migrants across the border by this means resulted in multiple deaths when the truck crashed or when they crossed miles of desert without air conditioning to the back of the truck. Scores of migrants suffocated to death (Department of Homeland Security 2018). In Laredo, in 2018, unauthorized migrants were found being smuggled in duffle bags in the backs of trucks. In Tucson, 18 undocumented immigrants, including two children, were discovered in a utility truck that had no light, ventilation, air conditioning, or water, nor a means of escape from the inside. In January and February 2018 alone, the CBP rescued 448 unauthorized immigrants being smuggled in tractor trailers in the South Texas corridor. In July 2017, a tractor trailer filled with 90 migrants was discovered in a Walmart parking lot in San Antonio, Texas, with temperatures over 101 degrees Fahrenheit. Ten of the migrants had died of severe dehydration and lack of oxygen, and 20 more were found to be in "dire condition," having suffered a heatstroke. Authorities have a daunting task given that an estimated five million cars and trucks travel through the border daily.

The DHS estimates that half a million unauthorized immigrants enter the United States annually, although the number of apprehensions at the border has dropped steadily since 2005 (from 1,171,396 in 2005 to 303,916 in 2017). Since 2010, the numbers have consistently remained beneath 500,000 (Department of Homeland Security 2018; LeMay 2015, 2019).

The attempt by the U.S. Border Patrol to "blockade" the illegal immigration traffic has led to a shift in that traffic from San Diego and El Paso to the Arizona desert. This "man-made" shift of the migrant flow has resulted in literally thousands of deaths in the desert (Ellingwood 2009; Martinez 2006). Ciudad Juarez and Tijuana have become centers for the smuggling of people, weapons, and drugs across the borders; violence has escalated so much due to the narco-wars since 2009 that one study has described it as a near all-out civil war between rival narcotics cartels and gangs as well as between the cartels and the Mexican government. These criminal operations are likely related to the ruthless and systematic murder of hundreds of women in Ciudad Juarez (Martinez 2006; Vulliamy 2010).

Ever since the often coyote-guided unauthorized immigrant flow shifted to New Mexico and Arizona, it has disrupted life in the small towns along both sides of the border. On the U.S. side, it has led to angry, gun-toting ranchers and a spike in vigilantism. Arizona ranchers decry the trails of trash left by the thousands of unauthorized immigrants trekking across their ranch lands. Vigilante groups like the Minutemen patrol the border trying to stop the illegal immigrant flow (Ellingwood 2009; Gaynor 2009).

The harsh realities of the change in immigration policy since 2001 and the resulting "war on terrorism" and "war on drugs" has negatively impacted the lives of Border Patrol agents. It has greatly increased the risks they face, since they are often "out-gunned" by the narcotics traffickers. The increasingly lethal weaponry available to the drug cartels has fuelled a sort of "arms race." The Border Patrol has increasingly been militarized and uses Black Hawk helicopters supplied by the Department of Defense. Heavily armed response teams are like Swat (special weapons and tactics) teams, with military-grade automatic rifles, night-vision goggles, unmanned drones, and manned light aircraft. They have installed electronic and radar surveillance systems at the border to augment the border fence (Gaynor 2009; Hernandez 2010).

However, there seems to be no real solution to the problem of drug, gun, and human smuggling. Border control measures and the militarization of the border and of the Border Patrol have all failed to stop the flow. While there is demand for drugs and cheap unauthorized immigrant labor in the United States, or for women and even children for the sex trade, and as long as the supply of drugs and humans is readily available in Mexico, the best that policymakers can hope for is mitigation of the flow and not its cessation. The strategy of apprehension and deterrence simply has not worked (Vulliamy 2010).

Economic Cycles of Booms and Busts

As described in the first chapter, the Mexico-U.S. border region has experienced considerable economic development since 1848, but that development has come in distinct stages of booms and busts. A border boom occurred between 1890 and 1930, when border communities first flourished and railroads were built connecting northern Mexican states with the United States. The region's population on both sides of the border grew significantly. There was a considerable spike in Mexico's mining economy and, indeed, in the Mexican economy overall. This was followed by the first border bust, which happened between 1930 and 1940, the decade of the Great Depression. The region was affected by the prohibition (of alcohol) movement in the United States in the 1930s. A smaller boom took place during the Bracero Program years (1942–1964), when the border economy was impacted by the U.S. build up for World War II, the migration patterns set by the Bracero Program, and the growing post war trend in globalization (Lorey 1999). The most recent boom has been going on since 1994, triggered by the NAFTA and the growing globalization of the economies of Mexico and the United States.

Critically important for the economy of the border region was the development of the maquiladoras (Chatzkey, McBride, and Sergie 2020; Lorey 1999). The border region has been shaped by expanding capitalism and the exercise of state power, by both Mexico and the United States (St. John 2012). This section concentrates on the problems experienced in the region, especially on the Mexican side of the border, since 1964 and the advent of the maquiladoras program. A second point of focus is the period of economic development since 1994 and the negotiation and implementation of NAFTA (Chatz-key, McBride, and Sergie 2020).

A maquiladora is a manufacturing operation or factory established in Mexico, near the border, that imports raw materials and equipment for assembly, processing, or manufacturing. Critics of maquiladoras refer to them as sweat shops, especially those that make clothing for the U.S. market. The products of the maquiladoras are exported to Canada and the United States under trade agreement programs that grant them tax breaks and other trade benefits. Maquiladoras in Mexico produce electronic equipment, clothing, plastics, furniture, appliances, and auto parts, and they also assemble automobiles. Their impact on the Mexican economy is second only to that of oil production.

They were launched in 1964 with the Maquiladora, Manufacturing and Export Services Industry (IMMEX) program. They were designed to attract foreign investment, create jobs, foster industrialization, and boost Mexico's economy along the U.S. border. IMMEX is jointly administered by Mexico and the United States and offers foreign manufacturers tax incentives to invest in production and labor in Mexico. Investing companies benefit from lower production costs while maintaining control of their offshore production. The raw materials and production equipment are imported tax-free, so long as the final products are exported.

Between 1964 and 1994, some 2,000 maquiladoras were established on the Mexican side of the borderlands. These factories employed about 500,000 workers. Since 1994, and the implementation of NAFTA, maquiladoras have more than doubled and now employ more than one million Mexicans along the border. About 80 percent of all goods in Mexico are shipped to the United States, and about 65 percent of Mexico's exports are produced by maquiladoras.

The program provides many advantages to companies including duty-free import and export; a skilled labor force; low labor costs; low shipping costs (to the United States) and quick delivery; and reduced trade risks. The program's challenges include trade and customs compliance, finding and retaining skilled workers, accounting compliance, a changing political landscape (in both Mexico and the United States), and the financing of maquiladoras in Mexico. Critics also contend that they have negatively impacted the environment in Mexico and contributed to nearly unrestrained and poorly developed urbanization in the region, apart from contributing to both legal and illegal migration flows as well as negative impacts from NAFTA.

NAFTA was established in January 1994. It eliminated most tariffs on products traded between Canada, Mexico, and the United States. NAFTA fundamentally reshaped economic relations in North America. It implemented unprecedented integration between the developed economies of Canada and the United States and the developing economy of Mexico. NAFTA was negotiated under the administration of President George H.W. Bush, and it was implemented under the administrations of Presidents Bill Clinton, George W. Bush, and Barack Obama. In December 2019, the administration of President Donald Trump negotiated its replacement (or amendment, depending on who was assessing the new agreement) by the U.S.-Mexico-Canada Agreement (USMCA).

Economists generally credit NAFTA with benefiting all three North American economies. Regional trade increased from roughly $290 billion in 1993 to more than $1.1 trillion in 2016 (Chatzkey, McBride, and Sergie 2020). The two largest trade partners to whom the United States ships its exports are Canada and Mexico, respectively. Economists have estimated that NAFTA added $80 billion to the U.S. economy since 1995, as a result of several billions of dollars of growth per year. Critics of NAFTA point out that it has moved production to Mexico, widened the trade deficit, and cost an estimated 600,000 U.S. jobs. Environmentalists argue that it appreciably worsened the environment on both sides of the border, but especially contributed to pollution and environmental degradation on the Mexican side.

As to its impact on Mexico, economic analysts assess that NAFTA boosted Mexican farm exports to the United States three-fold and added hundreds of thousands of auto manufacturing jobs (parts and assembly) to the Mexican economy. Critics contend that poverty in Mexico remains at the same level as it was in 1994. They note that the per capita income in Mexico rose just 1.2 percent annually, a slower growth rate than that of Latin American countries like Brazil, Chile, and Peru over the same period. It cost Mexican small-scale farmers heavily, and it was a driving force of both legal and illegal immigration from Mexico to the United States, including the immigration of middle-class Mexicans. Economic development on the Mexican side of the border depended largely on proximity to the United States. A study of the cross-border economic development notes the disparate industrial growth and living standards and the income gap between the regions on either side of the U.S.-Mexico border (Anderson and Gerber 2009).

Given the great gap between the economies of Mexico and the United States, problems of booms and busts are likely to continue despite economic and trade policies and, some might say, because of those policies. There is a good deal of truth to the observation that when the U.S. economy "sneezes," the Mexican economy suffers a cold. President Donald Trump was critical of NAFTA and felt it generated insufficient benefits to the United States. He viewed the negotiation of USMCA as a solution to the problems of the United States caused by unforeseen consequences of NAFTA. However, until USMCA is implemented for some time, it is simply too early to assess the degree to which it offers any solutions to the problems associated with NAFTA, and to the boom-and-bust economic cycles experienced by the two economies.

Environmental and Water Problems

The U.S.-Mexico borderlands region, at 1,954 miles long and 200 miles wide, is complex in terms of environmental issues. The region has diverse terrains that are home to a variety of flora and fauna, several of which are endangered by their living in fragile ecosystems. The region is populated by people of varied races and ethnicities who differ in their perceptions of the environment and of man's relationship with the environment. The region's environmental issues are made more complicated by the need to reach binational agreements on vexing issues such as the management and distribution of shared resources, limited water supplies, preservation of fragile ecosystems, and an increasing degree of air and water pollution due to population growth and industrialization.

These problems or issues are also changing in terms of their impact due to population growth, climate change, and changes in government policy over a century, all of which have increased environmental disparities between the two neighboring countries. The building of border fences and walls and river engineering, as well as the installation of surveillance infrastructure, have all reshaped the natural landscape and complicated environmental issues (Alvarez 2019). The disparate industrial growth and the income gap it helps create between the regions on either side of the U.S.-Mexico border further complicates the environmental challenges that the region faces (Anderson and Gerber 2009).

Some of the more notable environmental issues of the region concern toxic waste, overuse or inequitable distribution of scarce water resources, reduction of aquafers, air pollution, and the endangerment of species by the fragmentation of ecosystems caused by barrier construction. These environmental problems have varying impacts on the region's indigenous communities, on U.S. residents, and on Mexican residents (Byrd and Mississippi 1976; Ebright 1994; Ebright and Hendricks 2019; Lusk, Staudt, and Moya 2012; Wilken-Robertson 2004).

Many of these environmental issues have been addressed by various binational and multinational treaties, conventions, and agreements that have directly impacted the border region. The most significant of those are the binational Banco Convention (1905), the bilateral executive agreement (1942) that began the Bracero Program, the bilateral Treaty for the Utilization of Waters of the Colorado and Tijuana Rivers and the Rio Grande (1944), the La Paz Agreement (1983), the multilateral trade agreements of NAFTA (1994), and the USMCA (2020).

A "banco" is land surrounded by bends in the river that are segregated by a cut-off due to changes in the river channel. Since the border line is often defined by rivers dividing the two countries, as the river channel changes, bancos are created and come into boundary dispute as to which country they belong to, and therefore whose environmental regulatory laws and regulations apply to the farmland located on the banco. They were first dealt with by the Convention of November 12, 1884, and then by the Convention of March 1, 1889, that established the International Boundary Commission (IBC), later amended to International Boundary and Water Commission (IBWC). The Banco Convention was a binational agreement signed in 1905 and ratified in 1907. It resulted in the exchange of hundreds of bancos created by the meandering of the channels of the Rio Grande, Colorado, and Tijuana rivers.

The bilateral executive agreement of August 4, 1942, the Farm Labor Agreement, began what became known as the Bracero Program. It was an agreement between U.S. president Franklin Roosevelt and Mexican president Manuel Avila Camacho (who served from December 1, 1940, to November 30, 1946). As an executive agreement, it was binding only during the terms of the two presidents who negotiated and signed it. However, in the case of the Bracero Program it was extended and replaced by the Act of October 31, 1949 (63 Stat. 1052; LeMay and Barkan 1999, 217–218). The Agricultural Act of 1949 codified prior provisions of the temporary agricultural workers agreement and lasted until 1964. The Bracero Program brought hundreds of thousands of agricultural workers north from Mexico into the United States and significantly impacted the environment of the U.S. side.

The Treaty for the Utilization of Waters of the Colorado and Tijuana Rivers and the Rio Grande was negotiated and signed on November 14, 1944 (IBWC 2012). It covered the Rio Grande (Rio Bravo in Mexico) from Fort Quitman, Texas, to the Gulf of Mexico. It was aimed at obtaining the most complete and satisfactory use of the river waters. It modified the IBWC (created in 1889), responsible for the diversion and storage of river water and flood control by establishing upper and lower international dams and reservoirs. The treaty had significant environmental impact on both sides of the border, and its water usage affected Anglo, Latino, and Native American farmlands and communities (Alvarez 2019; Ebright 1994; Ebright and Hendricks 2019).

The Agreement on Cooperation for the Protection and Improvement of the Environment in the Border Area, known as the La Paz Agreement, was signed into law on August 14, 1983 (EPA 2015). Four subsequent programs were implemented under the agreement, each designed to cope with environmental destruction in the border region resulting from the maquiladora industries, the population growth they triggered, the lack of infrastructure to accommodate this population, the lack of environmental regulations for air and water pollution in Mexico, and the United States' environmentally destructive tendencies. It has remained the major agreement for bilateral cooperation on environmental protection in the border region ever since it came into being.

The IBWC was created in 1889, with two sections, one located in El Paso, Texas, and the other in Ciudad Juarez, Chihuahua. It was modified in 1944 to include water regulations and to focus on sanitation, distribution, and flood control of natural river waters and to regulate the distribution of boundaries between the United States and Mexico. IBWC covers water distribution of the rivers Rio Grande, Colorado, Tijuana, and Santa Cruz, and of the tributaries that flow into them. In addition to flood control, the IBWC deals with pollution and waste flowing into these rivers, and water treatment plants, dams, and levee systems. The Border 2012 agreement was the third program under the La Paz Agreement. It completed 400 projects using a community-based approach that addressed the most serious environmental and public health concerns reported by residents and workers along the shared border region (IBWC 2012).

More recently, developing problems that have had significantly negative impacts on the border environment are those associated with the U.S. policies enacted to "control the borders"—the Secure Fence Act of 2006, and Executive Order 13767 to build a border wall.

The construction of about 700 miles of high-security fencing along the U.S.-Mexico border has resulted in fragmentation of the habitat of wildlife, including some protected and endangered species (Alvarez 2019; Anderson and Gerber 2009). Environmentalists argued that extending fencing, or building the wall demanded by President Trump in 2017 would have adversely effected plants and animals in the Sonoran Desert, and disrupted the migration of animals for water, plants, and habitat resources that they need to survive. Except for high-flying birds, most animals cannot move along their usual ranges along the border areas. This would especially affect javelinas, ocelots, the Sonoran pronghorn and bighorn sheep, the Mexican gray wolf, and the cactus ferruginous pigmy owl. According to the Center for Biological Diversity, 30 animals living in the Arizona and Sonora would be endangered by the border wall, including 93 threatened and endangered species. Even the much fewer miles of border fence that the Trump administration did manage to build have harmed or destroyed the critical habitat of 25 species. A true "border wall" of hundreds of miles length would have unquestionably harmed border communities, perpetuated human suffering, destroyed thousands of acres of habitat, and halted the cross-border migration of dozens of animal species (Greenwald et al. 2017, 13–16; Center for Biological Diversity n.d.).

The construction of a true border wall (as opposed to a fence) would increase greenhouse gas emissions due to the enormous amount of concrete manufacturing required. Construction of a wall along the entire 2,000-mile border would affect more than 800 species, of which 140 are endangered and cost many billions of dollars.

A solution to the problem is stopping construction of a border wall. Mitigating the effects of the border fence has been one of the aims of the Lower Rio Grande Valley National Wildlife Refuge and the Sabal Palm Audubon Center and Sanctuary.

The La Paz Agreement requires hazardous waste created by U.S. corporations in Mexico to be transported back to the United States for disposal. However, only 91 of 600 manufacturing plants located along the Texas-Mexico border have returned hazardous (toxic) waste to the United States since 1987. Maquiladora industries on the border often dump or burn wastes thereby causing water and air pollution, and industrial accidents at the plants have killed eight workers and injured many others (Kelly 2007).

Air pollution is endemic in the region, created by vehicular and industrial emissions. According to the Bureau of Transportation Statistics, in 2016, 87,462,517 vehicles went through the border (trucks, cars, buses, and trains) (Bureau of Transportation Statistics n.d.).

Transborder environmental problems disproportionately and negatively impact indigenous communities and border tribes who depend on the natural environment for sustenance, survival, and ritual ceremonies. Indian reservations are affected by air pollution, traffic congestion, the extraction of natural resources (mining), and the burning or dumping of solid and hazardous waste (Ebright and Hendricks 2019; Nitze et al. 2001). They have been found to be especially susceptible to the COVID-19 pandemic, with infection and death rates three to four times that of people in off-reservation areas. Border tribes depend on river water and groundwater basins. The Tohono O'odham Nation has six indigenous villages on both sides of the border, and they have opposed the Trump border wall for its fragmentation of their community and their ancestral lands (Ebright and Hendricks 2019). Native tribes (Pueblos) have had some success in using courts and land and water rights claims to fight negative environmental impacts.

Foreign Policy Issues

Foreign policy refers to the conduct of relations between and among nation-states. Tensions between countries arising from conflicting national interests create problems and issues between them. Sometimes these problems lead to war. The solution to war is generally achieved by a peace treaty, such as the Treaty of Guadalupe Hidalgo of 1848. More often, problems can be solved (or at least temporarily "resolved") when two nations work together to reduce disequilibrium (Henderson 2011). Nation-states tend to want to dominate their territory and region of influence and try to limit the mobility of people crossing it without authorization. Often, people work around such "borderline defining" and cross the border with relative impunity, which is certainly the case for the U.S.-Mexico border, one of the more porous borders in the world (Nichols 2018).

The fact that the United States and Mexico share a 2,000-mile border means that the two must cope with problems and misunderstandings through economic and political relations, often formalized by conventions, executive agreements, and treaties (O'Neil and O'Neil 2013). Misunderstandings of the law and the interpretation of conventions, protocols, and treaties are generally resolved in courts (Reich 2017). Of course, the disparity between the two nations in terms of economic, military, and political power and in terms of the relative sizes of their economies and populations gives a decided advantage to the United States when it comes to achieving foreign policy goals through diplomatic relations.

This section discusses more than a dozen international agreements, each of which can be viewed as negotiating a "solution" to the problems of the region and between the two sovereign nation-states. They consist of bilateral treaties and conventions, bilateral agreements, and two multilateral treaties. They are briefly discussed here in the order of their date of their adoption.

The Adams-Onis Treaty of 1819 was negotiated between Spain and the United States to settle the disputed boundary between the United States and New Spain. The demarcation of the boundary did not last long, legally less than a decade, because Mexico became independent of Spain and so the treaty was no longer binding. However, Mexico essentially negotiated the same boundary line by the Treaty of Limits (January 12, 1828).

Tensions between the two countries over border issues and the annexation of Texas resulted in the Mexican-American War. The war was settled by the Treaty of Guadalupe Hidalgo (February 2, 1848, effective May 30, 1848). The treaty ended the war but forced Mexico to cede about half of its territory (all of what was then called Northern Mexico) to the United States.

The United States wanted some additional land in dispute after the Treaty of Guadalupe Hidalgo, which it settled by the Gadsden Purchase. That treaty was negotiated on December

30, 1853, and took effect on June 8, 1854. It transferred some 30,000 acres of land to the United States. Another treaty that settled a dispute between the two countries was the McLane-Ocampo Treaty of 1859. It is named after Robert McLane, U.S. ambassador to Mexico, and Melchor Ocampo, minister of foreign affairs. It is known as the Treaty of Transit and Commerce as it gives U.S. citizens the right to safe transit across the Isthmus of Tehauntepec and across Northern Mexico to the Gulf of California and the lower Rio Grande.

The next significant agreement was the Banco Convention of 1905. It was agreed to on March 20, 1905 and took effect on June 5, 1907. It settled disputes over hundreds of bancos—lands created by the meandering of the Rio Grande/Rio Bravo river. The convention modified prior ones on the matter—one signed on November 12, 1884, and the other being the Convention of March 1, 1889—that had established the International Border Commission.

Mexico experienced a revolution in the 1920s that required two settlements. The first was the De la Huerta-Lamont Treaty, which was negotiated by the 45th president of Mexico, Adolfo de la Huerta. It was signed on June 16, 1922, and took effect on September 22, 1922, but expired on June 30, 1924. It was an initial step toward normalizing foreign relations between Mexico and the United States and became the basis for several decades of Mexican foreign financing agreements. The second was the Convention of Claims, also known as the Bucareli Treaty of 1923. It was concerned with compensation for losses suffered by U.S. citizens or by U.S. companies operating in Mexico because of the Mexican Revolution. It was negotiated by Mexican president Alvaro Obregon and U.S. president Warren Harding, but it was never formally ratified and was later cancelled by Mexican president Plutarco Elias Calles.

The United States–Mexico Convention Relating to Final Adjustment of Certain Unsettled Claims was signed on November 19, 1941. Mexico agreed to pay the United States

$40 million for damages, losses, and the destruction or inter-ference of property of the nationals of either country.

On August 4, 1942, a bilateral executive agreement was reached, known as the Farm Labor Agreement. It was between U.S. president Franklin Roosevelt and Mexican president Manuel Avila Camacho and began what became known as the Bracero Program, authorizing (and legalizing) the temporary immigration of Mexican farm laborers to the United States. It was formalized legislatively by Congress in 1949, and the program ran until 1964. Hundreds of thousands of Mexican laborers went north to the United States, the vast majority to the borderlands region. They forged chain-migration patterns that affected the region and the migration of both legal and unauthorized immigrants to the United States, effects that per-sist to this day.

On November 14, 1944, a treaty was signed regarding the management of surface boundary waters of rivers in the bor-der zone. It took effect on February 3, 1944 and is known as the Treaty for the Utilization of Waters of the Colorado and Tijuana Rivers and the Rio Grande. It covered the use of waters of the Rio Grande (Rio Bravo) from Fort Quitman, Texas, to the Gulf of Mexico to obtain the most complete and satisfac-tory utilization of the waters. It was signed by Mexican presi-dent Francisco Castillo Najera and it modified the IBWC with regard to diversion of water, storage of water in reservoirs, and flood controls by upper and lower international dams. It was modified again by the Border 2012 Program, signed April 1, 2003 (IBWC 2012).

In 1970 a Boundary Treaty was signed that transferred 823 acres from Mexico to the United States for banco-type lands created by the shifting of the Rio Grande River.

The La Paz Agreement of August 14, 1983, as mentioned earlier in the chapter, is the most comprehensive treaty between the two nations regarding cooperation for the protection and improvement of the environment in the Border Area. It has governed water usage and land issues since then.

Finally, a trilateral free-trade treaty between Canada, Mexico, and the United States took effect on January 1, 1994. Known as NAFTA, it created a trilateral trade bloc. It was initiated during the presidential administration of Ronald Reagan. It was negotiated by the administration of U.S. president George H.W. Bush, Mexican president Carlos Salinas de Gortari, and Canadian prime minister Brian Mulroney. It governed free trade (no tariffs) from 1994 to 2020. President Donald Trump was unhappy with the terms of the treaty and the impact it had on U.S. trade deficits. He forced the renegotiation or amendment of the treaty, which resulted in the USMCA being signed on July 1, 2020. As discussed in the earlier sections, NAFTA had a great impact on the U.S.-Mexico border region. This aspect will be discussed further in the next section, which concerns problems and issues arising out of the trend toward a global economy.

Global Economic Issues

Globalization has been described as a complex process that brings about interaction and integration among peoples, companies, and governments worldwide. With globalization, organizations, particularly businesses, begin operating on an international scale. The globalization process has been categorized into four types—cultural, economic, political, and social (Bacon 2004; Danelo 2008; Ganster and Lorey 2008; Staudt, Payan, and Kruszewski 2009).

Critics of globalization emphasize its negative effects—increased transportation and a global shift in pollution-causing manufacturing resulting in environmental degradation. With respect to the borderlands zone, critics attribute the following to globalization: (1) the exploitation of child and women laborers, (2) an increase in sexual and labor trafficking, (3) a rapid increase in deplorable housing conditions outside cities like Tijuana and Ciudad Juarez, (4) the retaliation against union organizers by maquiladora corporations, and (5) growing economic inequality in the region (Bacon 2004; Ganster 2015; Tiano, Murphy-Agular, and Bigej 2012).

The many negative effects of globalization for businesses include: (1) increased risks and uncertainties brought about by the high degree of integration of markets, (2) intensification of competition, (3) increased imitation, (4) price and profit swings, and (5) business and product destruction (Mourdouk-outas 2011).

Todd Miller notes that the global industrial complex influences and sustains the lines that divide the globe. He argues that the U.S.-Mexico border really extends well beyond the frontier line of 100 miles that the DHS considers the border zone. Through interviews of residents on both sides of the border line, Miller tracks the influence of the border region on immigrants from countries as far away as Guatemala and Honduras to the Caribbean, Israel, the Philippines, and Kenya (Miller 2019).

The clearest evidence of the trend toward globalization in the border zone is found in the development of maquiladoras and NAFTA. Critics of both these developments draw a devastating, in-depth portrait of the effects of maquiladoras and NAFTA on border workers and the border region: (1) the extremes of poverty and wealth, (2) repression and struggle, and (3) the exploitation of child labor in the Mexico Valley. Critics trace the emergence of a new social consciousness in the region, and how organizations on both sides of the border are forming transnational social networks by joining together to search for economic and social justice, and in the process of doing so, are creating transnational social networks and social spaces (Ashbee, Clausen, and Pederson 2007; Bacon 2004; Ganster 2015).

NAFTA, as described earlier, increased the flow of global migration to the border region. NAFTA provided a spur to the maquiladora industries on the Mexican side of the border. The maquiladoras, in turn, brought about (1) rapid, massive, and largely uncontrolled urbanization, (2) the exploitive treatment of Central Americans, (3) a substantial and sustained increase in illegal immigration, (4) a blatant abuse of human rights and gender violence, and (5) drug-cartel turf wars in Mexican border cities like Tijuana, Nogales, Ciudad Juarez, and Nuevo Laredo.

All four of these cities experienced very rapid growth and population density. Tijuana, Baja California, Mexico has a population over 2 million and a population density of nearly 7,000 per square mile; Nogales, Sonora Mexico has a population of nearly 250,000 and a population density of about 1,000 per square mile; Ciudad Juarez, Chihuahua Mexico has a population of about 1.5 million and a density of more than 10,500 per square mile; and Nuevo Laredo, Tamaulipas Mexico has a population of about 650,000 and a density of about 1,260 per square mile. The increase in population and density has contributed to increased air and water pollution and related environmental degradation (Ashbee, Clausen, and Pedersen 2007; Danelo 2008; Ganster 2015; Mehta 2019; Staudt, Payan and Kruszewski 2009; Tiano, Murphy-Agular and Bigej 2012).

On the U.S. side, the rapid growth and increased immigration flow (of both legal and undocumented immigrants) have exacerbated concerns over border security, the cultural identity of their Hispanic population, and Hispanic political incorporation or integration. San Diego's population rose from just over 1.2 million in 2000 to an estimated 1.4 million in 2019. San Diego has a population density of 4,441 per square mile and 32 percent of its population is Hispanic. Nogales, Arizona, at just over 20,000 in population, has a density of 974 people per square mile; 10 percent of its population is Hispanic. El Paso, Texas, with an estimated population of 682,000 in 2019, has a population density of 2,663 people per square mile. El Paso's population is just under 83 percent Hispanic, 1.3 percent Asian, and about 4 percent Black. Laredo, Texas, has a population of just over 260,000 in its metropolitan area, a population density of 2,250 people per square mile, and a population that is 95 percent Hispanic.

Like the Mexican side, the U.S. side also shows considerable and pronounced negative effects attributed to globalization and NAFTA: (1) precarious and low-paying jobs, (2) questions of Mexican identity, (3) troubling social policy, (4) an increase in anti-immigrant backlash associated with the increase in undocumented immigrants from Central America to both sides of the border region, (5) an exacerbation of concerns over border security and border violence, and (6) an increase in the detention and deportation of undocumented immigrants from Mexico and Central America by both the Mexican and U.S. governments (Ashbee, Clausen, and Pederson 2007; Mehta 2019; Danelo 2008; Ganster 2015; Staudt, Payan, and Kruszewski 2009; Lusk, Staudt, and Moya 2012; Regan 2016).

Solutions to problems associated with globalization remain elusive. The amendment to the NAFTA agreement (USMCA), negotiated by the Trump administration, was justified by an attempt to address problems, especially the trade deficit issue of NAFTA, attributed to globalization. Negotiations were aimed specifically at unanticipated consequences of NAFTA. It remains to be seen whether the new agreement materially affects those entrenched problems. Most of the social changes that are needed to resolve—if not solve—the vexing and persistent problems associated with globalization and NAFTA, as evident in the border region, will likely require the cooperation of local and regional governments spurred by reforms advocated by nongovernmental advocacy organizations (Danelo 2008; Ganster 2015; Staudt, Payan, and Kruszewski 2009; Tiano, Murphy-Agular, and Bigej 2012).

The effectiveness of such social change spurred by cooperation of local and regional governments seemed unlikely as recently as 2018. However, the global COVID-19 pandemic may change the equation as to the likelihood of substantial social change. One predicted impact by experts coping with the pandemic is a long-term slowing down if not a reversal in globalization. The disruption in supply chains of personal protective equipment and COVID-19 diagnostic and antibody tests have spurred an increasing number of nation-states to rebuild their own manufacturing and distribution chains of such products rather than relying, for example, on supply from China.

Facing the common enemy called coronavirus has raised awareness of our common humanity, and this may change the social dynamics that previously entrenched and fuelled the racial/ethnic divisions so evident in the border region. Some observers of the remarkably quick calls for and enactment of social/racial reforms advocated by social movements like #BlackLivesMatter have suggested that the COVID-19 pandemic has played a role in that social change. A result of the pandemic may be the forging of transnational and binational social networks essential to bringing about solutions to the social policy conundrums that have previously stymied effective reform. A direction for effective policy reforms that have previously been seen as highly unlikely, if not impossible, now seems at least possible. The facing of the common viral enemy has led to an unprecedented level of cooperation by governments, biomedical scientists, and biomedical corporations to find effective treatments and to develop the vaccines to battle the virus. That cooperation may spill over from medicine to other areas of social cooperation. The pandemic has also made ever more evident the problems of overreliance on globalization.

Illegal Immigration Flows

In the United States, there are two ways by which an immigrant ends up having unauthorized status. There are an estimated 10.5–11 million unauthorized immigrants in the United States. About 40–50 percent of all unauthorized immigrants come to the United States with documentation, that is, with a visa of some sort. They become unauthorized if they overstay the time of their conditional or temporary visa (e.g., a tourist visa). Another way they become unauthorized is by breaking a condition of their visa; for example, immigrants entering with a student visa who then accept employment while in the United

States. The most common way they end up having unauthorized status—and this is what most people associate with "illegal immigrants"—is by entering the United States without documentation. Roughly 55–60 percent of unauthorized immigrants are undocumented immigrants, and they are by far the type that most commonly resides in the U.S.-Mexico border region. The greatest numbers of undocumented immigrants are found in California and Texas (LeMay 2015, 3–4). The greatest numbers of undocumented immigrants are from Mexico although—as indicated by apprehensions at the southern border since 2010—undocumented immigrants from Central America (specifically from El Salvador, Guatemala, and Honduras) are now a close second (LeMay 2015, 220–222). In the four states along the U.S.-Mexico border, one can only estimate the number of individuals who are unauthorized immigrants, but they undoubtedly are a significant number and make up a sizable portion of the border-zone population.

California has 11 million immigrants (foreign-born), and among them, 52 percent are documented and 23 percent are undocumented. The remaining 25 percent have become naturalized citizens. From 2010 to 2017, the number of undocumented immigrants in California declined from 2.9 million to 2.4 million (Johnson and Sanchez 2019). Texas has an estimated 1.6 million undocumented immigrants, which is about 33 percent of the state's foreign-born population and about 6 percent of the state's total population. At least 1.4 million native-born citizens in Texas have at least one family member who is undocumented (American Immigration Council 2020). In New Mexico, there are about 85,000 undocumented immigrants who comprise about 37 percent of the state's foreign-born population, and about 4 percent of its total population. Mexico, contributing 72 percent of New Mexico's immigrants, is by far the leading nation-of-origin of the state's foreign-born population. At least 11 percent of the state's native-born population has at least one immigrant parent (American Immigration

Council 2020). Arizona has about 275,000 undocumented immigrants. They comprise about 28 percent of the state's foreign-born population and 4 percent of its total population. Within Arizona's foreign-born population, 55 percent are from Mexico, 4 percent from Canada, 4 percent from India, 4 percent from the Philippines, and 2 percent from China (American Immigration Council 2020).

Several people who fear and oppose undocumented immigrants believe that many of them, if not most, come to use U.S. welfare programs. However, the fact is that most of them come to the United States to work, and they comprise 8–10 percent of the U.S. labor force (LeMay 2015, 222). In Spanish, the undocumented from Mexico are called the *alambrista*. The term refers to those who cross into the United States via its border with Mexico (thus, it is used to refer to undocumented migrants who are Mexicans or Central Americans). It translates as "tightrope walker" or "wire crosser" in English (Cult and Carrasco 2004).

Undocumented immigration has been viewed as a major problem since the 1970s, and U.S. immigration policy has used various crack down at the border policies designed to prevent it through increasingly strict migration policing controls— that is, a policy of "deterrence" by the criminalization of immigration (Ackerman and Furman 2013; Bender 2012; Chacon and Davis 2006; De Leon 2015; Ellingwood 2009; Frey 2019; Gutierrez 1995; Hernandez 2010; Payan 2006). The resurgence of reactionary anti-immigrant politics and racist vigilante violence has failed to deter the flow. The most problematic effect of Border Patrol blockades is that it has driven those seeking to cross to rely on coyotes and dramatically increased (to the thousands) the number of deaths in the Sonora desert (De Leon 2015; Ellingwood 2009; Frey 2019; Levario 2012; Martinez 2006).

As the statistics cited above indicate, a problem related to the illegal immigration flow is the number of "split" families, where some or even most members of the family are in the United States legally or are even native-born citizens but one or more of the family members is undocumented. The problem is especially poignant for the Dreamers who were brought here as children in illegal status but have often known no other country or home than the United States (LeMay 2019, 56–57; Regan 2016).

Efforts to deter the flow of the undocumented by the Trump administration's "zero tolerance" policy led to ICE and HHS detention centers being overwhelmed. This is illustrated by events at the massive Elroy Detention Center, a "for-profit prison" in Arizona. Elroy is in Pinal County, Arizona, and has had 15 detainee deaths (2003–2016) including five suicides. The increasingly draconian detention and deportation policies have expanded the police powers of the immigration law enforcement and have enriched the private prison system whose very profits are derived directly from human suffering, but they have failed to deter asylum-seekers, refugees, and undocumented immigrants (Regan 2016).

The root of the problem of illegal immigration flow and the failure of U.S. immigration policy to deter or stem the flow lies in the fact that undocumented immigrants are largely driven by push factors over which U.S. policymakers have little or no control. U.S. immigration policy primarily addresses pull factors, and they are simply no match for the force of push factors (LeMay 2015, 4–9).

The illegal immigration flow declined most dramatically during the "Great Recession" years—from 2008 to 2010—when apprehensions at the U.S.-Mexico border (the most often used metric for undocumented immigration) declined from nearly 900,000 in 2008 to 439,382 in 2010. It has remained under 500,000 annually since then (LeMay 2015, 220; LeMay 2019, 222).

Illegal immigration is a classic example of a public policy conundrum. Proposed solutions that have been tried have been politically popular but largely ineffective. Failed policy efforts to "solve" the illegal immigration problem once and for all include such notable attempts as Immigration Reform and Control Act of 1986, the Immigration Act of 1990, California's Proposition 187 initiative passed in 1994, and Illegal Immigration Reform and Immigrant Responsibility Act enacted in 1996 (LeMay and Barkan 1999, 282–310; Magana 2008); and since the 2001 terrorist attacks, policy efforts have included the USA Patriot Acts (I passed in 2001, and II passed in 2006), the Department of Homeland Security Act of 2002, and the Secure Fence Act of 2006. Attempts to solve the problem by a more progressive approach (DACA and DAPA, the various proposed Dream Acts and Comprehensive Immigration Reform bills, for instance) have been politically unpopular and to date have not been enacted. The failure to "solve" the illegal immigration problem has had its greatest impact on the border zone (LeMay 2019).

It may well be that the illegal immigration problem simply cannot be solved by U.S. immigration policy initiatives. A degree of "resolution" may be more of a result of economic trends and events. To get at the push forces of undocumented immigration, the United States has to use foreign policy that supports improvements in the economies of such sending countries as Mexico, El Salvador, Guatemala, and Honduras. Such policy initiatives require bilateral or multilateral diplomatic efforts. These policy efforts, moreover, have been politically unpopular or are often simply siphoned off by the corrupt governments receiving such aid. To the extent that the United States can do so, another approach to resolve the problem of immigration flow may be to help reduce the violence of the drug cartels in the sending countries, or the answer might lie in bringing about reforms to prevent the worst abuses of the maquiladora system. Again, the prospects for these policy changes are dim as they, too, are politically unpopular. A degree of resolution might simply need to wait until there is evidence that the Biden administration is capable of bringing about more substantial change.

Medicine, Medical Accessibility, and Medical Tourism

Economic and cultural disparities are at the heart of cross-border medical issues and concerns. The great differences between the economies of Mexico and the United States impact border medicine in several ways. This section will briefly discuss healthcare accessibility, public health concerns, and medical tourism related to economic disparities. It will also discuss the medical approach of *curanderismo* (folk healing) to cultural disparities.

The environmental degradation discussed earlier—in terms of air and water pollution and toxic and solid waste disposal—contributes to public health concerns, especially on the Mexican side of the border and especially in those areas where the maquiladoras predominate the local economy. Risks for incidents of epidemic disease outbreaks are increased and access to hospitals, clinics, and healthcare services lessened due to the conditions of poverty in the area. On the U.S. side, poor communities like the colonias (discussed previously) face similar concerns regarding access to health services and facilities. Among Indian Pueblo communities, often some of the poorest on the U.S side of the border zone, access to healthcare is a chronic issue (Jusionyte 2018; Ebright and Hendricks 2019; Hernandez 2018).

Solutions to problems of healthcare access and public health depend on changes in public policy priorities. Simply put, public health and healthcare access require greater public investment. A public policy shift to put a higher value on public health and on healthcare access is more likely with the election of President Joe Biden and his administration's approach to public health care, the vaccination against the pandemic virus. A dramatic shift in policy priorities that seemed so unlikely prior to late 2019 may be more possible now, given the apparent change in public attitudes regarding the value and importance of public health following the COVID-19 pandemic. The importance of preventive health measures has rather suddenly become more obvious and politically supported.

Sometimes the border divide affects the work of emergency responders, such as paramedic teams, who rush patients across country lines to save lives and prevent a disaster accentuated by the zone's often harsh terrain. Undocumented migrants climbing over walls and fences or crossing many miles of desert terrain cause an increase in medical crisis events. Over time, emergency responder organizations have developed binational arrangements to better cope with the need to save lives and work around politicized issues like border security, undocumented migration, and general public access to healthcare. Increasingly, paramedics take patients to the closest available facility without regard to border lines or the legal status of the individual (Jusionyte 2018; Romero 2008). Emergency responders as well as Border Patrol agents have had to deal with increased incidents of health emergencies (and deaths) as the militarization at the borders has led to increased traffic of undocumented migrants across the harsh desert terrain (Cult and Carrasco 2004; Ellingwood 2009; Hernandez 2018; and Levario 2012).

The solution to these problems seems to be having more of the informal arrangements between local governments on both sides of the border. A bilateral agreement, such as those negotiated for water usage issues, would be useful and probably preferable to informal arrangements, but such a solution is again very unlikely given the apparent strained relations between the United States and Mexico since 2017.

The disparity between the economies of the two countries is also responsible for the rise in medical tourism. As healthcare costs increase rapidly on the U.S. side, more Americans are crossing the border seeking prescription drugs in Mexico to reduce their medication costs. For residents who live along the southern border, a "vacation" trip across the border gives them access to prescription drugs that cost as much as four times less than they do if purchased in the United States (Eure 2020; Trevino 2018).

A solution would require a change in U.S. law regarding the importation of prescription drugs from Mexico (or from Canada, for that matter). However, given the lobby influence of "Big Pharma" in the United States that is politically unlikely even if legally possible. Again, however, the shift in U.S. public opinion on public health and preventive medicine may enable policy reforms in 2022 that seemed implausible in 2019.

Even routine healthcare visits across the border (for such services as dermatology, gynecology, and dentistry) can be at far lesser cost and usually at far lesser wait times than they entail if one were to see a doctor for the same services in the United States (Trevino 2018). In major Mexican cities that are well-known tourist destinations among English speakers (like the border cities of Tijuana and Mexicali but also those further from the border, such as Cancun, Guadalajara, and Puerto Vallarta), the quality of healthcare, if procured at private hospitals and clinics, is not very different from what is available in the United States. However, healthcare in these cities is considerably more affordable, especially given the strong U.S. dollar. A regular industry—medical tourism— has developed to meet the demand. Getting a dental crown, for example, can cost $175 in Tijuana compared to $500–700 on the U.S. side of the border. A routine office visit to a dermatologist in Mexico costs about $300, which is three to four times less than in the United States. Gastric bypass surgery in Tijuana costs under $5000, whereas in the United States, just across the border, such surgery typically costs $20,000–25,000 (Tessada 2020; Trevino 2018). Given the disparities in the economies of the United States and Mexico, it is likely that there is no real solution to medical accessibility and cost differential issues. It must be noted that this is not considered to be a problem for those Americans who live near the border and can readily avail themselves of access to healthcare services in Mexico.

The difference between the cultures of Mexico and the United States is at issue for what is called *curanderismo* (Hendrickson 2014). *Curanderismo* is a hybrid tradition of indigenous and Iberian Catholic pharmacopeias, rituals, and notions of self. It has been part of the border region for a long time. *Curanderismo* treats the sick person with a variety of healing modalities, including herbal remedies and intercessory prayer, body massage, and "energy manipulation." In the United States, it would be characterized as a "holistic" approach to medicine and medical treatments. The U.S. medical establishment views it with a skepticism that considers it bordering on quackery. *Curanderismo* entails an approach that treats the whole patient: body, soul, and community. It is accepted more easily within Native American communities and among a growing number of Americans open to metaphysical ideas like spiritualism, mesmerism, New Thought, New Age, and energy-based alternative medicines.

Curanderismo evolved from Mexican American religious healing traditions that developed at the end of the nineteenth century. It entered the U.S.-Mexico border region with Mexican immigrants and is found more often in communities with a high percentage of Mexican immigrants (e.g., San Diego, El Paso, and Tucson). From there, it spread to Anglo communities—particularly ones with multi-ethnic populations—outside the border zone. *Curanderismo* is a notable example of the influence of Mexican Americans on the cultural and religious practices found in the American West. It is less a problem than an issue. It is an example of transcultural exchange (Hendrickson 2014). Holistic approaches to medicine are increasingly recognized and accepted. The COVID-19 pandemic experience is causing a shift in cultural attitudes toward medicine in the United States (and, indeed, globally) and that shift may be the most likely source for a resolution of the issue.

Political Incorporation

Incorporation is the gradual inclusion of minority group members into the cultural, economic, social, and, finally, political structures of the majority society (LeMay 2009, 66). Latino political incorporation has followed four distinct pathways: (1) demands/protests (such as sit-ins, demonstrations, boycotts, etc.), (2) nonconfrontational political evolution (accommodation), (3) legal challenges to structural barriers, and (4) coalition politics (DeSipio 1996; Geron 2005, 13; LeMay 2009, 168).

Problems concerning political incorporation include structural barriers such as gerrymandering, voter dilution, and voter suppression. Gerrymandering is a form of de jure discrimination. It involves drawing electoral district lines in such a way that a social group (racial or ethnic) is disadvantaged. It is often done to split or dilute the votes of a racial or ethnic group so that they will be less able to elect one of their own to public office (LeMay 2009, 21). Gerrymandering takes place during the process of reapportionment and redistricting. Western states have a long history of racial (Black, Asian) and ethnic (mostly regarding Hispanics) redistricting struggles in which gerrymandering was used against Hispanic or racial minority voters (Moncrief 2011). The political battle against gerrymandering and voter suppression is ongoing (Daley 2020). Racial gerrymandering was ruled unconstitutional by the U.S. Supreme Court in *Gomillion v. Lightfoot* (364 U.S. 339, 1960; LeMay 2009, 371). It is, however, still used against Latino voters, especially in Texas. In 2017, a Texas redistricting plan was ruled unconstitutional in a district court but was subsequently upheld by the U.S. Supreme Court (PBS News Hour 2017). The major U.S. Supreme Court case concerning voter dilution was *Thornburg v. Gingles* (478 U.S. 30, 1986; Davidson 1984;

LeMay 2009, 373). In a 5-4 decision in 2019, *Rucho v. Common Cause* upheld the constitutionality of partisan gerrymandering.

Mexican Americans in the border region have had a long political struggle toward incorporation that has been more successful in California and New Mexico than it has been in Texas and Arizona (DeLeon and Griswold del Castillo 2012; Gonzalez 2009; LeMay 2009, 145–149; Massey et al. 1990; Navarro 2005).

Mexican American groups that used the strategy of legal challenges to overcome structural barriers to incorporation are well represented by the G.I. Forum and the League of United Latin American Citizens (LULAC) (LeMay 2009, 148; Ramos 1998; Strum 2010). Mexican American (Chicano) groups that used the demands/protest strategy that had relevance for the southwest border region include United Farm Workers (UFW), the Alianza Federal de Mercedes, the Brown Berets, the Crusade for Justice, and Mexicano Estudiente Chicano de Aztlan (MECHA) (LeMay 2009, 299–308). Groups using the non-confrontational political evolution pathway include La Raza Unida Partido (now UNIDOS) and the Community Service Organization (CSO). Groups using the coalition politics pathway include the Mexican American Nationalist Organization (MANO), the United States Hispanic Chamber of Commerce (USHCC), the Hispanic Congressional Caucus, and United We Dream (LeMay 2009, 145–150; Orr and Morel 2018).

The electoral strength of the Latino vote has yet to live up to its full potential. That, in part, is due to the structural barriers mentioned in the beginning of this section. But is also because of the way that low economic status decreases voter turnout. Another factor is that many Chicano families have one or more members in unauthorized status and the entire family keeps a low profile as a result (DeLeon and Griswold del Castillo 2012; DeSipio 1996; LeMay 2009; Moncrief 2011; Navarro 2005; Meeks 2008).

Largely since the 1980s, however, their success in using coalition electoral politics has been paying off. They have begun electing more mayors of major American cities (Orr and Morel 2018). In the border region, San Antonio has been most notable in this regard, having elected as its mayor Henry Cisneros, Edward Garza, and Julian Castro. In 1980, there were only six Hispanic members in the U.S. House of Representatives. In the 116th Congress (2019–2021), there are 47 Hispanic members. Among the four states in the region, Latinos in New Mexico have had the most electoral success— of 14 Latino governors, New Mexico has had 8 governors, including its most recent Latina governors Susan Martinez (R-2011-2019) and Michelle Lujan Grisham (D-2019–to date). In the 116th Congress, in the U.S. House of Representatives, New Mexico has two members—Ben Ray Lujan and Xochitl Torres Small. A further sign of the improving prospects of Hispanic voting power is exemplified by two Chicano politicians who have sought the presidential nomination of the Democratic Party: in 2008, Bill Richardson, former governor of New Mexico and former representative from New Mexico's 3rd Congressional District, and former secretary of commerce, and in 2020, Julian Castro, former mayor of San Antonio, Texas, and former HUD secretary.

For solutions to political incorporation issues, congressional action would be necessary to address the gerrymandering and voter dilution issues, given the Supreme Court's decision on the matter in 2019 (*Rucho v. Common Cause*). Several state governments are considering establishing a nonpartisan citizens' commission for redistricting, including in Texas where it is a much-needed alternative to a system that practices anti-Hispanic gerrymandering. In 2021, two bills were introduced in the Congress to deal with gerrymandering and various voter suppression laws passed by about a dozen states (the For the People Act and the John Lewis Voting Rights Advancement Act). Coalition politics remains the most promising option to resolve some aspects of the issue. Comprehensive immigration reform would help with the problem, especially if it includes a path to citizenship for Dreamers, but the political prospect for enacting comprehensive immigration reform remains poor (LeMay 2019, 122–123).

Social Change in the Borderland Region

A final problem evident in the border region that will be discussed here concerns the need for social change. The problems discussed in the previous sections, such as asylum and refugee issues, violence, the militarization of the border, drugs and human trafficking, environmental degradation, and so on, are all indications of a basic need for social change in the border region. Fortunately, a degree of social change seems to be an inevitable result of the migration across the border of goods and people, as migration tends to reduce the separation imposed by the border (Davenport 2004). Hispanics in the region have a different image of the southwest than do many Anglos, but their interactions in the border region are bringing about a change in the images that both populations in the region have of each other (Chavez 1984; DeLeon and Griswold del Castillo 2012; Donnan and Wilson 1999; Navarro 2005; Salee 2018; Sanchez 1993; Vila 2003).

Social change also comes about as the media and popular culture change. Popular culture, and all too often the stereotypical image of the Chicano, has changed from the very negative stereotypes of the 1950s and 1960s to a more positive image of Chicanos as persons adding to the rich cultural diversity of the region (Fox 1999; Gomez-Pena 2000).

Positive social change comes with the further incorporation of the region's minority populations into union, business, social, and political networks that span interactions at the grassroots level and create affective bonds. As the region's diverse population comes together through work and play, and increasingly through intermarriage, individuals shift their images of one another. They also change their view of the appropriate and respective roles to be played by women, by Hispanics, by Blacks, and by Native Americans. From their interactions, the region's population is increasingly forming a new and more common border identity (Hennessy 2013; Lim 2017; McClain and Steward 1995; Sandowski-Smith 2002; Segura and Zavella 2007).

Whenever and wherever two or more cultural groups come into sustained contact with one another, a degree of social change and exchange between the two cannot be avoided even if many members of both cultures desire to avoid it. This process is known as acculturation or cultural assimilation. It is the process by which members of one subculture gradually absorb the norms, values, and lifestyle of the dominant culture. But acculturation is a two-way street. Inevitably, the majority culture also absorbs some of the cultural norms, customs, values, and lifestyle aspects of the minority subculture. The two cultures begin to blend into a new culture—in this case into a distinctive border culture (think Tex-Mex cuisine, for instance). On both sides of the border region, productive connections are made that make the border more of a "seam" weaving the two together and blurring the boundary rather than being a barrier separating them. The interactions on both sides of the border resulting from a circular migration reshape communities on both sides of the border. The regionalism that binds them also works to construct a new identity and a new role for ethnicity in the very boundaries among them (Donnan and Wilson 1999; LeMay 2009, 28; Minian 2018; Salee 2018; Vila 2000).

Conclusion

This chapter discussed interrelated problems or controversies evident in the U.S.-Mexico border region. It discussed issues raised by asylum-seekers and refugees to the region and also possible solutions to the asylum/refugee problem. It discussed the installation of border barriers—fences and a wall—that have been used in association with the militarization of the border. It noted how that militarization has changed the flow of migration toward the desert areas of the border region, resulting in many more deaths and an increase in vigilantism and violence along the border. It discussed proposed solutions to reduce that militarization. It discussed the concept of colonization in the border region, the detrimental effects of colonization, and the processes by which colonization can be reduced.

Drugs, guns, and human trafficking were examined in the chapter, as were the devastating effects of these types of trafficking on residents on both sides of the border. The chapter related some proposed solutions to the trafficking problem, even while recognizing the likelihood that such solutions will fail.

The chapter examined problems and controversies associated with the cycle of booms and busts in the region's economic development and related foreign policy concerns. It discussed possible solutions to these economic trends and cycles. It also discussed the related problems arising from the global economy and some likely developments in the region that address the global economy and how events like the COVID-19 pandemic may slow down the trend toward a global economy.

The chapter discussed the vexing problem of illegal immigration flows and explained how virtually all prior attempts to solve the illegal immigration problem have failed. The chapter concluded that any solution to the illegal immigration flow will depend on changes in the push factors driving that migration and explained how little U.S. policy can do to resolve those push factors.

The chapter discussed the issue of border medicine and how medical tourism is impacting problems of access to medical care and public health. It described how informal arrangements among local governments on both sides of the border have developed to deal with those accessibility concerns. The chapter discussed incorporation of Hispanics into U.S. politics, and how that political incorporation is affecting politics in the borderland states.

Finally, the chapter discussed problems associated with social change in the region. It concluded with a discussion of the process of acculturation, and how that process is inevitable and will bring about social change.

The chapter's reference section provides readers with a wide range of academic research and resources to further their reading and study of the borderlands region and the multiplicity of problems facing residents of the region.

References

Ackerman, Alissa, and Rick Furman. 2013. *The Criminalization of Immigration: Causes and Consequences.* Durham, NC: Carolina Academic Press.

Aguilar, Julian. 2020. "Trump Administration Waives Environmental Safeguards to Fast-Track 69 Miles of Border Fence Construction." May 15, 2020. https://www .texastribune.org/2020/05/15/trump-wall-fence -regulations.

Alden, Edward. 2008. *The Closing of the American Border.* New York: Harper Collins.

Alvarez, C. J. 2019. *Border Land, Border Water.* Austin: University of Texas Press.

American Immigration Council. 2020. "State by State." https:// www.americanimmigrationcouncil.org/topics/state-by-state.

Amnesty International. 2016. "Fleeing for Our Lives: Central American Migrant Crisis." April 1, 2016. https://www .amnestyusa.org/fleeing-for-our-lives-central-american -migrant-crisis/.

Anderson, Joan, and James Gerber. 2009. *50 Years of Change on the U.S.-Mexico Border.* Austin: University of Texas Press.

Anton, Treuer, Karenne Wood, William Fitzhugh, George Capture, Theresa Fraizer, Miles Miller, Miranda Belarde-Lewis, and Jill Norwood. 2013. *Indian Nations of North America.* Washington, DC: National Geographic.

Ashbee, Edward, Helene Clausen, and Carl Pederson, eds. 2007. *The Politics, Economics, and Culture of Mexican-U.S. Migration: Both Sides of the Border*. New York: Palgrave/Macmillan.

Bacon, David. 2004. *The Children of NAFTA*. Berkeley: University of California Press.

BBC. 2020. "US-Mexico Border: 'Longest-Ever' Smuggling Tunnel Discovered." January 30, 2020. https://www.bbc.com/news/world-us-canada-51304861.

Bender, Steven. 2012. *Run for the Border*. New York: New York University Press.

Bobrow-Strain, Aaron. 2019. *The Death and Life of Aida Hernandez: A Border Story*. New York: Farrar, Straus, and Giroux/Macmillan.

Bureau of Transportation Statistics. n.d. "Border Crossing/Entry Data: Query Detailed Statistics." https://www.bts.gov/content/border-crossingentry-data.

Byrd, Bobby, and Susannah Mississippi, eds. 1976. *The Late, Great Mexican Border: Reports from a Disappearing Line*. El Paso: Cinco Punta Press.

Cantu, Francisco. 2019. *The Line Becomes a River*. New York: Penguin Press.

Casey, Edward, and Mary Watkins. 2014. *Up Against the Wall*. Austin: University of Texas Press.

Center for Biological Diversity. n.d. "No Border Wall." https://www.biologicaldiversity.org/campaigns/border_wall/index.html.

Chacon, Justin, and Mike Davis. 2006. *No One Is Illegal*. Chicago: Haymarket Books.

Chatzkey, Andrew, James McBride, and Mohammed Aly Sergie. 2020. "NAFTA and the USMCA: Weighing the Impact of North American Trade." Council on Foreign

Relations. https://www.cfr.org/backgrounder/nafta-and
-usmca-weighing-impact-north-american-trade.

Chavez, John. 1984. *The Lost Land: The Chicano Image of the Southwest.* Albuquerque: University of New Mexico Press.

Cult, Nicholas, and David Carrasco. 2004. *Alambrista and the U.S.-Mexico Border.* Albuquerque: University of New Mexico Press.

Daley, David. 2020. *Unrigged: How Americans Are Battling Back to Save Democracy.* New York: Liveright/W.W. Norton.

Danelo, David. 2008. *The Border: Exploring the U.S.-Mexico Divide.* Mechanicsburg, PA: Stockdale Books.

Davenport, John. 2004. *The U.S.-Mexico Border: The Treaty of Guadalupe Hidalgo.* Philadelphia: Chelsea House.

Davidson, Chandler, ed. 1984. *Minority Vote Dilution.* Washington, DC: Howard University Press.

Davidson, Miriam. 2000. *Lives on the Line.* Tucson: University of Arizona Press.

De Leon, Jason. 2015. *The Land of Open Graves.* Berkeley: University of California Press.

DeLeon, Arnoldo, and Richard Griswold del Castillo. 2012. *North to Aztlan, 2e.* Hoboken, NJ: Wiley Blackwell.

Department of Homeland Security. 2018. "The Perils of Illegal Border Crossing." July 19, 2018. https://www.dhs.gov/news/2018/07/19/perils-illegal-border-crossing.

DeSipio, Louis. 1996. *Counting on the Latino Vote: Latinos in a New Electorate.* Charlottsville: University of Virginia Press.

Donnan, Hastings, and Thomas Wilson. 1999. *Borders: Frontiers of Identity.* London: Routledge.

Dunn, Timothy. 1997. *The Militarization of the U.S.-Mexico Border, 1978–1992.* Austin: University of Texas Press.

Ebright, Malcolm. 1994. *Land Grant Law Suites in Northern Mexico.* Guadalupe: New Mexico Center for Land Grant Studies.

Ebright, Malcolm, and Rick Hendricks. 2019. *Pueblo Sovereignty.* Norman: University of Oklahoma Press.

Ellingwood, Ken. 2009. *Hard Line: Life and Death on the U.S.-Mexico Border.* New York: Vintage Books.

Environmental Protection Agency (EPA). 2015. https:// www.epa.gov/sites/default/files/2015--09/documents /lapazagreement.pdf.

Eure, Marian. 2020. "Buying Prescription Drugs in Mexico." February 15, 2020. https://www.verywellhealth.com /prescription-drugs-from-mexico-2966765.

500 Nations. 2018. "List of Casinos State-by-State: 474 Indian Casinos Across 29 States." https://www.500nations .com/Indian_Casinos_List.asp.

Fox, Claire. 1999. *The Fence and the River.* Minneapolis: University of Minnesota Press.

Frey, Juan Carlos. 2019. *Sand and Blood.* New York: Public Affairs Press.

Ganster, Paul. 2015. *The U.S. Border Today, 3e.* Lanham, MD: Rowman and Littlefield.

Ganster, Paul, and David Lorey. 2008. *The U.S.-Mexico Border into the 21st Century, 2e.* Lanham, MD: Rowman and Littlefield.

Gaynor, Tim. 2009. *Midnight on the Line.* New York: St. Martin's Press.

Geneva Declaration on Armed Violence and Development. 2015. http://www.genevadeclaration.org/measurability /global-burden-of-armed-violence/global-burden-of-armed -violence-2015.html.

Gerdes, Louise. 2014. *Should the U.S. Close Its Borders?* New York: Greenhaven Press.

Geron, Kim. 2005. *Latino Political Power.* Boulder, CO: Lynne Rienner Publishers.

Gomez-Pena, Guillermo. 2000. *Dangerous Border Crossers.* New York: Routledge.

Gonzalez, Manuel. 2009. *Mexicanos: A History of Mexicans in the United States, 2e.* Bloomington: Indiana University Press.

Gramlich, John. 2019. "How Americans See Illegal Immigration, the Border Wall, and Political Compromise." Pew Research Center, January 16, 2019. https://www.pewresearch.org/fact-tank/2019/01/16/how-americans-see-illegal-immigration-the-border-wall-and-political-compromise/.

Grandin, Greg. 2019. *The End of the Myth.* New York: Henry Holt.

Greenwald, Noah, Brian Segee, Tierra Curry, and Curt Bradley. 2017. "A Wall in the Wild: The Disastrous Impacts of Trump's Border Wall on Wildlife." Center for Biological Diversity. https://www.biologicaldiversity.org/programs/international/borderlands_and_boundary_waters/pdfs/A_Wall_in_the_Wild.pdf.

Gutierrez, David. 1995. *Walls and Mirrors: Mexican Americans, Mexican Immigrants, and the Politics of Ethnicity.* Berkeley: University of California Press.

Health and Human Services. 2020. "Unaccompanied Alien Children Information." https://www.hhs.gov/programs/social-services/unaccompanied-alien-children/index.html.

Henderson, Timothy. 2011. *Beyond Borders.* Hoboken, NJ: Wiley-Blackwell.

Hendrickson, Brett. 2014. *Border Medicine: A Transcultural History of Mexican American Curenderismo.* New York: New York University Press.

Hennessy, Rosemary. 2013. *Fires on the Border.* Minneapolis: University of Minnesota Press.

Hernandez, Kelly L. 2010. *Migra! A History of the Border Patrol*. Berkeley: University of California Press.

Hernandez, Roberto. 2018. *Colonality of the U.S.-Mexico Border*. Tucson: University of Arizona Press.

Hispanic Chamber of Commerce. 2021. https://www.ushcc
.com/advocacy1.html.

House of Representatives. 2004. "Deadly Consequences of Illegal Alien Smuggling." Hearing before the Subcommittee on Immigration, Border Security, and Claims. June 24, 2003. Washington, DC: Government Printing Office. https://www.govinfo.gov/content/pkg/CHRG
-108hhrg87993/html/CHRG-108hhrg87993.htm.

HUD Exchange. n.d. "State Community Development Block Grant Colonias Set-Aside." https://www.hudexchange.info
/programs/cdbg-colonias/.

Human Rights First. 2019. "Trump Administration's Third-Country Transit Bar Is an Asylum Ban That Will Return Refugees to Danger." September 13, 2019. https://www
.humanrightsfirst.org/resource/trump-administration-s-third
-country-transit-bar-asylum-ban-will-return-refugees-danger.

Human Rights First. 2020. "With Asylum Effectively Blocked at Southern Border, Those Seeking Safety Face Escalating Violence, Punishing Conditions." May 13, 2020. https://
www.humanrightsfirst.org/press-release/asylum-effectively
-blocked-southern-border-those-seeking-safety-face
-escalating.

IBWC. 2012 "The International Border and Water Commission." https://www.ibwc.gov/About_US
/About_US.html.

Johnson, Hans, and Sergio Sanchez. 2019. "Immigrants in California." Public Policy Institute of California, May, 2019. https://www.ppic.org/publication/immigrants
-in-California.

Jusionyte, Ieva. 2018. *Threshold: Emergency Responders on the U.S.-Mexico Border.* Berkeley: University of California Press.

Kang, S. Deborah. 2017. *The INS on the Line: Making Immigration Law on the US-Mexico Border. 1917–1954.* New York: Oxford University Press.

Kelly, Mary. 2007. "Free Trade: The Politics of Toxic Waste." North American Congress on Latin America, September 25, 2007. https://nacla.org/article/free-trade-politics-toxic-waste.

Kirkpatrick, Terry. 2012. *60 Miles of Border.* New York: Berkley Books.

Krauss, Erich, and Alex Pachedco. 2004. *On the Line: Inside the Border Patrol.* New York: Citadel/Kensington.

La Vere, David. 2013. *The Texas Indians.* Austin: University of Texas Press.

LeMay, Michael. 2006. *Guarding the Gates: Immigration and National Security.* Westport, CT: Praeger Security International.

LeMay, Michael. 2009. *The Perennial Struggle, 3e.* Upper Saddle River, NJ: Prentice Hall.

LeMay, Michael. 2015. *Illegal Immigration: A Reference Handbook.* Santa Barbara, CA: ABC-CLIO.

LeMay, Michael. 2018. *U.S. Immigration Policy, Ethnicity, and Religion in American History.* Santa Barbara, CA: Praeger Press.

LeMay, Michael. 2019. *Immigration Reform: A Reference Handbook.* Santa Barbara, CA: ABC-CLIO.

LeMay, Michael, and Elliott Barkan. 1999. *U.S. Immigration and Naturalization Laws and Issues: A Documentary History.* Westport, CT: Greenwood Press.

Levario, Miquel Antonio. 2012. *Militarizing the Border.* College Station: Texas A & M University Press.

Lim, Julian. 2017. *Porous Border.* Chapel Hill: University of North Carolina Press.

Lorey, David. 1999. *The U.S.-Mexican Border in the 20th Century: A History.* Lanham, MD: Rowman and Littlefield.

Lusk, Mark, Kathleen Staudt, and Eva Moya, eds. 2012. *Social Justice in the U.S.-Mexico Border Region.* New York: Springer Press.

Magana, Lisa. 2008. *Straddling the Border.* Austin: University of Texas Press.

Martinez, Oscar. 2006. *Troublesome Borders, 2e.* Tucson: University of Arizona Press.

Massey, Douglas, Rafael Alarcon, Jorge Durand, and Humberto Gonzalez. 1990. *Return to Aztlan: The Social Process of International Migration from Western Mexico.* Berkeley: University of California Press.

McClain, Paula, and J. Steward. 1995. *Can't We All Get Along? Racial and Ethnic Minorities in American Politics.* Boulder, CO: Westview Press.

Meeks, Eric V. 2008. *Border Citizens: The Making of Indians, Mexicans, and Anglos in Arizona.* Austin: University of Texas Press.

Mehta, Sukato. 2019. *This Land Is Our Land.* New York: Farrar, Straus and Giroux/Macmillan.

Miller, Todd. 2019. *Empire of Borders.* New York: Verso Books.

Minian, Ana Raquel. 2018. *Undocumented Lives.* Cambridge, MA: Harvard University Press.

Moncrief, Gary, ed. 2011. *Reapportionment and Redistricting in the West.* Lanham, MD: Lexington Books.

Mourdoukoutas, Panos. 2011. "The Good, the Bad, and the Ugly Side of Globalization." *Forbes*, September 11, 2011. https://www.forbes

.com/sites/panosmourdoukoutas/2011/09/10
/the-good-the-bad-and-the-ugly-side-of-globalization.

Native Languages of the Americas. n.d. "Native American
Tribes of Texas." http://www.native-languages.org/texas
.htm.

Navarro, Armando. 2005. *American Political Experience in
Occupied Aztlan.* Lanham: Alamira Press.

Newcomb, W. W., Jr. 1972. *The Indians of Texas: From
Prehistoric to Modern Times.* Austin: University of Texas Press.

Nichols, James D. 2018. *The Limits of Liberty.* Lincoln:
University of Nebraska Press.

Nitze, William, Jose Leyva, Sarah Sowell, Abraham Nehmad,
and Eike Duffing. 2001. "U.S.-Mexico Border XXI
Program Progress Report, 1996–2000." Washington, DC:
Government Printing Office.

O'Neil, Shannon, and Kathleen O'Neil. 2013. *Two Nations
Indivisible.* New York: Oxford University Press.

Orr, Marion, and Domingo Morel, eds. 2018. *Latino Mayors:
Political Change in the Post-Industrial City.* Philadelphia:
Temple University Press.

Payan, Tony. 2006. *The Three U.S.-Mexico Border Wars: Drugs,
Immigration, and Homeland Security.* Westport, CT: Praeger
Security International.

PBS News Hour. 2017. "Texas Gerrymandering
Discriminates Against Hispanics, Ruling Says." March 12,
2017. https://www.pbs.org/newshour/show/texas
-gerrymandering-discriminates-hispanics-ruling-says.

Ramos, Henry. 1998. *The American G.I. Forum: In Pursuit of
the Dream, 1948–1983.* Houston, TX: Arte Publico Press.

Regan, Margaret. 2016. *Detained and Deported: Stories of
Immigrant Families Under Fire.* Boston: Beacon Press.

Reich, Peter. 2017. *The Law of the U.S.-Mexico Border.*
Durham, NC: Carolina Academic Press.

Romero, Fernando. 2008. *Hyperborder*. New York: Princeton Architectural Press.

Salee, Andrew. 2018. *Vanishing Frontiers*. New York: Hachette Books.

Sanchez, George. 1993. *Becoming Mexican American: Ethnicity, Culture, and Identity in Chicano Los Angeles*. New York: Oxford University Press.

Sandowski-Smith, Claudia. 2002. *Globalization of the Line*. New York: Palgrave/Macmillan.

Segura, Denise, and Patricia Zavella, eds. 2007. *Women and Migration in the U.S.-Mexico Borderlands*. Durham, NC: Duke University Press.

Slack, Jeremy, Daniel Martinez, and Scott Whiteford. 2018. *The Shadow of the Wall*. Tucson: University of Arizona Press.

Spener, David. 2009. *Clandestine Crossings*. Ithaca, NY: Cornell University Press.

St. John, Rachel. 2012. *Line in the Sand*. Princeton, NJ: Princeton University Press.

Staudt, Kathleen, Tony Payan, and Anthony Kruszewski. 2009. *Human Rights Along the U.S.-Mexico Border*. Tucson: University of Arizona Press.

Strum, Philippa. 2010. *Mendez v. Westminster: School Desegregation and Mexican American Rights*. Lawrence: University Press of Kansas.

Taylor, Lawrence, and Maeve Hickey. 2001. *Tunnel Kids*. Tucson: University of Arizona Press.

Tessada, Gaston. 2020. "Gastric Bypass Costs in the U.S. vs. Mexico." January 25, 2020. https://www.oasisbariatrics .com/blog/2020/01/25/gastric-bypass-costs-in-the-203625.

Tiano, Susan, Moira Murphy-Agular, and Brianne Bigej. 2012. *Borderline Slavery*. Surrey, UK: Ashgate Publishing.

Torr, James D, ed. 2004. *Homeland Security*. San Diego: Greenhaven Press.

Trevino, Julissa. 2018. "Medical Tourism Is Booming in Mexico." January 9, 2018. https://psmag.com/economics/medical-tourism-is-booming-in-mexico.

Truax, Eileen. 2018. *We Built the Wall*. London and New York: Versa Books.

United We Dream. n.d. "About UWD." https://unitedwedream.org/about/.

U.S. Customs and Border Protection. 2011. "National Guard Supports Border Security Efforts." March 1, 2011. https://www.cbp.gov/newsroom/national-media-release/national-guard-supports-border-security-efforts.

Vila, Pablo. 2000. *Crossing Borders*. Austin: University of Texas Press.

Vila, Pablo. 2003. *Ethnography on the Border*. Minneapolis: University of Minnesota Press.

Vulliamy, Ed. 2010. *Amexica: War Along the Borderline*. New York: Farrar, Straus and Giroux.

Wilken-Robertson, Michael, ed. 2004. *The U.S.-Mexico Border Environment*. San Diego: San Diego State University Press.

3 Perspectives

Introduction

This chapter presents seven original essays on the U.S.-Mexico border region. Collectively, these essays provide an array of insights and perspectives on the different characteristics and challenges of the U.S.-Mexico border region—insights and perspectives that are different from those of the author.

Mexican Americans and the Long Fight against Segregation in the Southwest
David-James Gonzales

The Mexican American struggle against segregation in the American Southwest was a multi-decade effort led by several individuals and grassroots organizations, particularly in Texas, California, and Arizona. Comprising most of the 20th century, the movement centered on ending the *de facto* segregation of Mexicans and Mexican Americans in underserved schools and substandard housing, and from public amenities and private businesses. Initially, ethnic Mexicans lacked a national organization to centralize and coordinate these efforts. They primarily relied on newly formed regional and community organizations to fight Jim Crow–like conditions, known as

---

A U.S. inspection station on the border of the United States and Mexico in El Paso, Texas. The border between the United States and Mexico experiences the greatest number of legal and illegal crossings of people each year. (Salvador Burciaga/Dreamstime.com)

129

Jaime Crow throughout the Southwest. By the 1960s, these grassroots mobilizations developed into robust transregional civil rights organizations that brought the Mexican American struggle against segregation and other forms of discrimination into the national consciousness.

The segregation of ethnic Mexicans in the Southwest is rooted in the same sociocultural, economic, and political motives (namely racial capitalism and white supremacy) that led to the marginalization of people from Indigenous and African ancestry in the United States and throughout the Western Hemisphere (Ortiz 2018). Unlike African Americans, however, the segregation of ethnic Mexicans was based on customs and social practices that emerged from the aftermath of the Mexican American War rather than American law (San Miguel 1987; Montejano 1987; Donato 1997; Camarillo 2013). Nevertheless, the segregation of Mexicans and Mexican Americans was widespread, ranging from isolated rural colonias in southern Colorado and northern New Mexico to urban barrios in San Antonio, Denver, Tucson, and Los Angeles (Alvarez 1986; Gutiérrez 1995).

Perhaps, nowhere was this segregation more conspicuous than in public education. While the segregation of Mexican school children dates to the turn of the 20th century, it did not become common institutional practice in elementary schools throughout the Southwest until the 1920s and 1930s (San Miguel 1987; Montejano 1987; Lozano 2020). Following the large-scale migration of approximately 1.5 million Mexican immigrants from 1890 to 1929, school officials from south Texas to southern California began segregating ethnic Mexican children en masse. Despite the lack of statutory authority, teachers, principals, and district officials implemented a patchwork of both ad hoc and premeditated policies. Caving to pressure from white parents and relying on racially biased studies in the nascent field of progressive education philosophy, school officials either refused to admit Mexican children or separated them into different classrooms, or they built completely segregated "Mexican schools" (San Miguel 1987; Gonzalez 1990).

Indeed, the practice was so widespread that "by 1930, eighty-five percent of Mexican children in the Southwest were attending either separate classrooms or entirely separate schools" (Donato 1997).

From the outset, Mexican and Mexican American parents fought back against the segregation of their children by forming parent associations and community organizations (Gonzales 2017). Appearing before attendance clerks, principals, school boards, and judges, Mexican parents and community activists demanded that their children be provided equal educational facilities and instruction. In 1915 members of La Liga Protectora Latina (Latin Protective League), led by Adolpho Romo, objected to a new policy implemented by the Tempe school district in Arizona to segregate Mexican children in a different school away from "American" children (Muñoz 2013). In 1919, ethnic Mexican parents supported by members of the Pro Patria Club appeared before the Santa Ana Board of Education in Orange County, California to protest similar plans (Gonzalez 1990).

Although isolated, these early mobilizations foreshadowed the self-determined response exemplified by ethnic Mexican communities throughout the Southwest. These efforts led to the nation's first desegregation court victories in *Romo v. Laird* (1925), *Del Rio ISD v. Salvatierra* (1930), *Alvarez v. Lemon Grove* (1931), *Mendez et al. v. Westminster* (1947), *Delgado v. Bastrop ISD* (1948), and *Gonzales v. Sheely* (1951) (Trinidad 2018). Only in Texas did these victories result from the coordination of larger transregional organizations like the League of United Latin American Citizens and the American G.I. Forum, which also won legal battles against jury discrimination against people of Mexican descent and the segregation of Mexicans in cemeteries (San Miguel 1987; Allsup 1982; Orozco 2009; Garcia 2009).

In addition to education, ethnic Mexicans fought segregation in housing, public facilities, and private businesses. These efforts often involved forming interracial coalitions with other racial minorities. In 1943, five years before *Shelley v. Kraemer,* Alex and Esther Bernal retained the services of Jewish American lawyer David C. Marcus to fight a racially restrictive housing covenant on property purchased by the couple in Fullerton, California (Carpio 2012; Romero and Fernandez 2012). After winning the case, Marcus represented an estimated 8,000 Latinos—organized by a coalition of Mexican American grass-roots organizations—in *Lopez v. Seccombe* (1944). The courts sided with Marcus here as well, issuing a decision that deseg-regated the Perris Hill Plunge public swimming pool in San Bernardino County (Carpio 2012). In 1963, after decades of fighting segregationist practices in the real estate industry, eth-nic Mexicans joined Blacks, Asians, and Jews in successfully pushing the California legislature to pass the Rumford Fair Housing Act, making it illegal to discriminate on the basis of race in the rental or sale of housing in the state (Brilliant 2010).

Despite these unprecedented and improbable victories, the de facto segregation of ethnic Mexicans did not end; rather it evolved, leading to a new round of court battles during the 1960s and 1970s. Mexican Americans found a new form of civil rights mobilization that combined the struggle against seg-regation with a more militant push for progressive reforms that targeted the pervasive issues of poverty and economic exploi-tation, underserved neighborhoods and schools, and lack of political representation. Organizing around a new ethnic/racial identity and political ethos, the Chicanos—a term that became a popular expression of ethnic pride among many Americans of Mexican descent during the 1960s and 1970s—built a national movement out of new organizations like the Crusade for Jus-tice, La Alianza Federal de Mercedes, the Brown Berets, and La Raza Unida Party (Garcia 1997). Claiming the Southwest as an ethnic homeland (Aztlán), the Chicano Movement sought liberation from Anglo domination and demanded the self-determination of people of Mexican descent throughout the nation. Although short-lived, *el movimiento* inspired, trained, and mobilized a new generation of Mexican American activists, scholars, politicians, and professionals. Their experiences "cre-ated the foundation for the . . . immigrant rights movement and educational, criminal justice, and political reform movements nationwide" (Rodriguez 2015).

References

Allsup, C. 1982. *The American G.I. Forum: Origins and Evolution.* Austin: University of Texas Press.

Alvarez, R. R. 1986. "The Lemon Grove Incident: The Nation's First Successful Desegregation Case." *The Journal of San Diego History* 32 (2): Spring. https://sandiegohistory.org/journal/1986/april/lemongrove/.

Brilliant, M. 2010. *The Color of America Has Changed: How Racial Diversity Shaped Civil Rights Reform in California, 1941–1978.* New York: Oxford University Press.

Camarillo, A. 2013. "Navigating Segregated Life in America's Racial Borderhoods, 1910s–1950s." *The Journal of American History* 100 (3): 645–662. https://doi.org/10.1093/jahist/jat450.

Carpio, G. 2012. "Unexpected Allies: David C. Marcus and His Impact on the Advancement of Civil Rights in the Mexican-American Legal Landscape of Southern California." In *Beyond Alliances: The Jewish Role in Reshaping the Racial Landscape of Southern California,* edited by George J. Sanchez and Bruce Zuckerman, pp. 1–32. Lafayette, IN: Purdue University Press.

Donato, R. 1997. *The Other Struggle for Equal Schools: Mexican Americans During the Civil Rights Era.* Albany: State University of New York.

Garcia, I. 1997. *Chicanismo: The Forging of a Militant Ethos Among Mexican Americans.* Tucson: University of Arizona Press.

Garcia, I. 2009. *White but Not Equal: Mexican Americans, Jury Discrimination, and The Supreme Court.* Tucson: University of Arizona Press.

Gonzales, D. 2017. "Placing the *et al.* Back in *Mendez v. Westminster:* Hector Tarango and the Mexican American Movement to End Segregation in the Social and Political Borderlands of Orange County, California." *American Studies* 56 (2): 31–52. https://doi.org/10.1353/ams.2017.0018.

Gonzalez, G. C. 1990. *Chicano Education in the Era of Segregation.* Denton, TX: University of North Texas Press.

Gutiérrez, D. G. 1995. *Walls and Mirrors: Mexicans, Mexican Americans, and the Politics of Ethnicity.* Berkeley: University of California Press.

Lozano, R. 2020. "New Directions in Latino/a/x Histories of Education: Comparative Studies in Race, Language, Law, and Higher Education." *History of Education Quarterly* 60 (4): 612–622. https://doi.org/10.1017/heq.2020.43.

Montejano, D. 1987. *Anglos and Mexicans in the Making of Texas, 1836–1986.* Austin: University of Texas Press.

Muñoz, L. K. 2013. "*Romo v. Laird*: Mexican American Segregation and the Politics of Belonging in America." *Western Legal History: The Journal of the Ninth Judicial Circuit Historical Society* 26: 97–132.

Orozco, C. E. 2009. *No Mexicans, Women, or Dogs Allowed: The Rise of the Mexican American Civil Rights Movement.* Austin: University of Texas Press.

Ortiz, P. 2018. *An African American and Latinx History of the United States.* New York: Beacon Press.

Rodriguez, M. S. 2015. *Rethinking the Chicano Movement.* New York: Routledge.

Romero, R. C., and L. F. Fernandez. 2012. "*Doss V. Bernal*: Ending Mexican Apartheid in Orange County." *CRSC Research Report* 14: 1–5. https://www.chicano.ucla.edu/publications/report-brief/doss-v-bernal.

San Miguel, G. 1987. *'Let All of Them Take Heed': Mexican Americans and the Campaign for Educational Equality in Texas, 1910–1981.* College Station: Texas A&M Press.

Trinidad, M. 2018. "'To Secure These Rights': The Campaign to End School Segregation and Promote Civil Rights in Arizona in the 1950s." *The Western Historical Quarterly* 49: 155–183. https://doi.org/10.1093/whq/why033.

David-James Gonzales is assistant professor of history at Brigham Young University in Provo, Utah.

The Fourteenth Amendment, Incorporation Doctrine, and the U.S.-Mexico Border States
Timothy R. Johnson and Rachael Houston

Section 1 of the Fourteenth Amendment to the U.S. Constitution suggests that states may not abridge privileges or immunities of U.S. citizens, and must afford to them due process and equal protection of laws. One interpretation of this section is that the Bill of Rights applies to state governments as it does to the federal government—states may not encroach on the liberties explicated in the First through Eighth Amendments. The question is whether the U.S. Supreme Court has used such a literal interpretation of Section 1. The short answer is no. The longer answer—that the Court has only applied select liberties of the Bill of Rights to state governments—is the focus of this essay, which discusses the development of law concerning the incorporation of liberties outlined in the Bill of Rights at the state level. It examines how the Court has interpreted these Fourteenth Amendment clauses in a dozen important cases arising from challenges to laws of the four Southwest border states of California, Arizona, New Mexico, and Texas.

The Bill of Rights was originally applied only to the federal government. After all, it was a strong central government that the founders most feared. James Madison's first attempt at crafting the first Bill of Rights had 17 amendments, some of which provided limited protection from state encroachment on individual rights. As Madison wrote in Article 14, "No State shall violate the equal rights of conscience, or the freedom of the press, or the trial by jury in criminal cases." This section, however, was rejected by Congress, which some scholars interpret as an indication that the members of the first Congress did not intend for the Bill of Rights to apply to the states.

With the North's Civil War victory, the Thirteenth to Fifteenth Amendments were ratified with the intent of providing protection for emancipated slaves (and all African Americans). The Fourteenth Amendment was the most general of the three, providing that "no State shall make or enforce any law which shall abridge the privileges or immunities of citizens of the United States; nor shall any State deprive any person of life, liberty or property, without due process of law; nor deny to any person within its jurisdiction the equal protection of the law."

These three clauses of the Fourteenth Amendment gave attorneys an opportunity to ask the Supreme Court to apply the Bill of Rights to state governments as well as federal authority. The first avenue they chose—the Privileges or Immunities Clause—was quickly closed in the *Slaughterhouse Cases* (83 U.S. 36, 1873). The case focused on whether a state can control an entire industry (in this case, slaughterhouse operations in Louisiana). The Court ruled that the Privileges or Immunities Clause could not be used to protect the rights of citizens to conduct business, because the right to one's livelihood or the right to be protected against a monopoly is not specified in the Constitution. In the ruling, the Court gutted the Privileges or Immunities Clause and indicated it would never use this clause to nationalize the Bill of Rights.

Attorneys turned next to the Due Process Clause because, with a commensurate clause already in the Fifth Amendment, this path to incorporation of the Bill of Rights at the state level seemed intuitive. The Court took up this argument in *Hurtado v. California* (110 U.S. 516, 1884). *Hurtado* focused on the right to have a grand jury determine whether to issue an indictment. The case arose because California allowed prosecutors to use an information process rather than a grand jury. The state used this latter method to bring Hurtado to trial. He was subsequently found guilty of murder. Hurtado's lawyer argued he had a right to due process that applied to federal hearings under the Fifth Amendment and to state hearings under the same clause found in the Fourteenth Amendment. In its 7–3 ruling, the Court disagreed. In fact, it argued precisely the opposite. In particular, the majority argued that because due process protections are explicitly contained in the Fifth Amendment, the right to due process applies only to that amendment. It reasoned that inclusion of the term "due process" in the Fourteenth Amendment could not be used as the path to incorporate the entire Bill of Rights at the state level.

Between 1884, when the *Hurtado* decision was handed down, and 2011, when *Arizona Christian School Tuition Organization v. Winn* emerged as an important First Amendment case in Arizona, the Court issued a dozen rulings that addressed whether any of the Bill of Rights amendments could be applied to the states via the incorporation doctrine. The question these courts faced was whether the due process or equal protection clauses of the Fourteenth Amendment constituted "fundamental rights" that therefore could be legally incorporated, or applied, to state governments. Although these cases dealt with laws enacted by one or the other of the four border states along the Mexican border, by implication they affected all 50 states.

In *Miller v. Texas* (153 U.S. 535, 1894), the Court addressed whether the Second and Fourth Amendments applied to Texas under the Fourteenth Amendment. In *Miller*, the Court ruled that the plaintiff had not been deprived of due process and that the Texas gun law he broke had not violated the Fourteenth Amendment's privilege and immunities clause. Since Miller had not brought up the due process defense in his trial, the Court refused to apply it to Texas, ruling that the Second Amendment limited the national government, not the state of Texas.

Fast-forward to the 1960s, when a much more liberal Supreme Court under Chief Justice Earl Warren considered applying the Fifth Amendment to the states in *Miranda v. Arizona* (384 U.S. 436, 1966). By a 6–3 vote, the Court ruled in *Miranda* that the Fifth Amendment applied to the state via the Fourteenth Amendment's due process clause. States were required to read a person his rights upon arrest—that is, he was to be given what came to be called his Miranda rights.

Using the fundamental rights concept, the Court ruled 5–4 in *Cohen v. California* (403 U.S. 15, 1971) that the First Amendment's right to freedom of speech (in this case, symbolic speech written on a T-shirt) applied to the states via incorporation of the Fourteenth Amendment. A more nuanced ruling, however, impacted another California case, *Regents of UCLA v. Bakke* (438 U.S. 265, 1978). In this 5–4 decision, the Court ruled the state's use of racial quotas in admissions policy was unconstitutional but that the state's use of certain affirmative action provisions did not amount to a fixed quota. A California law was again at issue in *California v. Greenwood* (486 U.S. 35, 1986). In Greenwood, the Court held in a 6–2 vote that the Fourth Amendment does not prohibit warrantless search and seizures of evidence left in garbage outside the home.

Texas was another border state from which several cases challenged state laws on First Amendment rights via the equal protection clause of the Fourteenth Amendment. In *Texas Monthly Inc. v. Bullock* (489 U.S. 1, 1989) the Court ruled by a 6–3 vote that a Texas law granting tax exemptions to publishers of religious material promoted religion in violation of the First Amendment's establishment clause. That same year, in *Texas v. Johnson* (491 U.S. 397), the Court ruled against the state, declaring by a narrow 5–4 vote that a Texas law that criminalized the desecration of the flag violated First Amendment free speech protections. The court held that burning the flag was a fundamental freedom that protected "symbolic" speech. In 2003, in *Lawrence v. Texas* (539 U.S. 558), the Court ruled 6–3 that the right to privacy was fundamental and that a state law criminalizing homosexual behavior between consenting adults in the privacy of their home violated the equal protection clause of the Fourteenth Amendment. The *Lawrence* decision was a precursor to the far-reaching decision in *Obergefell v. Hodges* (2015) that ruled same-sex marriage laws were constitutional under the same rationale of a fundamental right protected by the equal rights clause.

New Mexico was the border state from which a First Amendment prayer case challenged a state's law. In *Santa Fe Independent School District v. Doe* (530 U.S. 290, 2000), the Court ruled 6–3 that a student-led and initiated prayer before a public high school football game violated the Establishment Clause of the First Amendment because the prayers were public speech on government property at government-sponsored events and authorized by government policy. Collectively, these factors were interpreted by the Court majority as unconstitutional government endorsement of prayer at public school events.

Arizona law came under constitutional scrutiny in *Arizona Christian School Tuition Organization v. Winn* (563 U.S. 125, 2011). *Winn*, like the Santa Fe case, challenged an Arizona state law on First Amendment Establishment Clause grounds via the Fourteenth Amendment's equal protection provision. In the *Winn* case, however, the Court ruled 5–4 that the residents did not have standing as taxpayers to challenge a program that provided tax credits for contributions to school-tuition organizations.

In the end, the U.S. Supreme Court has taken the approach it takes with many areas of the law—a legally conservative one. This means the Court has moved slowly to incorporate liberties (after more than 200 years it has still not applied the full Bill of Rights to the states). Time will tell whether U.S. citizens will be protected from state encroachment of the remaining rights that have not yet been incorporated.

Timothy R. Johnson is the Morse-Alumni distinguished professor of political science at the University of Minnesota.

Rachael Houston is a PhD candidate in political science at the University of Minnesota.

Indian Boarding Schools: A History Worth Remembering
Elizabeth M. Loomer

When you hear the term "boarding school," what images does your mind conjure? Do you envision beautiful stone corridors, antique scrolling woodwork, uniforms that function to show your house pride while still being edgy enough to be cool? Wait, are you thinking of Hogwarts? For those of Generation X and later years, these are most likely the first things that are recalled. Now what if I were to add the term "Native American" before boarding schools—what then? Do the same mental images appear? Probably not, because Native American boarding schools were grim institutions that became notorious for trying to assimilate "wild savage Indians" into civilized society—in part by scrubbing their minds and memories of their tribal histories and cultures. The first law providing for the creation of Native American boarding schools was passed in 1819, but many more followed in subsequent decades. Many of the methods used throughout this period were put in place by an army colonel known for his "reforms and adaptations" in military prisons. These practices were then implemented in the world of government-regulated reeducation for Native American youth. Colonel Richard Pratt, who served as headmaster of the first off-reservation boarding school, reflected a sentiment that many other white Americans shared when he declared that the country's duty to its Native American people was to "kill the Indian in him, to save the man" (Pratt 1892).

To get a clear understanding of how Indian boarding schools affected the areas along the current U.S.-Mexico border, it is critical to understand the high value Indigenous peoples place on their ancestral homelands. Many of these homelands were lost by Native American peoples during the 18th and 19th centuries. The United States, Spain, and Mexico engaged in military conflicts in the territories while waging war with pens and maps against tribes who were hundreds, if not thousands, of miles away. The disputed land consisted of approximately two-thirds of the United States as we know it today. The Indigenous peoples of the areas were viewed as nothing more than an obstacle to the expansion of each individual empire.

The sentiments that later drove the establishment of Indian boarding schools can be traced all the way back to the Civilization Fund Act of 1819, which was passed in Congress and signed into law by President James Monroe (Fifteenth Congress 1819).This act allocated funds—a sum of $10,000—to be used in the cause of "civilizing Indians." This legislation "directly spurred the creation of the schools by putting forward the notion that Native culture and language were to blame for what was deemed the country's 'Indian Problem'" (Pember 2019). When the act was passed, the United States consisted of 22 states and the territory of the Louisiana Purchase. Mexico had just gained independence from Spain in 1810, while Texans were attempting to declare themselves an independent country. In May 1824, the Bureau of Indian Affairs was established (BIA 1975). The "Indian Problem" was no longer directly overseen by the Department of War. The Indian Removal Act of 1830 was passed by Congress and signed into law by President Andrew Jackson (Library of Congress 1830). This act displaced tribes across the Southeast to the west of the Mississippi River to open their rich farmlands for European settlers. Twenty years later, in 1851, the Indian Appropriation Act passed by Congress and signed by President Millard Filmore forcibly moved all "Indians" onto the newly created reservations, where they were told to abandon their tribal practices and traditions and learn to farm. Herding Native Americans onto reservations also made it easier for the U.S. government to watch and control them. The Mexican-American War had ended in 1848 with the signing of the Treaty of Guadalupe

Hidalgo. This Treaty ceded to the United States the present-day states of Arizona, California, New Mexico, Texas, Colorado, Nevada, and Utah. The final land deal with Mexico that created the border that both countries acknowledge today was the Gadsden Purchase in 1853. Once the United States had laid claim to all this additional land and secured the necessary paperwork from Mexico, it quickly turned its attention to subduing and civilizing the "hostile Indians" still present on those lands. The newly drawn "boundaries" of the U.S.-Mexico border cut through the lands of 29 tribes, including the Tohono o'odham, Kickapoo, and Pueblo, and further north the Apache, Cheyenne, Arapaho, and Comanche.

In 1860 the first on-reservation school was established by the Bureau of Indian Affairs on the Yakima reservation in Washington Territory. In the years that followed, other on-reservation boarding schools were established but they did not produce the level of assimilation desired by the government. In 1879 the first off-reservation boarding school, Carlisle Indian Industrial School, was established in Pennsylvania. This shift in tactics was summed up by the sentiments of Congressman Thaddeus Pound, who said, "It is cheaper and better to teach a young Indian than to fight an Old One" (Laderman 2002). Native American boarding schools soon sprouted all around the country, dedicated to "civilizing" Indigenous children through military structure and discipline (and religious instruction, particularly in the case of schools operated by Catholic, Protestant, and other religious denominations) (Meriam 1928). This was achieved by cutting their hair, taking away their indigenous clothing, forbidding them from using their native language, forbidding them from practicing their native religious ceremonies, forcing them into isolation, and removing them from their families. All this was done in the hope of creating well-behaved, useful, patriotic citizens. A total of 367 Indian boarding schools were created; as of 2020, 73 were still open and 15 still boarded students (National Native American Boarding School Healing Coalition 2020).

Four boarding schools were created along or near the U.S.-Mexico border region—the Albuquerque Indian School (New Mexico, 1882), the Fort Mojave Indian School (Arizona, 1890), the Phoenix Indian School (Arizona, 1891), and the Perris Indian School (California, 1892; this school eventually became the Sherman Indian school, which continues to operate even today). These boarding schools did not just serve the immediate area. Native children were shipped from all over the country to different schools. It was never a single tribe represented at the off-reservation schools, there was always a cross section of tribes represented from across the nation. Anywhere from 1 to 30 different tribes could be represented at a single institution.

In 1928 a special report funded by the Rockefeller Foundation and produced by the Institute for Governmental Research was delivered to the Department of the Interior. The Meriam Report was highly critical of the U.S. government's policies toward Native Americans, including its boarding school program. It showed that schools were able to stay open only due to the labor of the children, having half the day for labor and the other half for learning skills, which primarily meant learning a trade. Most commonly, the trades were carpentry for the boys and sewing or domestic work for the girls. The Meriam Report also said that Native American children at these schools were often malnourished, poorly educated, and subject to harsh punishments (Meriam 1928).Yet, it was not until the Indian Self-Determination and Education Assistance Act of 1975 that the official mission and orientation of the schools changed. This act placed the power to oversee the boarding schools with the appropriate Native American tribe. It also provided for Native Americans to have a majority control over the Bureau of Indian Affairs (BIA). "Following the passage of ISDEAA, BIA's off-reservation boarding schools were no longer in the business of promoting assimilation; rather, their purpose was transformed to support and respect tribal self-determination and sovereignty" (Department of the Interior 2019).

Native American boarding schools have survived through more than 160 years of war, displacement, assimilation attempts, massacres, pandemics, and legislation. Today, however, they are managed in a different context. There are still 73 schools in operation, but instead of assimilation the goal is preservation and acceptance of unique Native American cultures (Partnership with Native Americans 2021).

For most non-Natives, this chapter of U.S. history is not something encountered until college. Even then, it is typically only skimmed over in a history or an education class. This is unfortunate since this means that the majority population remains unaware of this grim but important chapter in the history of America's first inhabitants. The U.S. government abused the doctrine of Manifest Destiny, and that abuse created a tragic legacy for Native Americans. Many aspects of that legacy, such as the seizure of their lands and resources, are better known than are the Native American boarding schools. But the establishment and growth of the schools in the late 19th and early 20th centuries shows that even after the United States had stopped killing Native Americans on the field of battle, it was still at war against Native American culture.

References

BIA. 1975. "Self-Determination." https://www.bia.gov /regional-offices/great-plains/self-determination.

Department of the Interior. 2019. "Indian Boarding Schools." https://www.doi.gov/ocl/indian-boarding-schools.

Fifteenth Congress. 1819. Library of Congress. https://www .loc.gov/law/help/statutes-at-large/15th-congress/session-2 /c15s2ch85.pdf.

Laderman, Scott. 2002. "'It Is Cheaper and Better to Teach a Young Indian Than to Fight an Old One': Thaddeus Pound and the Logic of Assimilation." *American Indian Culture and Research Journal* 26 (3): 9–10.

Library of Congress. 1830. "Research Guide." Library of Congress. https://guides.loc.gov/indian-removal-act/introduction.

Meriam, Lewis. 1928. *The Meriam Report: The Problem of Indian Administration.* Baltimore, MD: John Hopkins University Press.

National Native American Boarding School Healing Coalition. 2020. "American Indian Boarding Schools by State." https://boardingschoolhealing.org/education/resources/.

Partnership with Native Americans. 2021. "History and Culture." http://www.nativepartnership.org/site/PageServer?pagename=PWNA_Native_History_boardingschoolsSW.

Pember, Mary Annette. 2019. "Death by Civilization." *Atlantic Magazine*, March 8. https://www.theatlantic.com/education/archive/2019/03/traumatic-legacy-indian-boarding-schools/584293/.

Pratt, Richard H. 1892. "'The Advantages of Mingling Indians with Whites,' Americanizing the American Indians: Writings by the 'Friends of the Indian.'" http://historymatters.gmu.edu/d/4929/.

Elizabeth M. Loomer is a Public History and Museum Studies graduate student at the University of Wisconsin–Milwaukee.

Social Justice and Injustice in the U.S.-Mexico Border Region
Mark Lusk

From a perspective of human rights and social justice, the U.S.-Mexico border region is confronted by daunting challenges as well as boundless opportunities. The region, which sits at the periphery of American society, far from the centers of economic and political power, is characterized by the politics of exclusion. While the border region is affected by health disparities and economic inequality, the most critical social justice issues in the area concern exclusionary immigration policies and hyperaggressive border enforcement, which had intensified during the Trump administration.

American immigration policy limits the rights of forced migrants, refugees, and families of mixed immigration status. Immigration policy during the Trump administration placed severe limits on authorized admission to the United States. Since the Trump administration, it had become increasingly difficult for immigrants to qualify for admission under employment-based visas, family unification, diversity visas, and international student admissions, and all but impossible to qualify for refugee status (Krogstad and Gonzalez-Barrera 2019; American Immigration Council 2020/January 8). Those legally eligible for refugee status were routinely denied access despite facing serious and life-threatening dangers if deported to their country of origin (Lusk et al. 2019; Schwartz 2019). Unauthorized crossings were criminalized under the Trump administration's "zero tolerance policy." Improper entry was a federal misdemeanor punishable by as much as six months in prison. A second unlawful entry was a felony punishable by two years in prison (American Immigration Council 2020/January 10). Many of these sentences were and still are served in for-profit private prisons with substandard and dangerous conditions (Serwer 2019).

Increasingly aggressive immigration enforcement occurred at the U.S.-Mexico border where thousands of immigration officials arrested, detained, and deported immigrants from Latin America. As of 2019–2020, nearly 17,000 border agents were stationed at the 1,954-mile southern border, 690 miles of which are walled with the remainder covered by electronic and aerial surveillance (Southern Border Communities Coalition 2020). Deportations grew markedly under the Trump administration. During the fiscal year 2019–2020 there were over 850,000 migrant apprehensions, many of whom were seeking legal protections (Gramlich 2020).

Such was the level of physical barriers and aggressive border enforcement that undocumented migrants often stayed away from border crossings and cities to make the journey through the Sonoran Desert of southern Arizona. Thousands of migrants, often fleeing violence in Mexico and Central America, have attempted this deadly crossing. Between 1998 and 2020, at least 8,000 border crossers died in the desert from hyperthermia, dehydration, and accidents, which is a death rate average of one migrant per day over the two decades (Verini 2020).

Border militarization was embodied in the war metaphor used to justify the combat technology deployed at the border, including armored vehicles, omnipresent helicopters, body armor, war-grade automatic weapons, and military-style drones. It was also exemplified by a border enforcement culture that envisions migrants as an enemy comprised of criminals and terrorists (Slack et al. 2016). The technology and language that border enforcement had at its disposal were more suited to warfare than to the humanitarian management of human movement.

The authoritarian engineering of chaos was about more than barbed wire structures and agents dressed in riot gear; it was about the forced separation of child migrants from their parents, prolonged detention and, even migrant women undergoing forced hysterectomies (Hope Border Institute 2020). A nation of immigrants and their descendants had become "Fortress America" grounded in xenophobic exclusion.

Lost in the rhetoric and reality of exclusionary immigration enforcement was any recognition of why migrants leave their countries of origin to risk a dangerous journey in which there is a high likelihood of them being arrested, detained, and deported upon arrival. In contrast to the dominant American media narrative that framed immigrants at the southern border as a national security threat, the primary drivers of undocumented immigration into America are humanitarian crises in the primary countries of origin—Mexico and the "Northern Triangle" nations of Central America (Guatemala, El Salvador, and Honduras). Several factors were at play. First among them were high rates of violence and crimes that are committed with impunity in Mexico and the Northern Triangle. With limited law enforcement due to government and police corruption, the region was and still is adversely affected by organized crime, including drug cartels and notoriously dangerous gangs such as M-18 and Mara Salvatrucha that victimize and terrorize the public (Cheatham 2020). Complicating the situation was extreme food insecurity associated with economic inequality and years of drought and crop failure (Bermeo 2019). Faced with such an environment, many opted to undertake the journey to the United States, even though the border crossings were fraught with peril, including the potential for even more violence and trauma (Lusk et al. 2019).

Instead of spending billions on a military model of border enforcement, a viable alternative is to invest in improving conditions in the countries of origin through targeted foreign assistance and social investments in education and jobs. Immigration and Customs Enforcement (ICE) spends upwards of $8 billion annually. Customs and Border Enforcement, which includes the Border Patrol, spends over $17 billion annually (American Immigration Council 2020/July 7).

To ameliorate the "push factors" that currently impel migrants to flee their home countries, a wiser policy would be to invest a fraction of that budget toward improving food security, expanding school enrollment, and restoring justice to the police and the courts in Mexico and other Central American countries. A nation that invests in human security over homeland security creates the social and economic conditions that promote social well-being and bring an end to the need to flee for one's life and safety.

References

American Immigration Council. 2020, January 8. "An Overview of U.S. Refugee Law and Policy." https://www

.americanimmigrationcouncil.org/research/overview
-us-refugee-law-and-policy.

American Immigration Council. 2020, January 10.
"Prosecuting People for Coming to the United States."
https://www.americanimmigrationcouncil.org/research
/immigration-prosecutions.

American Immigration Council. 2020, July 7. "The Cost
of Immigration Enforcement and Border Security."
https://www.americanimmigrationcouncil.org/research
/the-cost-of-immigration-enforcement-and-border
-security.

Bermeo, S. 2019. "Could Foreign Aid Help Stop Central
Americans from Coming to the U.S.? Here's What You
Need to Know." *The Washington Post*, June 18. https://www
.washingtonpost.com/politics/2019/06/18/trump
-administration-threatened-cut-foreign-aid-if-central
-american-countries-dont-stem-migration/.

Cheatham, A. S. 2020. *Central America's Turbulent
Northern Triangle*. Washington, DC: Council on
Foreign Relations. https://www.cfr.org/backgrounder
/central-americas-turbulent-northern-triangle.

Gramlich, J. 2020. "How Border Apprehensions, ICE Arrests
and Deportations Have Changed Under Trump." Pew
Research Center, March 2. https://www.pewresearch.org
/fact-tank/2020/03/02/how-border-apprehensions-ice
-arrests-and-deportations-have-changed-under-trump/.

Hope Border Institute. 2020, September 28. "World Day of
Migrants: Forced to Flee." https://mailchi.mp/hopeborder
.org/fd-09282020?e=2805d99927.

Krogstad, J. M., and A. Gonzalez-Barrera. 2019, May 17. *Key
Facts about U.S. Immigration Policies and Proposed Changes*.
Washington, DC: Pew Research Center. https://www
.pewresearch.org/fact-tank/2019/05/17/key-facts-about
-u-s-immigration-policies-and-proposed-changes/.

Lusk, M., S. Terrazas, J. Caro, P. Chaparro, and D. Puga.
2019. "Resilience, Faith and Social Supports among
Migrants and Refugees from Central America and Mexico."
Journal of Spirituality in Mental Health. https://doi.org/10
.1080/19349637.2019.1620668.

Schwartz, S. 2019. "Sending Refugees Back Make the
World More Dangerous." *Foreign Policy*, November
27. https://foreignpolicy.com/2019/11/27/
sending-refugees-back-makes-the-world-more-dangerous/.

Serwer, Adam. 2019. "A Crime by Any Name." *The Atlantic*,
July 3. https://www.theatlantic.com/ideas/archive/2019/07
/border-facilities/593239/.

Slack, J., D. E. Martinez, A. E. Lee, and S. Whiteford. 2016.
"The Geography of Border Militarization: Violence Death
and Health in Mexico and the United States." *Journal of
Latin American Geography* 15 (1): 7–32.

Southern Border Communities Coalition. 2020. *Border
Militarization.* San Diego: Alliance San Diego.
https://www.southernborder.org/border_lens
_border_militarization.

Verini, J. 2020. "How U.S. Policy Turned the Sonoran
Desert Into a Graveyard for Migrants." *The New York
Times*, August 28. https://www.nytimes.com/2020/08/18
/magazine/border-crossing.html.

*Mark Lusk is professor emeritus in the Department of Social Work
at the University of Texas, El Paso.*

Understanding Political Inactivity in the Border Region
Maria Antonieta Reyes

The U.S.-Mexico border is greatly influenced by its geography. It is at once a physical, social, economic, and political line marking an area of both division and unity between the United States and Mexico. It spans 1,933 miles from the Pacific

Ocean to the Gulf of Mexico and is comprised of desert, rocky, and mountainous terrain, sprawling and densely populated urban areas, and approximately 1,255 miles of the river Rio Grande. The geography of the border makes it impossible to erect a continuous man-made physical barrier between the two countries, but those who live on either side of the border are aware of the inhospitable terrain that prevails along much of its length. Historically, many land disputes between Mexico and the United States led to much of this area being deemed a "no man's land" and contributed to a strong culture of survival and self-sufficiency among people living along the border. This attitude of self-sufficiency, given the land's limited water resources particularly, has created an inactive political culture, even when it comes to socioeconomic priorities.

Border politics and border-control policies are key functions of the state; together, they form a basic element of state sovereignty (Gravella 2018, 107). Sovereignty centers on control of migration and related economic concerns. It concerns the relationship of the state with the environment. It further concerns the state's role in the world. Sovereignty dominates the conceptualization and construction of physical barriers (Madsen 2011, 547, 553).

Border barriers form the tangible, physical demarcation of where one nation's power ends and another's begins. They also reflect the cultural landscapes of a diverse sociopolitical environment along the border (Madsen 2011, 548, 553). The border region consists of four states on the American side (California, Arizona, New Mexico, and Texas) and six states on the Mexican side (Baja California, Sonora, Chihuahua, Coahuila, Nuevo Leon, and Tamaulipas). The region has 15 sets of "twin cities"— towns and cities that sit directly across each other along the U.S.-Mexico border. Generally speaking, residents of these twin cities often cross the border daily to work or to shop. The twin cities are: San Diego–Tijuana, Calexico–Mexicali, Yuma–San Luis Río Colorado, Nogales–Nogales, Naco–Naco, Douglas–Agua Prieta, Columbus–Puerto Palomas, El Paso–Ciudad

Juárez, Presidio–Ojinaga, Del Rio–Ciudad Acuña, Eagle Pass–Piedras Negras, Laredo–Nuevo Laredo, McAllen–Reynosa, Weslaco–Río Bravo, and Brownsville–Matamoros. These towns and cities share a binational reality in which their communities exist amid a constant exchange—with one another—of commerce, politics, culture, people, and more. Each of these cities experiences the border not just as a social or political barrier but as a constant physical and symbolic barrier that contributes to cultural and political conceptions of the people on the other side as alien "others" (Lopez 2020, 243; Madsen 2011, 547).

With every shift in the political environment in the two countries, the nations "reinterpret the barriers accordingly" (Madsen 2011, 548). On the one hand, borders can strengthen sociopolitical ties by emphasizing cooperation between the members of the two nations concerned. Porous borders can also provide opportunities for exchange and openness in such areas as politics, culture, marriage, family ties, traditions, labor, commerce, and exchange of goods and services (Lopez 2020).

On the other hand, the border is a division, a barrier, a demarcation mostly felt by transnational actors (understood as citizens who are living outside their borders, and organizations or groups involved in politics, commerce, and expanding social relationships that take place between residents in border regions), by citizens at the local level, and by those seeking to migrate to the United States (Lopez 2020, 243). For citizens living at the border, the demarcation is a "physical structure" that is both imposing and arbitrary (Lopez 2020). The border is the area where agents of state authority decide who enters the country as well as when and how they do so. This decision is a categorical discrimination that establishes the potential of illegality based on class and race differences that factor into some individuals being classified as "illegal aliens" when they migrate to the United States without legal documentation to do so (Lopez 2020).

This process "creates an extended regime of spatial and social segregation where the nation-state through the border exercises physical power, disciplining power, and punishing power" (Lopez 2020). One of the ways that *physical power* is established and exercised is through the creation of physical barriers. Although these barriers have changed in form—from fences to walls—according to changes in political priorities and power in Washington, D.C., the fact remains that they are always present, just as electronic surveillance systems and border agents are always present. Interactions with these physical powers occurs daily (Garfield 2017).

Disciplining power is the power exercised by the nation-state and its border-control agency to make applicants follow complex and arcane procedures decided by and brought into effect by the state. Each step of the process is established and decided by the authority of the state, and not following the steps precisely entails punishment (Lopez 2020, 250–251). *Punishing power* is the power of the state to deny entrance to an immigrant in a reality that denotes immigration as an opportunity. Here, denial of entrance is in many ways the placing of a person in a space that is neither a nation nor a culture nor a social structure (like a family). It is the placing of humans in a kind of purgatory or "no man's land" (Lopez 2020, 252–254). This means that while each nation may view the border as a space of opportunity, it is the transnational actors and the locals who carry the burden of disconnection. Migrants from Central American countries (particularly Guatemala, Honduras, and El Salvador) who come to the border seeking asylum are forced to remain in Mexico until hearings are scheduled, but many of them don't learn about the timing and scheduling of those hearings for weeks (Lopez 2020, 242).

The discussion of politics regarding the U.S-Mexico border includes a certain level of practicality that attempts to maintain an established political reality even if that reality is unacceptable to certain democratic values. Daniel Elazar, in his book *The American Cultural Matrix* (1972), distinguished three main political cultures, which he developed according to the original groups of immigrants to the United States. These political cultures aim at facilitating understanding of politics in any given geographical area. Elazar noted that while areas can have more than one political culture, there is one culture that is dominant. It defines not only the political priorities of an area but also who participates in politics and how the process of politics is practiced. Two of these political cultures operate in the U.S.-Mexico border region: Traditionalistic Political Culture (TPC) and Individualistic Political Culture (IPC).

TPC views the government as a tool to maintain order. The culture promotes acceptance of an established hierarchy where the commonwealth is protected by a paternalistic power personified by an elite class. Order is maintained by limiting who gets involved in politics, leaving the activity only to those members of society established as belonging to a certain kind of political class. These members are presumed to know what is best for the community and established as belonging in that class, or having that privileged status, due to their familial ties or social status. In this context, the remaining citizens are expected to play the role of inactive citizens who only participate when it may be deemed necessary for them to do so by those in power. This establishes elections and the process of politics as consisting of transactions and exchanges of favors—the main means by which inactive members can move up into active roles. TPC extends to organizations that have been established and maintained to serve the public (such as city hall, the police department, the fire department, and the utilities department). These agencies and departments are sometimes perceived as an impediment by those in power because bureaucracies tend to be responsive to the law, not to politicians.

IPC views the government as a tool to serve the individual politician in their pursuit of happiness, which in this culture is defined as enrichment, gain, or profit. The IPC views society as a marketplace. The competition of ideas and approaches leads to political power and once obtained, that political power is accepted as dominant. Dominant ideas or approaches then confer the right to lead, which in this culture is manifested in the area's economics. The language and priorities are all expressed in terms of profit and economic gain. In this context, the rest of the citizens are expected to play the role of inactive citizens who only participate when the competition is open and only if they are considered worthy opponents, meaning they have sufficient wealth.

This makes elections and the process of politics a competition for dominance that fosters division between the dominant group and those who do not agree with the dominant group's ideas or methods. It also promotes politics as an activity in which not everyone should get involved. When this culture is extended to public organizations, it also perceives them as an impediment to the pursuit of happiness, as red tape. This culture sees governance as a business enterprise. Political activity is then seen as recognition that government is only a tool to serve specific interests. Similarly, politics is not understood as a mechanism for consensus building but as the basis for contracts and trade-offs between the state and its dominant political ideas, individuals, and organizations.

The border emerged with a strong spirit of "frontierism," a sense of endless opportunity coupled with an absence of government. Frontierism and the history of border disputes enhances a kind of pride in self-reliance (Mendoza 2011). Land and water disputes left the border in a type of "neutral zone," a "netherworld," where different groups fought to gain control because neither country would officially recognize the border area (Mendoza 2011, 131). Citizens having to fend for themselves resulted in the emergence of local trading posts, commerce centers, and import and export trading operations (Mendoza 2011, 129).

In 1953, the U.S. Department of Justice adopted a law that established the jurisdiction of the Border Patrol to 100 miles from the border. According to this law, certain constitutional protections against government abuse of power do not apply in these regions, particularly in the first 25 miles on either side of the border. While this has resulted in high levels of government presence, it has also reinforced the sense that the border does not wholly belong to either Mexico or the United States. Alexander Mendoza notes that "national allegiance and identity could be part of a two-way exchange in which [one] could negotiate what that loyalty could be in order to further [one's] own interests" (2011, 126–127). In other words, questions of economic survival can heavily impact considerations of national allegiance and identity.

When one attempts to understand politics at the U.S.-Mexico border, it may be easy to attribute insights to voting or polling results and trends. However, it is important to note that understanding particular socioecological systems requires knowledge of local personal practices, leadership, levels of trust, reciprocity, and collective action. Individual, personal practices may reveal more for an overall understanding of politics in the border area (Toledo 2013). If we accept that the border is a different socioecological system than the rest of the nation, then we should accept that results in the two areas may not be the same. If one looks at election maps, regardless of state politics, cities along the U.S.-Mexico border tend to be blue and are therefore presumed to adhere to Democratic Party politics or to the liberal side. However, traditional practices of submission to power (which emphasizes certain presumptions of power as might- and gender-based), to economic interests (what will be seen as making my economy more stable or to grow; thereby creating jobs), and to the importance of religious traditions has made other stretches along the border more conservative and Republican. The interest of self-sufficiency and economic gain surpasses democratic practices. In the border region, then, politics is about self-sufficiency and economic gain and power. An analysis of U.S. border city voting by Adkisson and Saucedo (2011) revealed that democratic values in the cities vary and that voting may be influenced not only by rhetoric but, most importantly, by the uniqueness of life on the border. Activities in the border region between the two nations involve personal activities and experiences, with economic, security, and immigration issues here differing from those experienced by citizens outside the border. Most border citizens are more invested in the socioeconomic dimension of their society than in the political dimension.

Both TPC and IPC highlight that those active in governance do so for their own interest—to maintain control of order and power. The geographical imposition of border towns as bridges between two nations has emphasized their economic prioritization. This makes those in power exercise such power in terms of IPC and those inactive to accept reality in terms of TPC. The border is thereby both an area of opportunity for unity and a reinforcement of otherness and division.

References

Adkisson, R. V., and E. Saucedo. 2011. "Voting for President in the U.S.-Mexico Border Region." *The Social Science Journal* 48 (2): 273–282. https://doi.org/10.1016/j.soscij.2010.12.003.

Elazar, J. D. 1972. "The American Cultural Matrix." In *American Federalism: A View from the States*. 2nd ed. New York: Thomas Y Crowell.

Garfield, L. 2017. "Trump's $25 Billion Wall Would Be Nearly Impossible to Build, According to Architects." *Business Insider*, January 14. https://www.businessinsider.com/trump-wall-impossible-build-architects-2017-1.

Gravella, T. B. 2018. "Politics, Time, Space, and Attitudes towards US-Mexico Border Security." *Political Geography* 65: 107–116.

Kelin, C. 2018. "Everything You Need to Know About the Mexico-United States Border." History.com, December 26. https://www.history.com/news/everything-you-need-to-know-about-the-mexico-united-states-border.

Lopez, J. L. 2020. "Together and Apart: Transnational life on the U.S. Mexico Border Region." *Journal of Ethnic and*

Migration Studies 46 (1): 242–259. https://doi.org/10.1080 /1369183X.2018.1523003.

Madsen, K. D. 2011. "Barriers of the US-Mexico Border as Landscapes of Domestic Political Compromise." *Cultural Geographies in Practice* 18 (4): 547–556.

Mendoza, A. 2011. "'For Our Own Best Interest': Nineteenth-Century Laredo Tejanos, Military Service, and the Development of American Nationalism." *The Southwestern Historical Quarterly* 115 (2): 125–152. http://www.jstor.org/stable/23059197.

Toledo, D. 2013. "Socioecological Systems along the US/ Mexico Border." *Frontiers in Ecology and the Environment* 11 (2): 106–107. https://www.jstor.org/stable/23470530.

Maria Antonieta Reyes is an Auburn University PhD graduate, a professor, and a Loredo, Texas political candidate.

Changing Labor Dynamics on the U.S.-Mexico Border: Agricultural and Domestic Workers in Historical and Contemporary Perspectives
Mark Saka

The U.S.-Mexico border is characterized by long-standing economic, demographic, cultural, and ecological interdependence. This interdependence is complicated by great disparities between the two nations—in terms of wealth, of political and social balances of power, and of labor systems. Labor systems on both the Mexican and U.S. sides of the border region are built having a low-wage and expendable labor force across many economic sectors. Those sectors include agricultural and migrant workers, domestic female workers, construction workers, and since 1965, a manufacturing labor system in Mexico under the maquiladora factory regimes and spurred by the 1994 North American Free Trade Agreement. This essay seeks to examine the past, present, and future of the work force in the border region by focusing on workers in the agricultural and domestic-help sectors.

At the turn of the 20th century, Mexican migrant agricultural labor indirectly subsidized the growth of the American industrial economy and the American consumer. Low-wage and labor-intensive migrant work helped maintain an ample supply of vegetables, fruits, and meats for Americans, apart from serving as a brake on inflationary food prices. Over the course of the 20th century, Mexican agricultural workers functioned as a "transnational reserve army of the poor" as the American agricultural sector "pulled" them into the Southwest during the decades 1900–1930. The United States expelled those same workers during the Great Depression repatriation drives of the 1930s, but when it needed cheap agricultural labor after World War II it used the Bracero Program (1942–1965) to draw new generations of Mexicans back to U.S. fields and orchards. The demise of the Bracero Program also marked the beginning of the era of the "illegal alien," which remains an important source of cheap labor for American agriculture and various low-wage industries.

Multiple transnational forces gave rise to this agricultural labor regime, including the transition of the American working class from agricultural labor to a Southwestern and Midwestern industrial work force and professional class; the tremendous growth of the American metropolitan Southwest; the emergence of a post-industrial U.S. economy based increasingly on healthcare and the hospitality service sector; and the growth of specialty agricultural products in northern Mexico and the American Southwest—crops that tend to be labor intensive and grow only within short-term growing and harvesting seasons. In Mexico, these economic forces and the magnet of the U.S. economy gave rise to sustained demographic growth during 1940–1982, with a fertility rate of 3.5 percent. It also gave rise to a lack of labor-intensive manufacturing job growth. It impacted the Mexican political economy as one dependent on the North American economy.

Exploited and expendable, Mexican agricultural workers are expected to decline sharply in numbers in 2020 to 2030, due to macroeconomic and demographic forces, the same ones that gave rise to the borderland labor systems. Mexico's declining fertility rate (from 3.5 percent in 1982 to less than national replacement levels of 2.1 percent by the first decade of the 21st century), the rise in its per capita income and a shift in the Mexican labor force from farm jobs to non-farm jobs, the rise in Mexican agricultural labor productivity, the growth of the manufacturing and automobile industrial sectors, and the rising level of education in Mexico among the rural population have all contributed to the decline of Mexican agricultural workers in the U.S.-Mexico border region and the American Southwest in general. As a result, farm economies on the U.S. side of the border region may increasingly be forced to rely on Central American or Asian African workers, an increasing mechanization of Southwestern agriculture, or a shift away from labor-intensive crops. The age of the Mexican agricultural worker toiling away in American fields—supplementing the American consumer's dinner table with low-wage, exploited, and expendable labor—is markedly declining.

The trend lines are moving in the opposition direction for Latinx (U.S. Latinx, Mexican, and Central American) women providing domestic labor in the U.S.-Mexico border region. Instead of declining, as in the case of migrant agricultural workers, demand for domestic labor is expected to expand rapidly due to the aging of the U.S. population and the increasing need for healthcare, the lack of childcare for American working-class and even middle-class families that increasingly work multiple jobs for economic survival, and the demand among more affluent Americans for in-home house-cleaning services. Domestic women workers represent the most vulnerable of border workers as the intersectionality of class, race, and gender leave them vulnerable to a number of exploitive labor practices and economic and personal forces, and that too in a far less regulated home and private environment than other industries. Numerous studies have focused on this vulnerability in such areas as food and housing insecurity, wage theft, irregular pay and schedules, long and extended work hours without overtime pay, lack of workers' compensation, potential solvent and chemical exposure, workplace injuries, verbal and physical abuse and potential sexual assault, and the overall fear of deportation, even as the lack of citizenship rights and proper documentation hangs as an albatross over the necks of undocumented workers. Although a significant percentage of Latinx domestic workers are U.S. citizens or hold worker's permits, inadequate worker protection and an anti-immigrant and anti-Latinx hostility from America's chauvinistic and xenophobic political culture may combine to leave this "invisible" segment of the border-region workforce nearly as vulnerable as undocumented domestic workers.

Another factor in conceptualizing domestic workers' exploitive labor and personal situation is the fact that two-thirds of the 1,933-mile U.S.-Mexico border lies along the state of Texas. Texas is a state that is home to the lowest-paid workers in the country and contains a border region saddled with impoverished "colonias" where infant mortality rates and health and welfare indicators rank below many regions of the "third world." This region's rankings in these areas parallel that of deeply impoverished Native American reservations. Texas also has an aggressive state legislature that openly encourages state law enforcement officials to coordinate repressive and deportation-focused immigration policies with federal law enforcement agencies.

Unlike the declining role of Mexican agricultural labor in the U.S.-Mexico border region, however, the role of domestic Latina workers in the American economy is expected to increase over the 2020–2030 decade due to escalating demand, and they will represent the most vulnerable segment of the inequitable political, economic, and social labor force due to the intersection of class, race, and gender in oppressive systems of repression and discrimination.

References

Burnham, Linda, Lisa Moore, and Emilee Ohia. 2018. *Living in the Shadows: Latina Domestic Workers in the Texas-Mexico Border Region*. New York: National Domestic Workers Alliance.

Charlton, Diane, and J. Edward Taylor. 2013. "Mexicans Are Leaving Farm Work: What Does It Mean for U.S. Agriculture and Immigration Policy." *Agriculture and Resource Economics* 16 (4): 1–4.

Holder, Sarah. 2018. *The Process of Domestic Workers' Invisible Labor in U.S. Border Towns*. New York: National Domestic Workers Alliance.

Massey, Jorge Durand, and Nolan Malone. 2002. *Beyond Smoke and Mirror: Mexican Immigration in an era of Economic Integration*. New York: Russell Sage Foundation.

Taylor, J. Edward, Diane Charlton, and U. C. Davis. n. d. "U.S. Farms and the Dwindling Labor Supply from Mexico." Policy Brief. Center for Poverty Research, volume 1, number 5. https://poverty.ucdavis.edu/policy-brief/us-farms-and-dwindling-labor-supply-mexico.

Mark Saka is chair of behavioral and social sciences and professor of history and political science at Sul Ross State University in Alpine, Texas.

The Apache Wars and the U.S.-Mexico Border
David Zeh

During the 19th century, the U.S. government was eager to expand its territory and develop the lands to the west, in part to accommodate the seemingly endless numbers of people emigrating from Europe to American shores. Americans of European descent believed it was their duty to settle on and tame the wilderness of the American West, even though it was already occupied by hundreds of Native American tribes. They convinced themselves that Native Americans were improperly using the land and that it was up to Europeans to teach them how to be "civilized." This idea that the West was destined to be tamed and converted for America's use came to be known as Manifest Destiny, and it was used to justify the horrible treatment and displacement of Native Americans throughout the 19th century. One Southwestern tribe, called the Apache, acted as a thorn in the side of both the U.S. and Mexican governments during these decades. The Apaches were so notorious for their raids on Mexican and American villages and towns that the governments of both countries dispatched armies to deal directly with the tribe. This essay will demonstrate how the defiance of one small band of Chiricahua Apaches, however, led to their removal from their ancestral homelands in the Southwest—and how subsequent depictions of the Apache people in American media, particular in popular films, complicated their fight to reclaim the land taken from them.

The ancestral homelands of the Apache are congregated around the modern-day U.S.-Mexico border. The Chiricahua Apache, or Western Apache, are linguistically associated with the Eastern Apache, but they have a different system of kinship. They lived primarily in the mountain landscapes of New Mexico and Arizona on the U.S. side, and Chihuahua and Sonora on the Mexican side. Their land had both defensive and spiritual purposes (Arreola 2012, 113–117). During the Spanish colonial era, the government in Mexico implemented the *reduccion* system. This government policy forced Native Americans to resettle on mission-based villages in the hope that it would encourage a more agrarian lifestyle. While many tribes accepted and came to terms with the arrangement, the nomadic lifestyle of the Chiricahua Apache, combined with the mountainous landscape of their homeland, made it difficult for the Spanish to keep the Apache within the *reduccion* process, unlike the other tribes in the region (Arreola 2021, 119–121).

The Chiricahua Apache were notable for their raids on settlements and villages in both Mexico and the United States. The main goals of these raids are still debated, but historians believe they helped young warriors prepare for warfare, provided the tribe with supplies, and bolstered their numbers by adopting captives into the tribe. In 1821, the Spanish government recognized Mexico as an independent nation. This transition of power led the Chiricahua to return to their settlements in the mountains and to continue their raids on neighboring villages. The violence between the Apache and the Mexicans became so horrific that in 1835 it led to the states of Sonora and Chihuahua implementing scalping laws that placed a bounty on Apaches. Authorities in these states accepted the scalps of Apaches as proof of a "kill" (Arreola 2012, 122). Unfortunately, the violence in the border region only worsened throughout the mid-1800s, as more American settlers arrived from the East.

In 1861, Lieutenant George Bascom accused the leader of the Chokonen band of the Chiricahua Apache, Chief Cochise, of raiding a farm within his territory. Cochise denied any knowledge of the event, but Bascom believed he was lying and took Cochise's family hostage after Cochise escaped from Basom's camp (Apache Wars, Part I). This event led to a 24-year conflict between the U.S. government and the tribe that came to be known as the Apache Wars. They were part of the larger Indian Wars taking place all over the Western United States with the intent of pushing Native Americans onto reservations—many of which were established on land of limited or no commercial value—to make way for settlers who could "make better use of the land" that had once belonged to the Indigenous people. Many of the tribes fought to maintain their sovereignty, risking everything against an army with vastly superior supplies of resources and soldiers. Eventually, the tribes were left with no other choice but to agree to the terms set by the U.S. government. This was true even for the Apaches, except for a small band of Chiricahua led by the infamous Geronimo. His band fought back against the invaders with such tenacity that it altered the way the Apache were depicted in the U.S. mass media for the next century.

Geronimo was one of Cochise's most reliable warriors and he shared the belief that his people deserved freedom and the right to stay on their land. His legendary status began after he lost his family to a massacre when he was still a young man (Apache Wars, Part II). Geronimo's changed outlook on life made him an exceptionally dangerous opponent since he did not care whether he lived or died. After the death of Cochise in 1874, Geronimo led the remaining Chiricahua, who were still willing to fight the U.S. government and unwilling to give in to its demands. Geronimo's continuous raids in the United States and Mexico led both governments to form an agreement whereby their soldiers could travel across the border to try to stop the Chiricahua. However, the agreement proved to be of little use since the relationship between the two countries was still strained as a result of the Mexican-American War. On one occasion, for example, a U.S. army lieutenant was shot and killed by Mexican soldiers when he tried to pursue Geronimo and his band of warriors.

After years of brutal conflict, U.S. president Grover Cleveland appointed General Nelson Miles to deal with Geronimo. General Miles placed a whopping $25,000 bounty on Geronimo's head, but the warrior and his small band of followers continued to evade capture by the 5,000 U.S. soldiers, 3,000 Mexican soldiers, and around 1,000 volunteers who were tasked with getting his surrender. In 1886, General Miles finally managed to get Geronimo to surrender by maliciously arresting 434 Chiricahua members on the San Carlos Reservation and moving them to Florida. The forced relocation of the members of his tribe to distant Florida prompted Geronimo to surrender (Apache Wars, Part II). Following Geronimo's surrender, the Chiricahua Apache were completely removed from their homeland along the border, and to this day they have no federally recognized land in the region.

Geronimo's legendary leadership and use of guerrilla-warfare tactics during the Apache Wars made the Apache popular antagonists in Western movies filmed during the mid-20th century. These films seldom addressed the fact that the Chiricahua were defending themselves against assimilation and the loss of their ancestral lands. In the John Wayne movie *Rio Grande,* for example, the mission of the U.S. Army is to make the region safe for "civilized" society and prevent the Apache from crossing the U.S.-Mexico border on the river Rio Grande (Lahti 2013, 57). Western movies like *Rio Grande* conveyed the idea that the Apache were standing in the way of progress, thereby reinforcing the belief in Manifest Destiny and ignoring the plight of Native Americans. These insensitive, negative, and oftentimes racist media portrayals of the Apache made it difficult for the tribe to gain public support when fighting to reclaim their ancestral homelands.

Despite such offensive media depictions, the Apache still hold ties to their homeland through place names throughout the Southwest. Places like Cochise Head, a mountaintop in the Chiricahua Mountain range, keep alive the legacy of the Chiricahua Apache, even though few Chiricahua now live in the region.

In 2011, the tribe established a 30-acre reservation near Akeia Flats in New Mexico. While this reservation is tiny in comparison to the land they once called home, the Chiricahua Apache proudly advertise their land on a billboard off the interstate highway that proclaims, "Apache Homeland." Places allow people to form attachments and memories that make the land much more than just a place. Memories give places life and meaning. When these important places are taken away from people by force, they end up losing a central part of their cultural identity as well.

References

"The Apache Wars Part I: Cochise." *National Park Service.* U.S. Department of the Interior. https://www.nps.gov/chir /learn/historyculture/apache-wars-cochise.htm.

"The Apache Wars Part II: Geronimo." *National Park Service.* U.S. Department of the Interior. https://www.nps.gov /cnhir/learn/historyculture/apache-wars-geronimo.htm.

Arreola, Daniel D. 2012. "Chiricahua Apache Homeland in the Borderland Southwest." *Geographical Review* 102 (1): 111–131.

Lahti, Janne. 2013. "Silver Screen Savages: Images of the Apache in Motion-Pictures." *The Journal of Arizona History* 54 (1): 51–84.

David Zeh is a graduate student at the University of Wisconsin– Milwaukee. He focuses in particular on Native American history and culture in the university's museum studies program.

4 Profiles

Introduction

This chapter profiles some of the organizations and people involved in the U.S.-Mexico border region—impacting its culture, economy, environment, policies, and politics as well as influencing social change in the region. These organizations and people are key stakeholders involved in advocating policy for or against changes in the borderland region. They exemplify both government and nongovernment affiliations. Although many dozens of such organizations and people could be appropriately profiled here, space considerations have limited our selection. The ones that have been profiled have been selected to illustrate organizations and persons using the four pathways to incorporation discussed in Chapter 2: (1) demands/protests, (2) nonconfrontational political evolution, (3) legal challenges to structural barriers, and (4) coalition politics (Geron 2005; LeMay 2009).

Organizations

Alianza Federal de Mercedes

Initiated in New Mexico on February 2, 1962, Alianza Federal de Mercedes (the Federal Land Grant Alliance) was a coalition

Border patrol officers drive their all-terrain vehicles along the rugged border between the United States and Mexico. The border patrol also uses trucks, drones, and planes to patrol the border. (James Tourtellotte/U.S. Customs & Border Protection)

of groups. It was also known by the names Alianza de Pueblos y Pobladores (the Alliance of Towns and Settlers) and Alianza de Pueblos Libres (the Alliance of Free Pueblos). It was an organization that began as an accommodationist-style advocacy group that used federal court litigation as the pathway to pursue its incorporation objectives. It has been compared to the National Alliance for the Advancement of Colored People (NAACP) in that regard. The motto of Alianza Federal de Mercedes was "Justice is our creed, and the land is our heritage" (Gardner 1970; LeMay 2009; 148, 303–305; Steiner 1969, 88; Tijerina 2001). It had affiliates in Tierra Amarilla, New Mexico, and San Luis, Colorado. The Alianza used federal courts to assert claims to land that had been taken illegally from Mexican settlers living in Texas and New Mexico after the Treaty of Guadalupe Hidalgo. In particular, they challenged the land grabs of the 1870s and 1880s that were perpetrated by Thomas Benton Catron and others of the infamous Santa Fe Ring (Ebright 1994).

The Alianza was led by the fiery Reies Lopez Tijerina, known as "El Tigre" (the Tiger) (Oropeza 2019; Tijerina 2001). The Alianza argued that land rights were based on treaty rights established by the law of nations. The land grants comprised millions of acres across Texas, New Mexico, Arizona, California, Nevada, Utah, and Colorado (LeMay 2009, 303–304).

Records of land grants were often destroyed, but they were known to number as high as 1,700 and enormous profits were made by Anglos who had seized land grant property, often employing legal chicanery to do so. For example, Thomas Catron had acquired 593,000 acres with a single "patenting claim" brought to the Court of Private Land Claims (Ebright 1994; LeMay 2009, 304). Hispanic settlers, many of whom were traditional shepherds, lost their land to cattle ranchers and to the U.S. Forest Service, often in what became known as the "Sheep Wars" of the 1880s and 1890s. When the Alianza's litigation efforts failed, its members turned to the tactics of direct-action protest. On June 5, 1967, in Tierra Amarilla, a small town in southern New Mexico, members seized the town's courthouse, holding it for several hours during which time shots were fired and two deputies were wounded. The state government responded by sending in some 400 National Guard troopers and 200 state troopers apart from using armored tanks. The Guard and state troopers were called in by New Mexico's governor David Cargo (Republican, 1967–1971). The state troopers arrested the leadership of the Alianza on a charge of kidnapping, which was later reduced to false imprisonment (LeMay 2009, 304; Steiner 1969, 41; Tijerina 2001). Reies Tijerina was sent to jail, and while he was in jail the Alianza offices were attacked, in April 1968; the attacks were led by a former sheriff's deputy. Persons perpetrating the attack were associated with the vigilante Minutemen organization. They bombed the Alianza headquarters. The likely Minutemen member, a former deputy, bungled the job and blew off his right hand. Police followed the bloody trail and arrested him, but a grand jury cleared him of the more serious charges, and he was sentenced to a mere 16 hours of community service. An Alianza car was tear-gassed while members were still in it, but no arrests were made. As was all too often the case, the local police were complicit if not actively involved in the discrimination against Hispanics and Native Americans in the border region.

The paramilitary vigilante group Minutemen was caught by the Federal Bureau of Investigation (FBI) near Albuquerque. The FBI seized a large cache of weapons, ammunition, bombs, and maps of land grant villages. Minutemen's leader, Robert De Pugh, was caught along with Walter Peyson, the alleged assassin-to-be of Tijerina. The cache of seized weapons was so large that it took 24 single-space typed pages of the police report on the raid to list all the items seized. Someone in local law enforcement, however, warned the Minutemen membership that the raid had caught DePugh and Peyson, had confiscated the weapons, and had seized documents that included a membership list of the Minutemen. The chief of security of Alianza was warned that Reies Lopez Tijerina had been marked for assassination. Although no assassination was attempted—perhaps because Peyton had been seized—Tijerina's house was bombed three times, once while his wife and children were inside (LeMay 2009, 305; Steiner 1969, 89). Tijerina's health declined while in prison and to be released early, he agreed not to hold any leadership position in Alianza. The Alianza organization declined without Tijerina's fiery leadership. In 1979, the federal courts did consider the land grant issue, but no legal victories were won, and the organization faded. In 2015 in El Paso, Texas, Tijerina died at the age of 89 (Oropeza 2019).

Center for Biological Diversity

The Center for Biological Diversity (CBD) is a 501(c)(3) nonprofit membership organization working to protect endangered species through litigation, scientific studies, creative media campaigns, and grassroots activism. It was founded in 1989 by Kieran Suckling, Peter Galvin, Todd Schulke, and Robin Silver. It is headquartered in Tucson, Arizona, but has staff and offices in New Mexico, Nevada, California, Oregon, Illinois, Minnesota, Alaska, Vermont, Florida, and Washington. It sponsors an e-network of volunteers. It exemplifies the coalition pathway to incorporation as well as being a think-tank organization.

The CBD began with a small grant from the Fund for Wild Nature. Its initial objective was to protect endangered species and habitats in the southwestern United States. It began advocating against the U.S. Forest Service for its failures in protecting endangered species from logging, grazing, and mining operations (all of which provide funds to the Forest Service). Today, the CBD addresses concerns regarding global threats to biodiversity and climate change. It uses litigation extensively and claims a 93 percent success rate in its lawsuits. The CBD was highly critical of President George W. Bush's administration for its failure to enforce the Endangered Species Act and for the environmental degradation effects of the border fence projects. It also fought the Trump administration's proposal for a border wall and expansion of the border fence (Center for Biological Diversity n.d.). The CBD has conducted several studies and issued reports on the detrimental biological effects on the environment in the borderland region, particularly in southern Arizona, and on the devastating impact that building the border wall would have on hundreds of endangered species along both sides of the U.S.-Mexico border. Its reports have focused particularly on the Sonora Desert region and the plant and animal species in that region; they have focused on how extension of the border fence or barriers would adversely affect Pueblo communities, the habitats of dozens of species of wildlife and plants in the border region, and colonia communities on the U.S. side of the border.

Center for Land Grant Studies

The Center for Land Grant Studies (CLGS) is a 501(c)(3) nonprofit organization devoted to research, education, and the distribution of books and other archival materials about the Southwest. It is a good example of the "think-tank" approach to advocacy concerning for a policy problem area. A think tank is a public policy center or institute comprised of experts who provide advice and ideas on specific political or economic problems. It performs research and advocacy on topics ranging from social policy, political strategy, and economic policy to military matters, technology, and culture. It is a term used to describe private nonprofit policy research organizations (Hagedorn and LeMay 2019, 169–172).

CLGS was founded in 1979. It lays emphasis on land and water rights issues concerning traditional communities in New Mexico (pueblos and colonias). It focuses on Spanish and Mexican land grants that were made to Hispanics and Native Americans as well as on genealogical materials connected with the rural communities of New Mexico. Among its important books on the area are *Pueblo Sovereignty: Indian Land and Water Rights in New Mexico and Texas* (2019); *Advocates for the Oppressed: Hispanos, Indians, Genizaros, and Their Lands in New Mexico* (2014), *Four Square League* (2014), and *Spanish and Mexican Land Grants and the Law* (1989). There is also a research paper called "The Tierra Amarilla Grant: A History of Chicanery." Another CLGS book *Land Grants and Lawsuits in Northern New Mexico* (2008), by Malcolm Ebright, is considered the definitive book about land grants.

The CLGS also maintains a land grant database from archives in New Mexico. It has archived the complete text of the Treaty of Guadalupe Hidalgo. It has on file excerpts from various land grant lawsuits; it also has a critique of the U.S. General Accounting Office report on the Treaty of Guadalupe Hidalgo that has a list of community land grants in New Mexico. Importantly, the CLGS maintains an online database of all New Mexico land grants that is broken down by county for easier research and analysis. The CLGS has census transcriptions from Rio Arriba for the years 1860–1900. The CLGS is an invaluable resource for research and analysis related to land grants that were, or are, within the U.S.-Mexico border region, as well as for cultural-social issues facing Hispanic and Latino communities in the region.

Chicanos Por La Causa

Chicanos Por La Causa (CPLC) is a nonprofit advocacy organization founded in 1969 to confront discrimination faced by Latinos in the Phoenix, Arizona area. It has now grown to service Latino communities throughout the southwestern states. It was earlier associated with Cesar Chavez, Dolores Huerta, and the United Farm Workers (UFW) movement that began in the early 1960s and practiced peaceful protest politics into the 1970s. CPLC is headquartered in Phoenix but has grown to become one of the largest nonprofits in the Southwest. It evolved from the politics of protest to the strategy of coalition politics. It promotes stronger and healthier communities throughout the borderland region. CPLC assists more than

375,000 individuals in Arizona, Nevada, and New Mexico. It advocates in bilingual and bicultural services for health and human services, housing, education, and economic development. CPLC is incorporated in Arizona. It serves low- to moderate-income individuals and families. It promotes cultural and linguistic competencies and advocates for economic and political empowerment and self-sufficiency. The term "Chicanos" in the organization's name refers to persons who navigate the Mexican and American worlds. The name was popularized during the Hispanic civil rights movement of the 1960s and 1970s. "For the cause" refers to the organization's combat against discrimination. CPLC advocates for equal opportunity for all people—regardless of racial or ethnic background. It owns and manages some for-profit businesses to help sustain its charitable initiatives.

CPLC addresses the changing needs of the communities it serves, including all age groups from infants to seniors. Its integrated programs aim at helping the whole person. While it helps people of all backgrounds, it has a special competence in meeting the needs of Southwest Latino communities in Arizona. "Si, se puede!" (Yes, we can!), the phrase made famous by the UFW and later popularized by President Obama's campaigns in 2008 and 2012, was coined by Cesar Chavez and Dolores Huerta at the CPLC headquarters in Phoenix in 1972 (Chicanos Por La Causa 2020; Dimas 2019).

Human Rights First

Human Rights First (HRF) is an independent advocacy and action organization that is nonpartisan, nonprofit, and an international human rights institution with offices in New York, Washington, D.C., Houston, and Los Angeles. It was founded in 1978 by Marvin Frankel and Michael Posner. It accepts no government funding. It challenges U.S. society and government to live up to American ideals expressed in the country's founding documents. It exemplifies an organization using the legal challenges to structural barriers pathway to incorporation. HRF vigorously opposed, for example, the Trump administration on several executive actions and policy proposals that, it believed, would have very adverse effects on the U.S.-Mexico border region. It opposed the Trump administration's inhumane treatment of migrants, especially children, in the detention centers run by the Border Patrol and the Office of Refugee Resettlement. It strongly criticized the "zero tolerance" policy approach of the Trump administration announced by then attorney general Jeff Sessions. It supported litigation against the Trump administration's decision to essentially end asylum and refugee admissions to the borderland region (Human Rights First 2020a).

HRF promotes American leadership in the global struggle for human rights, pressuring the U.S. government and private corporations such as the maquiladoras to respect human rights as well as the rule of law and due process of law. It demands reform, accountability, and justice. It is an especially strong advocate of the rights of asylum-seekers, immigrants, and refugees. It exposes and protests injustices, advocating for public policy solutions to ensure consistent respect for human rights. It pursues goals to protect the rights of all persecuted minorities, and with respect to the borderland region, the rights of Hispanic and Indigenous communities.

HRF conducts campaigns urging policy makers at all levels of government to hear from citizen champions of human rights without regard to their legal status. Since its inception in 1979, it has built a bipartisan coalition of frontline activists and lawyers to take on challenges to human rights through litigation and the pressure of public opinion. It seeks to promote American leadership in protecting human rights and the moral obligations that it considers to be vital to U.S. national interest. For example, HRF strongly opposed the Trump administration's use of a report by the Center for Disease Control as a pretext to ban refugees and asylum-seekers. HRF characterized the use of the CDC report as a sham for the Trump administration to pursue its wider anti-immigration policy that so greatly impacts the border region. HRF maintained that the administration's policy was really aimed directly at Central Americans seeking refuge or asylum. The draconian approach of the Trump administration, they argued, was designed to deter asylum-seekers from even trying. HRF was highly critical of U.S. Customs and Border Protection (CBP) and Border Patrol agents regarding their use of the COVID-19 pandemic for their own ends, as evident in the lack of use of personal protective equipment (PPEs) by agents and by their lack of effort at providing even basic health protections for those held in their detention centers at the southwest border in 2019 and 2020 (Human Rights First 2020a, 2020b).

HRF considers America to be strongest when its governmental policies (including administrative rules and regulations as well as laws enacted) match American values. As of June 2021, its president is Michael Breen (Human Rights First 2020b; LeMay 2019, 169).

League of United Latin American Citizens

The League of United Latin American Citizens (LULAC) was founded in Corpus Christi, Texas, in 1929. It exemplifies a Latino organization that uses the nonconfrontational politics pathway to incorporation. From its inception it has followed an assimilationist ideology and is considered one of the most conservative minority groups operating in American politics. Its approach, particularly prior to the 1960s, was like that of the NAACP's approach for the Black civil rights movement; LULAC, too, relied heavily on litigation before federal courts to pursue its policy objectives (LeMay 2009, 299–300; Marquez 2003; Strum 2010). It supported scholarships for Hispanic youth, helping about 18,000 of them per year.

LULAC aims at promoting the advancement of Latino citizens in terms of economic status, educational attainment, political influence, decent housing, and access to healthcare; it also aims at promoting the civil rights of Hispanic citizens. It believes that Mexican Americans can best improve their socioeconomic status through assimilation into American culture (Marquez 2003). LULAC is structured as a nationwide council and has chapters in 32 states, including the four in the U.S.-Mexico border region. LULAC claims a membership of about 132,000. It has long supported the role of women in politics, and it sponsors many programs and conferences for women (Orozco 2009).

It fought against the mass deportation of Mexicans during the Great Depression years, particularly because those mass deportations likely deported many U.S. citizens swept up in the anti-Mexican sentiment inherent in the campaign. LULAC was founded by a group of American veterans returning from service in World War I, such as Ben Garza, Manuel Gonzales, Andres de Luna, Alfonso Perales, Rafael and Juan Galvan, Samuel Hinojosa, Vincente Lozano, Jose Canales, Mauro Machado, Luz Saenz, and Juan Solis (Marquez 2003; Strum 2010). It quickly spread from Corpus Christi to establish other chapters in the border region, for example, in Brownsville, McAllen, Mission, La Grulla, Encino, San Diego, Del Rio, Eagle Pass, Rio Grande City, Roma, Hebbronville, Kingsville, Sarita, San Angelo, Ozona, and Sonora (Orozco 2009).

When the civil rights movement of the 1960s began to influence the rise of many alternative Hispanic organizations, most of which appealed to younger and more militant Hispanics, LULAC began to support the use of public protests. It used its political influence to seek government funding and grants to assist support for LULAC as well as for other Hispanic youth organizations (LeMay 2009, 299–300).

In using litigation, it targeted segregated public education that was particularly prevalent in Texas. LULAC had several notable cases that were partially successful (and likely helped pave the way for *Brown v. Board of Education* in 1954), such as *Del Rio Independent School District v. Salvatierra* (1930), *Mendez et al. v. Westminster* (1947), and *Minerva Delgado v. Bastrop*

Independent School District (1948) (Marquez 2003; Strum 2010).

After World War II, LULAC opposed the Bracero Program, consistent with its support for limits on legal immigration. It also spread its presence and influence across more of the United States and beyond the U.S.-Mexico border and the broader Southwest region. For example, by 1965, LULAC had 146 Councils in 21 states. By 1988, it had over 600 Councils and state offices in 32 states, Washington, D.C., and Puerto Rico, as well as in the Upper East Coast and Florida (Marquez 2003). By the 1990s, LULAC was a strong partner with the Congressional Hispanic Caucus in the U.S. House of Representatives, its most notable member being Edward Roybal who for a time was chair of the Hispanic Caucus. LULAC campaigned against California's Proposition 187 in 1994, and when the initiative passed, LULAC sued in federal court, arguing that the law was unconstitutional. It won that case: *LULAC et al. v. WILSON et al.* (November 20, 1995, 980 F. Supp. 755, CD Cal; LeMay and Barkan 1999, 296–301).

As of June 2021, LULAC's president was Roger Rocha, a healthcare analyst from Laredo, Texas, elected in 2015 in Salt Lake City, Utah. In 2017, he led LULAC's fight against a Texas Senate bill that ended sanctuary cities in Texas. That fight claimed the proposed measure was specifically created to target Latinos. LULAC opposed the Trump administration's rescinding of Deferred Action for Childhood Arrivals (DACA) and Deferred Action for Parental Accountability (DAPA), and President Trump's executive order against sanctuary cities, his ban on asylum-seekers, and the drastic reduction in the number of refugees legally allowed to enter the United States (LeMay 2019, 16–17).

Mexican American Legal Defense and Education Fund

The Mexican American Legal Defense and Education Fund (MALDEF) began in San Antonio, Texas, in 1968. It exemplifies a Latino civil rights organization that uses the legal challenge to structural evolution pathway to incorporation (Geron 2005; LeMay 2009, 309, 375; Meier and Gutierrez 2000). It is a national nonprofit organization—a 501(c)(3) organization—that is headquartered in Los Angeles, California, with regional offices in Sacramento, San Antonio, Chicago, and Washington, D.C. It is managed by a president and general counsel and a 30-member board of directors. MALDEF works with other nonprofit organizations serving Hispanics, minorities, and underserved communities (LeMay 2015, 196).

MALDEF was initially funded by a Ford Foundation grant of $2.2 million, with the help of LULUC and the NAACP. It models itself on the NAACP's Legal Defense Fund. In using the litigation pathway, MALDEF claimed some important legal victories in which it filed amicus briefs. MALDEF's first litigation case was *San Antonio Independent School District et al. v. Demetrio P. Rodriguez et al.* (411 U.S. 1, 1973), a school funding case. Its first important victory was in *White et al. v. Regester et al.* (412 U.S. 755, 1973), which concerned a single member voting district system (used for county boards, city council, and school district boards) in which the Texas law setting up at-large voting districts was found to have egregiously weakened Hispanic voting power.

MALDEF's president in 1974, Vilma Martinez, set up the Chicana Rights Project (Orozco 2009). It focused on Mexican American women's legal issues. MALDEF opposed California's Proposition 187 in 1994, and the Illegal Immigration Reform and Immigrant Responsibility Act (IIRIRA) in 1996, and proposed English-only state laws and several similar bills proposed in Congress. It opposed the Obama administration's, the Trump administration's and the Biden administration's use of expedited removal as both anti-immigrant and anti-Hispanic executive orders.

MALDEF won a class action suit against Texas's discrimination against Mexican Americans in south Texas because of unequal and inadequate funding. As a result of the case, Texas set up the South Texas Initiative to improve Texas system schools in Brownsville, Edinburg, San Antonio, El Paso, Corpus Christi, Laredo, and Kingsville. The Border Region Higher Education Council helped enact legislation and oversee the program's process. It won a major victory in *Edgewood Independent School District v. State of Texas* (777 S.W.2nd 391, Texas, 1989). The Edgewood case established what came to be called the Robin Hood school financing system in which wealthier school districts had to help fund poorer districts (the majority of which were in Southwest Texas's poor Hispanic districts). MALDEF supported the GI Forum by an amicus brief in *GI Forum of Texas v. Perry* (2005). That case was consolidated with *LULAC et al. v. Perry* (548 U.S. 399, 2006). MALDEF won a challenge against a Texas redistricting plan that was overtly gerrymandering, resulting in new lines being drawn for Texas's 23rd Congressional District, which straddles the border with Mexico's Coahuila state from San Antonio to El Paso, Texas. It opened the way for the Chicano communities in the district to elect a Chicano representative to the U.S. House of Representatives.

MALDEF was an important coalition participant (with LULAC, GI Forum, MAPA, and the ACLU) in the fight against passage of Arizona's 1070 law passed in 2010. It won its legal challenge against the law in *Arizona v. United States* (132 U.S. 2491, 2010) that struck down the law as unconstitutional (LeMay 2015, 33). The Arizona law was considered the most blatantly anti-Hispanic illegal immigration law that the state had ever passed. Similarly, MALDEF won the case that overturned the 2004 Arizona law that restricted voter registration by requiring proof of citizenship (known as Proposition 200) in *Gonzales v. State of Arizona, et al.* (2020).

In 2014 President Obama appointed former mayor of San Antonio Julian Castro, who MALDEF had supported, as secretary of housing and urban development. This exemplified the efficacy of MALDEF'S use of strategy and tactics that has produced policy results important to the U.S.-Mexico border region.

Mexican American Political Association

The Mexican American Political Association (MAPA) is a Chicano political advocacy organization formed in Fresno, California, in 1960. It uses the nonconfrontational and evolutionary political pathway to incorporation that developed into the coalition politics approach (Geron 2005; LeMay 2009). It advocates for the interests of Mexican Americans, Mexicanos, Latinos, Chicanos, Hispanics, and asylum-seekers from Central America. It emerged out of the Hispanic civil rights movement of the 1960s and sister organizations like the Political Association of Spanish-Speaking Organizations (PASSO) (LeMay 2009, 299–300; Navarro 2005). It campaigned to elect Mexican Americans to public office, exemplified by its first president, Edward Roybal (D-CA), who was elected to the U.S. House of Representatives and served from 1963 to 1993. Roybal had earlier been a member of the Los Angeles City Council (1949–1962). His daughter, Lucille Roybal-Allard, served the same district (CA-34th) from 2003–2013, and after redistricting, CA-34th, since 2014. Like her father, she is a prominent member of the Congressional Hispanic Caucus (LeMay 2009, 311).

MAPA assisted Cesar Chavez and the UFW, and in the early 1960s MAPA grew to 36 chapters. It helped California governor Pat Brown win election and convinced him to abolish the Bracero Program in 1964. In the 1970s it campaigned for his son, California governor Jerry Brown.

MAPA is a grassroots organization working for political empowerment, self-determination, and the economic sustainability of the Latino community. Since 2004, MAPA has declined in membership and political activity. Like many of the

Hispanic civil rights movement organizations of the 1960s and 1970s following the coalition politics approach, it focused on electing Chicanos to elective office, registering and getting-out-the-vote campaigns, raising-political-awareness campaigns, and grassroots-level community organizing. It has been successful in those efforts, and in part its relative decline reflects that its primary organizing goals have been achieved (Geron 2005; Marquez 2003; Martinez 2008; Meier and Gutierrez 2000; and Navarro 2005).

In 2010, MAPA supported a boycott of the 2010 census, and its then president, Nativo Lopez, was charged with voter fraud. The organization is officially nonpartisan, but its members have routinely been strong coalition partners of the Democratic Party. It continues to be relevant to the U.S.-Mexico border region, however, in assisting Hispanics throughout the region to seek and often win elective office. It vigorously opposed the Trump administration's policies regarding immigration, illegal immigration, asylum, and refugee goals. It successfully opposed the 2020 census plan of the Trump administration to include a question on citizenship status. MAPA has worked with Dreamers, and the United We Dream organization, to support comprehensive immigration reform and in advocating for a path to citizenship for undocumented immigrants. It strongly supported President Obama's DACA and DAPA executive orders; and it has equally strongly opposed President Trump's efforts to abolish or rescind those programs and his increased use of expedited removal. It is equally critical of the Biden administration for not forcefully push through Congress legislation to provide a path to citizenship for Dreamers, and for the Biden administration's continued use of expedited removal and continuation of the Trump administration's deportation back to Mexico of undocumented immigrants arrested in the United States. An estimated 700,000 to 800,000 undocumented immigrants are Dreamers, and many of them reside in the Southwest border region. About 700,000

Dreamers belong to mixed-status families, many of whom live in the border region.

Mexican American Youth Organization

The Mexican American Youth Organization (MAYO) was formed in 1967 in San Antonio, Texas by Jose Angel Gutierrez, Willie Velasquez, Mario Campean, Ignacio Perez, and Juan Patian—known as Los Cinco (the five) (Navarro 2005, 24). In turn, MAYO founded a political organization, the La Raza Unida Party. La Raza played an important role in the Chicano civil rights movement of the late 1960s and early 1970s, and MAYO and La Raza were part of the larger Chicano movement in the United States. MAYO exemplifies the protest/demand approach to Hispanic incorporation (Geron 2005; LeMay 2009). It was heavily involved in voter registration in South Texas. It notably staged school walkouts to achieve equality for Mexican Americans, took over seats on Texas school boards, and staged major walkouts in Crystal City, Kingsville, and San Antonio, Texas. By joining previously all-white school boards, the members of MAYO participated in changing school policy to reflect Chicano interests (Adams 2018; Garcia 1997, 2015).

MAYO helped create the La Raza Unida Party—a third party movement that took control of Crystal City, Texas, and spread to other states (Orozco 2009; Steiner 1969). It helped coin and to popularize the practice of referring to Mexican Americans as "Chicanos," and like the Black Power movement within the Black civil rights movement, MAYO emphasized Brown Power and Brown Pride within the Chicano movement. MAYO was later integrated into the youth arm of the La Raza Unida Party (LRUP). MAYO advocated a more militant style and approach to the Chicano civil rights movement than did, for example, LULAC, which MAYO members considered too soft in its approach to achieve equality for Mexican Americans. MAYO earned its reputation of being the militant arm of the Chicano movement (Navarro 2005; Steiner 1969).

One of MAYO's founders, Willie Velasquez, was posthumously awarded the Presidential Medal of Freedom in 1995 by President Bill Clinton in recognition of his work with voter registration. Although MAYO did excellent work in getting Chicanos registered, they were not as successful in getting Hispanic youth to turn out and vote (DeSipio 1996; LeMay 2009). Another of MAYO's founders, Jose Angel Gutierrez, went on to earn a PhD in political science as well as a law degree and became an attorney and a professor at the University of Texas at Arlington. Gutierrez founded the Center for Mexican American Studies there. He authored several books, notably *The Making of a Chicano Militant* (1998), and he coauthored, with Reies Lopez Tijerina, *They Call Me King Tiger* (2001).

Movimiento Estudientil Chicanx de Aztlan

The Movimiento Estudientl Chicanx de Aztlan (MEChA) has gone through a couple of name changes since it was founded in Santa Barbara, California, in 1969. It first used the term "Mexicano" and changed that to "Movimiento" at a 2010 conference in Seattle (Garcia 2015). "Chicano" was changed to "Chicanx," to be gender neutral, at a 2016 conference in Tucson, Arizona. In 2019, the group's leadership voted to drop the words "Chicano" and "Aztlan" from its name.

MEChA is a student-based organization that uses somewhat radical student activism and the protest/demand pathway to incorporation. It is one of the more militant Chicanx organizations ("x" to indicate a gender-neutral organization open to men and women, Chicanos and Chicanas, Latinos and Latinas) (Garcia 1997). It is found most often on college campuses but has many chapters at high school and junior college campuses. MECha is considered the most militant among Hispanic student groups such as the Political Association of Spanish-Speaking Organizations (PASSO), the Mexican American Political Association (MAPA), the Mexican American Youth Organization (MAYO), and United Mexican American Students

(UMAS). In recent years, MEChA's approach may be better described as following the coalition politics pathway to incorporation. For example, it has joined a coalition of groups to support proposed bills for earned legalization, comprehensive immigration reform, and the various Dreamer bills (LeMay 2009, 306–309; LeMay 2015, 44).

It grew out of a conference called by Corky Gonzales of the Denver-based Crusade for Justice. The conference was attended by members of MAYO, an organization founded in San Antonio, Texas, in 1967 that used the tactics of the Black civil rights movement organization Student Nonviolent Coordinating Committee (SNCC). MAYO also became involved in the creation of the La Raza Unida Party. Another group whose members attended the conference were the Brown Berets, a Los Angeles youth group that fought against police brutality in East Los Angeles and helped form UMAS; it was also known for using protests called Blowouts.

An activist from San Diego formed the Chicano Coordinating Committee on Higher Education (CCHE) as a network to pressure adoption and expansion of equal opportunity programs in California's colleges and universities. In April 1969, they met at the conference called by Corky Gonzales at the University of California-Santa Barbara, from which MEChA formed, emerged, and quickly spread among California schools, and then from there to high schools, junior colleges, and college campuses in other states. MEChA has roughly 400 loosely affiliated chapters that sponsor educational and social activities and support tutoring and mentorship, folklore and poetry recitals. Many chapters employ political actions, lobbying administrators for expanded bilingual education and Chicano or Latino studies programs, celebrating Cinco de Mayo, and participating in sit-ins, hunger strikes, boycotts, rallies, marches, and other political activism events. MEChA protested policy violence (in today's jargon, excessive use of force) reminiscent of the violence by police and military members against Hispanics in the Zoot Suit Riots of June 5–8, 1943, in the Los Angeles metropolitan area. In the Zoot Suit riots gangs of military members attacked Latino youth wearing zoot suits, beating and stripping them. The police arrested more than 500 Latinos for disturbing the peace rather than any of the rioters who had violently attacked them.

In the 1970s and 1980s, MEChA spread throughout the Southwest and was a principal sponsor of Cinco de Mayo celebrations on college campuses throughout the country. It became involved in the establishment of the La Raza Unida movement, the La Raza Unida Partido, which is now UNIDOS US (LeMay 2009, 306).

Since the late 1990s MEChA has increasingly worked in coalition with other civil rights organizations. It actively opposed the Trump administration's immigration policy, the rescinding of DACA and DAPA, the zero-tolerance policy, and the ending of asylum and reduction of refugees. It works with Dreamers (e.g., with United We Dream) to promote a pathway to citizenship for undocumented immigrants, many of whom reside in the Southwest border region.

National Alliance for Hispanic Health

National Alliance for Hispanic Health (NAHH) began in 1973 in Los Angeles, California, as the Coalition of Spanish Speaking Mental Health Organizations (COSSMHO). As its name implies, it is an example of an organization using the coalition politics approach to Hispanic incorporation (Geron 2005; LeMay 2009).

NAHH is a 501(c)(3) nonprofit and nonpartisan advocacy organization for improving the health and well-being of Hispanics. It expanded into a national organization, moved its headquarters to Washington, D.C., and changed its program objectives to respond to the changing needs of the people and communities it serves. It was and continues to be a coalition organization important to Hispanic communities in the borderland region, such as the colonias in Arizona, New Mexico, and Texas. NAHH is a major science-based and community driven organization that focuses on the best health for all. Community-based members provide services to more than 15 million Hispanics throughout the United States annually, and the national organization provides services to more than 100 million people annually.

NAHH incorporates the best of science, culture, and community development and improvement in its varied programs: (1) by listening to the individual, (2) by investing in leading community-based organizations, (3) by working with a coalition of national organizations, (4) by examining and improving the resources and systems available to Hispanic communities; and (5) by working to make health a part of each person's life. NAHH works to close gaps in health services in Hispanic communities in the Southwest, and especially in colonias of the border region that are underserved communities. That work became all the more relevant as the COVID-19 pandemic so devastatingly impacted the Hispanic communities of the borderland region.

The president and CEO of NAHH is Dr. Jane Delgado. NAHH is governed by a board of directors comprising 13 members that includes Lourdes Baecondi-Garbanati as its chair and Juan Cuellar as vice-chair. NAHH has provided more than 104,000 health screenings and $2.375 million in scholarships awarded to 175 students over five years. For example, it provides annual STEM Scholarships to 10 high school students. It has held Hispanic Family Health Lifestyle events in 10 cities, and its Demonstration Programs promote enrollment in Medicaid, Affordable Care Act (ACA), the Children's Health Insurance Program (CHIP) of the Medicaid program, and other social welfare programs. It promotes local health and human service providers for diabetes prevention, apart from working to change the United States Department of Health and Human Services' (HHS) "public charge" rule and working to get Congress to prevent online sale of e-cigarettes to children; it opposes HHS rules that get rid of protections for many Hispanics, especially in the Southwest border region; it supports cancer prevention, Alzheimer's awareness, and enactment of the Personal Care Products Safety Act.

Since the late 1980s, NAHH has been at the forefront of working with the federal government to improve health data research for Hispanic populations in the United States and to find more complete health and demographic data on Native Americans, Asian Americans, and Hispanics. It has worked with Child Trends.org, which in its 2020 study of the racial and ethnic composition of the child population (under 18), found that the nation's largest racial/ethnic group of children was made up of Hispanics (Child Trends 2020).

Among its notable lobbying efforts, NAHH supported the Medicare Modernization Act and the expansion of the Children's Health Insurance Program. It advocated for clean air and water in Hispanic communities—critically important in the borderland region. In 2007, it partnered with Research America to field the first national public opinion survey of Hispanics on health issues and established an online action network, Vote for Your Health, that delivers election-day text messages reminding its members to vote. NAHH's health information services to Hispanic communities include topics such as obesity, diabetes, heart health, high blood pressure, mental health, fitness, physical activity, healthy eating, Alzheimer's disease, Parkinson's disease, environmental health, and health insurance. In 2012, it partnered with the University of Southern California to create a sister organization, Healthy Americans Institute, housed at the Keck School of Medicine.

National Hispanic Institute
The National Hispanic Institute (NHI) began in the late 1970s, and since then it has designed, tested, and researched means to experience transformative leadership concepts, experiences,

and skills. It exemplifies an organization using coalition politics as the pathway to incorporation, but it also has the characteristics of a think-tank organization. It seeks to provide a reservoir of skilled and educated youth from which the organized sectors of Latino community life can draw its future leaders. NHI viewed the Latino community leadership as drained by the civil rights era of the 1960s. It adopted as its mission the development of a pool of potential leaders to replace an aging leadership base.

NHI has grown to become a leading organization fostering community leadership for the expanding Latino community throughout the United States and Latin America, although it is still largely focused on the borderland region. It seeks to engage youth (high-school-age and college-age groups) in community leadership roles. It uses community leadership and social entrepreneurship as transformative learning experiences to develop youth as community leaders, to promote academic excellence, and to foster a commitment to personal development.

NHI draws 3,000 young people annually to its 14 leadership conferences that are held in Texas, Colorado, California, Pennsylvania, New York, Florida, Illinois, and Panama City, Panama. It owns and operates a Victorian-style home in Central Texas and draws its conference attendees from the Rio Grande Valley (Hidalgo and Starr Counties), Brownsville, El Paso, San Antonio, Corpus Christi, Houston, Laredo, Dallas, and Austin. NHI helped establish an 80-member college and university consortium for admission purposes. It recognized the increased career and business opportunities opening up among the Latino communities of the Southwest region.

NHI promoted pilot projects to develop high-school-age and college-bound youth by engaging them in extended periods of self-learning and helping them to acquire tools for self-assessment and self-change. NHI is headquartered in Maxwell, Texas. It was founded by Ernesto Nieto and Gloria de Leon. It has developed projects like the Lorenzo de Zavala Youth

Legislative Session, the Collegiate Leadership Network, and the JFL Fellows.

New Mexico Center on Law and Poverty

The New Mexico Center on Law and Poverty was established in 1996 to deliver systemic legal advocacy that other legal service organizations in New Mexico were barred from performing. It is a good example of an organization that uses the third path to incorporation, that of legal challenges to structural barriers (Geron 2005; LeMay 2009). The center was established in response to opponents to civil legal aid in Congress who imposed restrictions on all legal service organizations preventing them from receiving federal funding through the Legal Services Corporation (LSC). Those restrictions barred grantees from initiating or participating in class action lawsuits, engaging in direct or grassroots lobbying on behalf of clients, representing many categories of immigrants, conducting litigation on behalf of prisoners, and challenging welfare reform measures, making the performance of such services unconstitutional or otherwise illegal (provisions in the IIRIRA of 1996; LeMay and Barkan 1999, 304–310).

Many civil legal aid systems within state governments formed independent agencies that would not be funded by the federal LSC to provide systemic advocacy and litigation for people living in poverty. The New Mexico Legal Services and Support Project was one such agency that was transformed into the New Mexico Center on Law and Poverty. New Mexico's governor Gary Johnson vetoed legislation that would have supported poor New Mexicans needing legal assistance. The center challenged Johnson's veto with a Writ of Mandamus for implementing the new welfare program without legislative approval and won before the New Mexico Supreme Court in *Taylor v. Johnson* (1998). The center went on to challenge administrative rules regarding public benefits by winning important improvements to the Temporary Assistance to Needy Families program.

The center launched training for civil legal service attorneys. The center's agenda expanded to address critical issues impacting New Mexicans living in poverty, such as providing access to hospital care for uninsured indigent patients, addressing insufficiencies in New Mexico's education system and expanding civil legal services to underserved populations (many of whom reside in the borderland region). Between 2002 and 2015, the center expanded its budget by more than $1 million and increased its staff by 300 percent.

The center advances economic and social justice in New Mexico through education, advocacy, and litigation. It recognizes that economic injustice and poverty are rooted in the state's historical, racial, and structural inequity. It works with a coalition of community partners to advance change in the courts, state legislature, and public institutions through a multipronged approach that involves collaboration with community members, advocates, and tribal leaders to identify systemic issues. The center works to advance a social movement to promote economic justice, education, and the health and well-being of children and families. It publicizes laws and policies that have an impact on poverty in New Mexico. It conducts in-depth research and analysis on laws, policies, and programs and investigates solutions to systemic problems. It represents clients in courts and administrative hearings to address systemic injustice and discrimination. The center conducts litigation to enforce rights and to hold the state accountable to following the law. It engages in ongoing monitoring to ensure that changes to laws and policies are successfully in place and operate for the long term (Adams 2018; Martinez 2008; Meier and Gutierrez 2000).

Office of Refugee Resettlement

The Office of Refugee Resettlement (ORR) is a part of the program of the Administration for Children and Families within the Department of Health and Human Services (HHS). It was

founded on April 1, 1980, by the Act of March 17, 1980—
The Refugee Act (94 Stat. 102; LeMay and Barkan 1999, 272–
275). It has a great—and critics will say negative—impact on
the borderland region through its administration of detention
centers on the border for undocumented immigrants, their
families, particularly unaccompanied alien children (UAC),
and most recently, asylum-seekers and refugees from Central
America who cross the southern border into the United States.
Its purpose under the Refugee Act of 1980 was to provide new
populations of refugees with the opportunity to achieve their
full potential in the United States—that is, cultural, economic,
political, and social incorporation into American society.
United States policy allows refugees of special humanitarian
concern entrance into the country, reflecting the American core
values and tradition of safe haven for the oppressed. It works
with state partners and with other federal agencies (Customs
and Border Patrol (CBP), Department of Homeland Security
(DHS), Department of Justice (DOJ), and the Department of
Agriculture (DOA), for example) that typically send refugees
to the ORR/HHS for detention while their legal status is clari-
fied by immigration, refugee, or asylum hearing.

It has program areas for refugees, asylees, Cuban and Hai-
tian entrants, special immigrant visa (SIV) holders, victims
of trafficking, survivors of torture, and oversight of refugees
with respect to the Affordable Care Act. In has been impacted
greatly since the war on terror in 2001 and the establishment of
the DHS in 2002, and by President Trump's executive order on
refugee resettlement in 2017. Those critical of the ORR argue
that the war on terror has been more often aimed at economic
refugees and families from Central America seeking jobs, safety,
and freedom in the United States (Frey 2019; Truax 2018).

On March 1, 2003, the Homeland Security Act of 2002
transferred responsibilities for the care and placement of UACs
from the commissioner of the Immigration and Naturalization
Service (INS) to the director of the ORR. Since then, the ORR
has cared for more than 340,000 children under provisions

established by the Flores Agreement in 1997, the Trafficking Victims Protection Act of 2000, and the reauthorization of those Acts, the William Wilberforce Trafficking Victims Protection Reauthorization Act of 2005, and 2008.

It has been their care—or lack thereof—of UACs apprehended by the DHS that has brought the greatest criticism to the ORR. Since the Trump administration's DOJ adopted the zero-tolerance policy, increased implementation of expedited removal, and separated children from their families at the border detention centers run by the ORR in 2017, several children have died in U.S. custody and the media exposed atrocious humanitarian conditions at the ORR and HHS detention centers.

The ORR responds to its critics by arguing that the numbers sent to them for care have simply overrun the ability of the ORR to adequately care for them. Under the Obama administration, the ORR routinely and promptly placed children with family members or others who could house and care for them in the least restrictive setting and in the best interest of the child. Under the Trump administration's 2017 directives, the ORR took into consideration danger to self, danger to the community, and risk of flight in case management and release decisions. After separation of thousands of children at the border detention centers run by the ORR, HHS was reluctantly forced to admit that it had no plans in place for their reunification with their families and that the ORR had lost track of hundreds to possibly thousands of children who were separated, in many instances after their parent or family member had been deported. Since the Biden administration came to power, the administration has addressed the issue and has developed a plan for reunification, and the first few families were reunited in early 2021.

Pew Research Center
Pew Research Center was founded in 2002 as a nonpartisan research organization (a classic example of a think tank) that

uses the nonconfrontational political evolution approach to Hispanic incorporation (Geron 2005; LeMay 2009). It is supported by the Pew Charitable Trust, a 501(c)(3) organization. Among its major research efforts, the Pew Research Center strives to improve understanding of the U.S. Hispanic population and to authoritatively chronicle Latinos' growing impact on the United States. Its research and data analyses are especially relevant to the U.S.-Mexico border region. Its research reports and public policy papers are noted for their timeliness, relevance, and scientific rigor and objectivity. It does not advocate policy positions but rather seeks to focus light on critical issues. It regularly publishes demographic data, immigration, and unauthorized immigration data, as well as data regarding UAC flow, the sources of that flow and how immigration trends change over time. It has studied and reported on the amount and impact of remittances of Hispanics in the United States sent to Mexico (and Central America) and the importance and impact of those remittances on the overall economy of those countries and on the communities within them (the same communities that Mexican and Central American immigrants come from).

The Pew Hispanic Forum, the Pew Hispanic Center, and the Pew Research Center are all funded by the Pew Charitable Trust Fund and are headquartered in Washington, D.C. Pew Research Center's published data and studies are regularly reported on by the mass media, thereby reflecting and influencing public opinion with respect to its issues and concerns (LeMay 2019, 175–176).

Sinaloa Cartel

The Sinaloa Cartel was formed in 1988 and is one of Mexico's most powerful and notorious drug cartels. Sinaloa is noted for its extreme violence and its criminal enterprises of drug trafficking, money laundering, weapons trafficking, murder, kidnapping, and bribery. It is also known as the Guzman-Loera

Organization, the Pacific Cartel, the Federation, and the Blood Alliance. The cartel was founded by Joaquin Guzman, Ismael Zambada Garcia, and Hector Luis Palma Salazar. It is based in Culiacan, Sinaloa State, Mexico, and is allied with the Gulf Cartel and the notorious MS-13 gang.

The Sinaloa Cartel can be traced back to the Guadalajara Cartel, which in 1985 had tortured a U.S. drug enforcement agent causing the U.S. and Mexican governments to crack down on them. The Guadalajara Cartel broke into various groups, including the Sinaloa Cartel, which quickly gained control over the marijuana and poppy crops. Joaquin Guzman Loera, better known as "El Chapo," emerged as its primary leader. A drug cartel is an illicit consortium of independent organizations formed to limit competition and to control the production and distribution of illegal drugs. Cartels are well-organized, well-financed, efficient, and ruthless criminal operations. Since the 1980s, various cartels have dominated the international narcotics trade and have been involved in the fentanyl/opioid crisis in the United States. The cartels in Mexico have fought for control of markets and territories, and the violence they perpetrate has been a major push factor in the migration of asylum-seekers, refugees, and undocumented migrants to the United States. The degree and expansion of violent conditions from cartel rivalries have been likened to civil war. The violence makes the Mexican side of the border very dangerous. Cartels have also corrupted the Mexican government, and some in the U.S. border patrol, and as a result, cartels operate with virtual impunity on the Mexican side of the border (Bailey and Godson 2000; Ellingwood 2009; Kirkpatrick 2012; Slack, Martinez, and Whiteford 2018; and Vulliamy 2010).

Sinaloa, a state in northwest Mexico, is bounded by the Gulf of California (or the Sea of Cortez), the Pacific Ocean, the state of Sonora to the north, the states of Chihuahua and Durango to the east, and the state of Nayarit to the south. In Mexico, the Sinaloa Cartel's territory of operations includes Sinaloa, Baja

California, Durango, Sonora, Chihuahua, Mexico City, Guadalajara, Tepic, Toluca, and Zacatecas. In the United States, the cartel's operations and influence are spread over California, Arizona, Utah, Alabama, Texas, Colorado, Illinois, New York, and Washington (Bailey and Godson 2000).

The Sinaloa Cartel operates all imaginable means and routes for smuggling people and drugs north into the United States and guns south into Mexico. They have created several "super tunnels," for example, from Agua Prieta to Douglas, Arizona, and from warehouses in Otay Mesa to San Diego. Their enterprises are extremely lucrative. Their marijuana, cocaine, heroin, and methamphetamine operations alone have been estimated as ranging from $3 to as high as $39 billion (Bailey and Godson 2000; Crosthwaite 2002; Kirkpatrick 2012). The cartel is suspected of being responsible for the disappearance and systematic murder of hundreds of women in Ciudad Juarez (Vulliamy 2010).

Joaquin Guzman, "El Chapo," was captured in Mazatlan, Mexico in 2014 but escaped in 2015. He was recaptured in 2016 in Los Mochis, Sinaloa, and extradited to the United States, where he was tried and found guilty in 2019. Guzman has been imprisoned in the United States since then. In February 2021, El Chapo's wife, Emma Coronel Aispuro, was arrested and has pled guilty to drug smuggling charges.

Unidos US

Unidos US began as the National Council of La Raza (NCLR) and has also been known as La Raza Unida. It is headquartered in Washington, D.C., and its president and CEO is Janet Murguia. It serves millions of Latinos through its more than 300 affiliates across the United States. Unidos US advocates in the areas of civic engagement, civil rights, immigration, health, and housing. The organization is a good example of one that started off following the protest/demand pathway to incorporation but now exemplifies and uses the coalition politics pathway (Geron 2005; LeMay 2009; Martinez 2008; Schaefer 2008). That is a transition in style and tactics that many Hispanic organizations have gone through since the 1970s. As NCLR, it has helped elect literally thousands of Latinx officials at the local level of government who have, in turn, advanced policies of cultural, legal, political, and social incorporation (Adams 2018; LeMay 2009, 374–375). Hispanic members of Congress grew from 8 in 1983 to 47 in 2019, and to 54 in 2021 (47 in U.S. H.R., 2 Delegates from U.S. territories, and 7 Senators) (Congress.gov 2021). Prominent among them is Joaquin Castro, who represents the 24th Congressional District of Texas (that includes San Antonio, Texas) and has represented it since 2014. In 2019, he was selected as chair of the Congressional Hispanic Caucus. His twin brother, Julian Castro, served as mayor of San Antonio from 2009 to 2014 and then was secretary of HUD in President Barack Obama's cabinet from 2014 to 2017. He ran for the presidential nomination of the Democratic Party in the 2020 elections, losing to former VP Joseph Biden.

Unidos US traces its origins back to the National Organization for Mexican American Students (NOMAS), which received a Ford Foundation grant to assist the Mexican American community in the Southwest. Following a conference held in El Paso, Texas in 1967, Jose Angel Gutierrez formed La Raza Unida Partido as a third party to contest local elections in Crystal City, Texas (LeMay 2009, 306). Through the Ford grant, the Southwest Council of La Raza was founded in Phoenix, Arizona in 1968. La Raza emerged as a coalition of Hispanic advocacy groups, such as Jose Angel Gutierrez–led Mexican American Youth Organization (MAYO), United Mexican American Students (UMAS), Mexican American Student Association (MASA), Movimiento Estudientil Chicanx de Aztlan (MEChA), the National Association of Mexican American Students (NOMAS), and the Association of Mexican American Educators (AMAE) (LeMay 2009, 148–151). La Raza organized the Southwest Voter Education Project in

1971. NCLR also sponsored school walkouts for Mexican Independence Day and Cinco de Mayo celebrations (LeMay 2009, 307–308).

In 1973 it moved its headquarters to Washington, D.C., and changed its name to National Council of La Raza. Its president and CEO from 1974 to 2004 was Raul Yzaguirre, a Latino civil rights lawyer and activist from San Juan, Texas, in the Rio Grande Valley. NCLR moved from protest politics to coalition politics and by the late 1980s saw Hispanic elected officials increase from fewer than 900 in the late 1970s to more than 3,400 by 1988 (Adams 2018; LeMay 2009, 309).

Unidos US is very active in the Southwest. It holds an annual conference at which it gives awards—including the prestigious Raul Yzaguirre President's Award—to Hispanic Americans for outstanding contributions in various categories (such as leadership and communications). In 2018, it operated on revenues of more than $59 million and had an endowment of more than $142 million. Since 2015, 85 percent of its funding comes from individuals, corporations, and foundations, and 15 percent from the government, of which, in 2018, 7 percent came from the federal government.

United Farm Workers

The United Farm Workers (UFW) was founded in 1962 by Cesar Chavez, Dolores Huerta, Gilbert Padilla, and Philip Vera Cruz. UFW is one of the best examples of an organization using the demands/protests path to incorporation that evolved into coalition politics (Geron 2005; LeMay 2009). Its impact on the U.S.-Mexico border region has been profound and long-lasting; it has influenced the border region's culture, economics, and politics. UFW was one of the leading organizations to use the word "Chicano" as a source of pride in the Chicano civil rights movement. Its motto, "Si, se puede!" (Yes, we can!), became the motto of the entire Chicano movement. It was coined at a rally in Phoenix, Arizona, at the founding of the Chicano Por La Causa organization. The phrase was even adopted by President Barack Obama for his 2008 and 2012 presidential campaigns. Chavez began to refer to his movement as "La Causa" in 1965, in Delano, California, during a strike by Hispanic and Filipino workers harvesting grapes. The strikers belonged to the Agricultural Workers Organizing Committee (AWOC), which expanded from Filipino workers to include Mexican migrant workers (LeMay 2009, 306).

They began using the term *la huelga*, the strike, which became "La Causa" as they evolved into a social movement that used strikes, boycotts against lettuce and grape growers, and marches and hunger strikes. UFW soon inspired the entire Hispanic or Chicano civil rights movement (Araiza 2014; Dimas 2019; Flores 2016; Ganz 2009; Gutierrez 1995; Orozco 2009; Meier and Gutierrez 2000; Navarro 2005).

By 1964–1965, the UFW was formed as a union of migrant workers, becoming the first enduring and largest farm workers union. The UFW organized in all the major agricultural sectors, chiefly in California, but notably in southern Arizona, New Mexico, and Texas, inspiring the Chicano movement throughout the border region. Thousands of farm workers unionized and won contract agreements protecting them from some of the largest berry, winery, tomato, dairy, and mushroom companies in the nation. More than 75 percent of California's fresh mushroom industry is now unionized under the UFW. The UFW sponsored laws and regulations to protect all farm workers in California, and in the Southwest, including those at non-unionized ranches. They won legislative victories to prevent deaths and illnesses from extreme heat, and in 2016, won passage of the first law in the country providing farm workers in California with overtime pay if they worked beyond eight hours a day. UFW continues to champion legislative and regulatory reforms for farm workers, covering issues such as worker protections, the use of pesticides, and immigration reform. During the COVID-19 pandemic, they actively pushed to acquire PPEs for farm workers who worked in the fields to harvest perishable crops as required "essential workers." In the Southwest border region, Latino communities comprised a dramatically higher percentage of those who tested positive for COVID-19 compared with other racial and ethnic groups (Center for Disease Control 2020).

United We Dream

United We Dream is the nation's foremost organization of the Dreamer youth—estimated at 800,000. It is an example of an organization pursuing the coalition politics approach to incorporation of the Dreamers (and of their parents). It conducted campaigns powered by immigrants, people of color, and their allies rejected and opposed President Trump's position on immigration policies. They advocated honoring and celebrating immigrant and refugee resilience by defiance to the Trump administration's policies. They advocated for undocumented-friendly classrooms and education. United We Dream promoted schools and campuses as sanctuaries and opposed the Trump administration's anti-sanctuary cities executive order. They defended sanctuaries as places promoting freedom of expression through dialogue and activism, where the dignity and integrity of every individual is respected and preserved.

United We Dream organizes sanctuaries to protect persons from deportation and prevent Immigration and Customs Enforcement (ICE) from "infecting" local law enforcement. It vigorously opposed the Muslim travel ban and opposed the establishment of a religious registry, surveillance, and harassment by the DOJ or DHS. It uses coalition politics to advocate against police brutality and abuse (with #BlackLivesMatter). United We Dream advocates against local police departments employing the stop-and-frisk policy. Its various chapters and affiliated organizations are united against misogyny and work to promote women's rights.

United We Dream is a major organization that has won the hearts and minds of Latino voters. It continues to promote a permanent solution to the Dreamer's legal problems, advocating for congressional enactment of a Dreamer bill and including Dreamer provisions within the various comprehensive immigration reform proposals. It celebrated the Supreme Court's 5–4 decision on June 18, 2020, that effectively blocked President Trump from ending DACA. That decision's majority opinion was written by Chief Justice John Roberts and was joined in by justices Ruth Bader Ginsburg, Stephen Breyer, Elena Kagan, and Sonia Sotomayor. The four dissenting justices were Clarence Thomas, Samuel Alito, Neil Gorsuch, and Brett Kavanaugh. The decision protected about 700,000 DACA recipients from deportation. It was a relief to the millions of mixed-status families, many residing in the border region, who were facing the threat of family separation due to the deportation of one or more family members who lacked legal status. The majority opinion described Trump's decision to rescind DACA as arbitrary and capricious. Since assuming office in January 2021, President Biden issued an executive order rescinding President Trump's DACA order.

United We Dream advocates policy reform that would provide a path to citizenship not only for Dreamers but for all undocumented immigrants. United We Dream focuses on actions at the state level, particularly on California, Arizona, New Mexico, and Texas and the border communities within them. It advocates that state governments should issue licenses to Dreamers and provide various benefits such as in-state tuition at state colleges and universities (LeMay 2019, 175–176).

Voto Latino

Voto Latino was cofounded in 2004 by Maria Teresa Kumar, Rosario Dawson, and Phil Colon. It is a 501(c)(4) nonprofit, nonpartisan organization that is headquartered in Washington, D.C. Voto Latino exemplifies the coalition politics approach to incorporation. The organization is a pioneering civic media group that seeks to transform America by organizing and recognizing Latinos' leadership. It uses innovative digital campaigns, pop culture, and grassroots activism to engage, educate, and ultimately empower Latinos to be agents of change in their respective communities, so many of which are located within the border region. Voto Latino advocates building a stronger and more inclusive democracy in the United States. In its early days it emphasized voter registration. It later expanded into civic engagement and Latino leadership development.

Voto Latino claims to have registered more than 500,000 voters by 2018, and it plans to register one million voters by the 2020 election by adding 500,000 more. As of October 19, 2020, it had registered 558,000 new voters (Shondaland.com 2020). Voto Latino introduced innovation in its voter registration drives with internet text messaging. It has helped count Latinos in the 2010 census. It is again advocating for Latinos to participate in the 2020 census, and has formed a partnership with the U.S. Census Bureau to do so. It cofounded the National Voter Registration Day.

Voto Latino started a LV Power Summit Conference to bring together young people and key leaders. It has contributed more than one-half million to young Latino innovators. Voto Latino estimates there are more than 27 million potential Hispanic voters in the United States. It has vigorously conducted voter registration and leadership development among Latino communities in the U.S.-Mexico border region. It currently advocates on a wide range of issues that are particularly relevant and important to the borderland region. These include healthcare and health accessibility and public health (critically important given the COVID-19 pandemic), police brutality (especially in barrios of the region and against abuses perpetrated by the CBP and Border Patrol agents), paid sick leave, a safe and clean environment (important in border communities impacted by the maquiladoras), gun violence prevention (again, in barrios and colonias), immigration (it vigorously opposed the anti-immigration policies of the Trump administration that so impact the border region), fair pay, reproductive justice, education, student debt, voting rights (and against ger-rymandering, voter dilution, and voter suppression), and the census. It supports enactment of the For the People Act and the John Lewis Voting Rights Advancement Act.

People

Brewer, Janet (1944–)

Janet Brewer was the 22nd governor of Arizona (R, 2009–2015). She first assumed the office when former governor Janet Napolitano resigned to become President Obama's secretary of homeland security. Brewer was then elected in 2010. A career politician, Brewer served as Arizona secretary of state from 2003 to 2009, on the Maricopa Board of Supervisors from 1997 to 2003, in the Arizona Senate from 1987 to 1997, and in the Arizona House of Representatives from 1983 to 1987. She exemplifies the nonconfrontational evolution political style of incorporation (Geron 2005; LeMay 2009).

Brewer was born in California. She attended Glendale Community College. She is a very conservative Republican politician who has backed and signed several legislative measures that impacted the U.S.-Mexico border region. For example, in May 2010, she signed into law a measure that banned the teaching of ethnic studies classes in Arizona public schools. In 2010, Governor Brewer signed into law SB 1070, a measure that was billed as the state's most anti-immigrant law ever enacted. Most of its provisions were later ruled unconstitutional. She used executive orders to prohibit state and local governments from providing any public benefits to undocumented immigrants. She supported deploying Arizona's National Guard along the southern Arizona border.

As governor, Brewer created the Human Trafficking Council in 2014 to study and suggest actions to oppose trafficking. She also created the Arizona Serves Task Force that worked through faith-based nonprofits. Brewer is the author of a best-selling book: *Scorpions for Breakfast: My Fight against Special Interests,*

Liberal Media, and Cynical Politicos to Secure America's Border (2011).

Bush, George W. (1946–)

George W. Bush served as the 43rd president of the United States (2001–2009). He claimed the title of wartime president after the 9/11 terrorist attacks, and his subsequent opening of the invasion of Afghanistan in 2001 (launching a U.S.-led war lasting until September 2021), and the Iraq war (March 2003–2011). During his term as president, George W. Bush had an impact on the U.S.-Mexico border region through executive actions, legislation signed into law, and administrative rules and regulations of several federal departments and agencies that have a considerable role in the border region.

Bush was born in New Haven, Connecticut. He worked on his father's Senate bid in 1964. He graduated from Yale University in 1968 and served in the Texas Air National Guard during the Vietnam War. He earned an MBA from Harvard Business School in 1975. In 1978, his first run for elective office turned out to be an unsuccessful campaign for the U.S. House of Representatives. He also worked on his father's campaign for president. He was a co-owner of the Texas Rangers baseball team in 1989. Bush served as the 46th governor of Texas from 1995 to 2000. He was elected president of the United States (POTUS) in 2000.

As POTUS, Bush declared a "war on terrorism" and his administration authored and passed in Congress the USA Patriot Act (2001) and the Department of Homeland Security (DHS) Act (2002). Bush appointed Tom Ridge as the first secretary of DHS and Michael Chertoff as its second. His administration was notable for its efforts to crack down on illegal immigration and for increasing the use of expedited removal. He was unsuccessful in getting a comprehensive immigration reform bill enacted during his presidency. Bush pushed for an expansion of a guest-worker program, again unsuccessfully, that would have had a significant impact on the border region. While serving as POTUS, Bush oversaw passage of the Secure Fence Act in 2006; he began building the first several hundred miles of the fencing, which as we have seen, had considerable negative environmental impact on the border area. Bush can speak some Spanish, and he won 40 percent of the Hispanic vote in 2004, a high point for Republican presidential candidates among Latino voters (De la Garza and DeSipio 2005; Suro, Fry, and Passel 2005).

Castro, Julian (1974–)

Julian Castro is the former U.S. secretary of the Department of Housing and Urban Development (16th, 2014–2017). He was the youngest cabinet secretary in President Barack Obama's administration. He has also served as mayor of San Antonio, Texas (D, 2009–2014), having won the office with more than 56 percent of the vote.

Julian Castro received his BA from Stanford University in 1996 and his JD from Harvard Law School in 2000. His twin brother, Joaquin Castro, also graduated from those schools and represents the 20th Congressional District of Texas (D-2013 to date). The Castro brothers are the sons of Maria Castro, a Chicana political activist who helped start La Raza Unida in Texas. The brothers started a law firm together before their political careers began. Julian was elected to the San Antonio City Council from the 7th district, which was 70 percent Hispanic in terms of population. He was elected mayor of San Antonio in 2009. While mayor, he was a strong supporter of the North American Free Trade Agreement (NAFTA), but by 2016 he agreed that it needed some reforming. He supported universal pre-kindergarten education and has proposed Medicare for All as the best solution to bring about essential healthcare reform.

Julian Castro was briefly considered as the possible vice-presidential candidate to Senator Hillary Clinton in 2016. He ran for his party's presidential nomination in 2019. His campaign's motto was "one nation, one destiny." Several of his campaign planks are relevant to the U.S.-Mexico border region. He advocated what was called the green new deal for the environment. He proposed a pathway to citizenship for most undocumented immigrants as well as the enactment of a Dreamer bill; he advocated the decriminalization of illegal entry, arguing that it should return to the prior status of being only a civil offense. He strongly opposed the building of a border wall. Julian Castro is the author of a memoir, *An Unlikely Journey: Waking Up from My American Dream* (2018). His life and career exhibit the nonconfrontational political evolution path to incorporation (Geron 2005; LeMay 2009).

Catron, Thomas Benton (1840–1921)

Thomas Benton Catron was a Republican senator from New Mexico and served in the U.S. House of Representatives from 1895 to 1897, and again from 1911 to 1917. Catron is arguably the most famous, prominent, and influential of the loose coalition of persons dubbed the "Santa Fe Ring" (Caffey 2014). He graduated from the University of Missouri at Columbia in 1860. He served in the Confederate Army from 1860 to 1864. He moved to New Mexico Territory in 1866. He studied law and was admitted to the bar in 1867. He practiced law in Las Cruces, on the Mexican border, and served as district attorney from 1866 to 1868. Catron was appointed attorney general of the New Mexico Territory, and then served as a U.S. attorney in the Grant Administration. He served on the Territorial Council from 1884 to 1909 and used his high-level political positions to promote his land claims schemes, amassing a fortune and acquiring hundreds of thousands of acres of land. He was elected as a Republican Delegate to the Congress (1895–1897). He ran for the seat again but lost the election in 1896 and resumed his private practice in Santa Fe.

When New Mexico was admitted as a state, Catron was elected to the U.S. Senate and served there from 1912 to 1917.

In the U.S. Senate, he chaired the Committee on Expenditures in the Interior. His activities in the notorious Santa Fe Ring had negative environmental impacts on the border region. However, he also helped the region's economic development, the construction and expansion of the railroads in the region, and the development of the mining industry. The mining industry was undoubtedly economically beneficial to the region but environmentally negative due to lax oversight of the industry by the state government, and subsequently by the U.S. Bureau of Mines.   Catron died in 1921 in Santa Fe, New Mexico (Caffey 2014).

Cuellar, Henry (1955–)

Henry Cuellar is the representative from Texas's 28th Congressional District (D-2005 to date). The district includes Rio Grande City, Laredo, Mission, and parts of San Antonio, Texas. The district lies along the U.S.-Mexico border and is within the border zone. Cuellar exemplifies the nonconfrontational political evolution path to incorporation (Geron 2005; LeMay 2009). Prior to his election to the U.S. House of Representatives, Cuellar briefly served as secretary of state of Texas (2001), appointed by Governor Rick Perry. He was a member of the Texas House of Representatives (D, 1987–2001), where he was a member of the Appropriations Committee and the Higher Education Committee. He was a member of two national legislative committees relevant to the border zone: the U.S.-Mexico Border Committee and the International Trade Committee. Cuellar first ran for the U.S. House of Representatives in 2002, for the Texas 23rd Congressional District but lost. After redistricting, the 28th Congressional District was created and Cuellar won in 2004 by a 20-point margin. He has been easily reelected ever since, often unopposed by a Republican. In June 2006, the U.S. Supreme Court ruled that the Texas legislature had gerrymandered districts to violate Latino voter rights.

Cuellar was born in Laredo, the son of Mexican American migrant workers who spoke no English. However, he went on to become highly educated. He earned an AA degree from Laredo Community College, where he later taught government courses. He earned a BS degree in foreign service from Georgetown University, an MA from Texas A&M University, and a JD and PhD from the University of Texas at Austin. He opened a law firm in Laredo in 1981. He was an adjunct professor at Texas A&M University teaching international commerce law from 1984 to 1986.

In the U.S. House of Representatives, Cuellar is a moderate/centrist and a member of the New Democratic Coalition. He is an active member of the Congressional Hispanic Caucus, the Blue Dog Coalition (conservative Democrats), the U.S. Congressional International Conservation Caucus, and the U.S.-Japan Caucus. He serves on the Appropriations Committee and is vice-chair of its Subcommittee on Homeland Security. Representative Cuellar is a member of the Homeland Security Committee and its Subcommittee on Border and Maritime Security. He was named the chief deputy whip in 2019. He is noted for his bipartisanship.

On issues relevant to the U.S.-Mexico border region, which his district spans, Cuellar is pro–gun rights. In 2008, he was an early supporter of the Hillary Clinton presidential campaign. He authored a bill to honor a slain ICE agent, Jamie Zapata; it was a "Border Security" bill against the smuggling of humans and drugs. In 2013, Cuellar voted against the building of a border fence along the Rio Grande, calling it an antiquated solution to a new-age problem. In 2014, he was the only Democrat to vote in favor of a bill making it easier to deport UAC from Central America, but he also released unauthorized photographs of the unsanitary conditions at Border Patrol detention centers. He consistently supported comprehensive immigration reform measures that would provide a path to citizenship for Dreamers. In 2015, Cuellar proposed a bill to add 55 more federal judges to deal with the overload of immigration cases (estimated at 450,000), which he urged were especially needed in South Texas and the Laredo area. In 2018, he was one of only three Democrats to vote for Kate's Law, which expanded maximum sentences for immigrants who reenter the United States after being deported. That year he also voted for legislation defunding jurisdictions that have sanctuary policies in place.

Geronimo (1829–1909)

Geronimo is arguably the most famous Apache warrior who fought both Mexican and Anglo settlers and was never defeated (he voluntarily surrendered three times to prevent starvation among his band). He exemplifies a person who is a "separatist," never accepting assimilation or acculturation. Geronimo was a Mescalero-Chiricahua Apache. He was a prominent leader (but not a chief) of the Apache tribe. Geronimo led numerous raids against Mexican and U.S. military in the northern Mexican states of Chihuahua and Sonora in what are today the border regions of New Mexico and Arizona. Geronimo was a medicine man of the Bedonkohe band of the Apache tribe, and he led numerous raids and retaliations between 1850 and 1886. The final series of conflicts occurred between 1876 and 1886. His band was also known as the Plains Apache or the Kiowa Apache.

Geronimo was born near Gila River, New Mexico. In 1858, 400 Mexican soldiers from Sonora attacked Geronimo's camp, while he was away, and killed his wife, children, and mother. Thereafter, Geronimo was an implacable foe of the Mexicans, killing them whenever possible. His chief, Mangas Coloradas (meaning "red sleeves"), sent him to the Cochise band. At that time, Mexico placed a bounty on Apache scalps, and from 1858 until his final surrender in 1886, Geronimo and several Apache bands that followed him raided settlers in reprisal for attacks on them, such as the Massacre at Casa Grande in 1873. He surrendered twice but resisted confinement to a reservation.

He led breakouts from the San Carlos reservation in Arizona in 1885, after which the U.S. Army branded him and his followers "renegade Apaches." The army used rival Apache band members as scouts to track him down, and his final surrender happened in 1886.

He was a prisoner of war from 1886 until his death in 1905. He was first sent to Fort Pickens in Florida, and then to Fort Sills in Oklahoma in 1894. While he and his warriors who had surrendered with him were imprisoned, Apache children were sent to Carlisle Industrial School in Pennsylvania to be forcibly acculturated.

Geronimo was displayed at various events in the late 1890s. He met President Theodore Roosevelt in 1905 and was featured in Roosevelt's inaugural parade. Geronimo died of pneumonia on February 17, 1909, at age 80. He reportedly told his surviving son that he never should have surrendered and instead should have died fighting to the last man (Haugen 2005; Utley 2012).

Grijalva, Raul (1948–)

Raul Grijalva represents Arizona's 3rd Congressional District (D, 2003 to date), previously numbered the 7th Congressional District. The district runs along the entire Arizona-Mexico border and includes Tucson, Yuma, and Nogales and peripheral parts of metropolitan Phoenix. Grijalva is the "dean" (meaning the longest-serving) of the Arizona congressional delegation. He has been a Democrat since 1974. Prior to 1974 he was a militant leader of La Raza Unida Party in Arizona (Navarro 2005). He exemplifies an individual who evolved from the protest/demand pathway for pursuing incorporation to follow the nonconfrontational political evolution path (Geron 2005; LeMay 2009).

Raul Grijalva is the son of migrant farm workers who came to Arizona in 1945 with the Bracero Program. He was born on the Canoa Ranch, about 30 miles south of Tucson. He earned a BA degree in sociology from the University of Arizona. In 1974, Grijalva was elected to the Tucson School District board and served on it until 1986. He was also a community organizer, serving as director of El Pueblo Neighborhood Center from 1975 to 1986. In 1987, he served as the assistant dean, Hispanic Student Affairs, at the University of Arizona. From 1989 to 2002 he was a member of the Pima County Board of Supervisors, including a term as its chair from 2000 to 2002.

In 2003, Grijalva was elected to the U.S. House of Representatives. In the House, he serves on the Committee on Education and Workforce, the Subcommittee on Civil Rights and Human Services, and the Subcommittee on Workforce Protection. He is a member of the Committee on Natural Resources, elected as its chair in 2019, and the Subcommittee on National Parks, Forests, and Public Lands. These positions shape his environmental policy positions of relevance to the U.S.-Mexico border region. Grijalva is a member of several caucuses in the House: (1) the Congressional Progressive Caucus, of which he is cochair; (2) the Hispanic Congressional Caucus; (3) the LGBT Equality Caucus, of which he is vice-chair; (4) the Arts Caucus; and (5) the Next Gen 9-1-1 Caucus.

Of importance to the border zone, he introduced a mining law reform bill and a bill to enhance oversight of offshore drilling rights. He introduced a bill to create a National Landscape Conservation System within the Bureau of Land Management. He was a vocal opponent of Arizona's SB 1070 and in 2010 he opposed deployment of some 1,200 National Guard troops at the U.S.-Mexico border calling it "political symbolism." He is pro-choice and was a strong supporter of the Affordable Care Act. As chair of the Progressive Caucus, he proposed a budget reform bill titled Budget for All. In 2010, he introduced a bill regarding oil rig safety following the Deep Water Horizon event. He proposed fossil fuel funding of climate-change studies. In 2007, Grijalva cosponsored the Assault Weapons Ban bill. Long involved in community health activism, he supports the Tucson El Rio Community Health Center. He

supported the various bills to pass a Dream Act and opposed
Arizona's Proposition 200 in 2004. He is a strong supporter
of Native American Sovereignty and in 2010 introduced a bill
titled RESPECT Act. He opposed Arizona SB 1070, calling it
"racial profiling." He was a sharp and outspoken critic of President Trump's immigration policy, zero tolerance, the Trump
administration's attempts to rescind DACA and DAPA, and
the 2020 regulations changes regarding asylum and refugee
policy (Navarro 2005).

Grisham, Michelle Lujan (1959–)

Michelle Lujan Grisham was elected as the 32nd governor
of New Mexico in 2019, the first Democratic woman to be
elected governor of the state, and the first Latina to be elected
chief executive in U.S. history. She previously served in the
U.S. House of Representatives (D, 1st CD, 2012–2018). Prior
to her service in the House, she was secretary of health in New
Mexico from 2004 to 2007 and Bernalillo county commissioner from 2010 to 2012.

Grisham was born in 1959 into the prominent Lujan political family that can trace their antecedents in New Mexico back
12 generations. She was born in Los Alamos, New Mexico. She
earned her BS degree from the University of New Mexico in
1981 and her JD there in 1987. She served as director for the
New Mexico Agency on Aging under three governors: Bruce
King (D, 1971–1975, 1979–1983, 1991–1995), Gary Johnson (D-1995–2003), and Bill Richardson (D-2003–2011).
Governor Richardson elevated the agency to a cabinet-level
department. Grisham won her seat to the U.S. House of Representatives in 2012 with 59 percent of the vote, and again by
the same margin in 2014. She won reelection in 2016 with
65 percent of the vote. In 2016, she was elected chair of the
Congressional Hispanic Caucus.

While in the House of Representatives, Michelle Grisham
served on the Committee on Agriculture and the Committee

on the Budget. She was a member of three Congressional Caucuses: Congressional Hispanic Caucus, the Congressional Native American Caucus, and the Caucus for Women's Issues. In 2019, she won the gubernatorial race with 56.9 percent of the vote. Of relevance to the U.S.-Mexico border region, as governor she signed an executive order for New Mexico to join the U.S. Climate Alliance. She exemplifies the nonconfrontational political evolution path to incorporation (Geron 2005; LeMay 2009).

Huerta, Dolores (1930–)

Dolores Huerta was born in 1930 in Dawson, New Mexico, where her family roots go back to the 17th century. She grew up in Stockton, California, after her family moved there. Huerta is the daughter of a miner and an agricultural worker. Her impact on the U.S.-Mexico border zone, and on the Chicano civil rights movement—not only in the border region but throughout the United States—has been profound.

In the 1950s, while helping to organize the Community Service Organization (CSO), Huerta met Cesar Chavez. When Chavez left the CSO in 1962, she left as well to organize farm workers in Delano, California. She cofounded the United Farm Workers (UFW) and spent most of the 1960s organizing migrant workers in Stockton and Modesto. She went to the UFW's central headquarters in Delano where she became Cesar Chavez's most trusted and valuable associate. In 1965, she was instrumental in securing Aid to Families with Dependent Children (AFDC) benefits for farm workers in California that had previously been denied to them. She played a central role in the five-year long Delano Grape Strike as well as in the ensuing lettuce strike in the Salinas Valley. Dolores Huerta and Cesar Chavez went to Phoenix, Arizona, in 1969 and helped found the Chicanos Por La Causa (CPLC). CPLC serves the Chicano movement not only in the Phoenix area but throughout southern Arizona's border region. It was at CPLC that Chavez and Huerta coined the phrase that became the Chicano movement's motto: Si, se puede! (Yes, we can!).

Huerta served as vice president of the United Farm Workers (UFW) from 1970–1973, and as the first vice-president emeritus of the UFW union within the American Federation of Labor-Congress of Industrial Organizations (AFL-CIO). Huerta was the national spokesperson for the union and developed its labor contracts. She was its chief negotiator, boycott strategist, and lobbyist. She exemplifies a civil rights activist using the direct-action, peaceful protest path to incorporation (Geron 2005; LeMay 2009). As an advocate for farm workers' rights, she has been arrested 22 times for nonviolent, peaceful union activities.

In 1924, the California Senate bestowed on her the Outstanding Labor Leader Award, and in 1993, she was inducted into the National Women's Hall of Fame and awarded the American Civil Liberties Union's (ACLU) Roger Baldwin Medal of Liberty. She also received the Eugene V. Debs Foundation's Outstanding American Award and the Ellis Island Medal of Freedom Award. She has been awarded numerous honorary degrees.

She continues to serve in leadership roles for the UFW, the California AFL-CIO, the Fund for the Feminist Majority, the Democratic Socialists of America board, Latinas for Choice, FAIR (Fairness in Media Reporting), and the Center for Voting and Democracy. In the past, Huerta has served on the federal commission for the Minority Apprentice Program, the Advisory Committee on Immigration, and the Commission on Agricultural Workers. She was a member of the California State Library Service, California's Industrial Welfare Commission, and University of California's Board of Trustees. In 1998, President Bill Clinton awarded her the Eleanor Roosevelt Award for Human Rights. In 2002, she founded the Dolores Huerta Foundation. In 2011, President Barack Obama awarded her the Presidential Medal of Freedom for Civil Rights (LeMay 2009, 301).

Jimenez, Cristina (1984–)

Cristina Jimenez is the cofounder and managing director of the United We Dream Network (UWD). She exemplifies an activist using the demands/protest path to incorporation who has increasingly combined that with using the coalition politics path (Geron 2005; LeMay 2009). Cristina Jimenez was brought to the United States from Ecuador as an unauthorized immigrant when she was 13 years old. She attended and graduated from high school and college. As an undergraduate student, she organized youth and workers for passage of various pro-immigrant policies at the local level and the national level; and she has been doing so for the past 20 years. United We Dream has been active and instrumental in organizing young Dreamers throughout the U.S.-Mexico border region, and in particular in reaching out to and involving those from Central America. Since 2016, UWD has advocated for more progressive asylum and refugee policies; it has been sharply critical of the Trump administration's policies and executive orders on asylum-refugee matters, and of the zero-tolerance policy of the DOJ and DHS. Cristina Jimenez was named by *Forbes Magazine* as one of the "30 under 30 in Law and Policy" and one of the "21 immigration reform power players." The *Chronicle of Philanthropy* selected Jimenez as one of five nonprofit organization leaders who will influence public policy. Jimenez cofounded the New York State Youth Leadership Council and the Dream Mentorship Program at Queens College. She served as an immigration policy analyst for the Drum Major Institute for Public Policy and as an immigrant rights organizer at Make the Road New York. Jimenez holds a master's degree in public administration and public policy from the School of Public Affairs at Baruch College, CUNY. She graduated cum laude with a BA in political science and business from Queens College, CUNY.

Jimenez led UWD's campaign to support President Obama's executive orders, DACA and DAPA, in 2012 and 2014. UWD was party to the June 18, 2020, class action suit before the U.S. Supreme Court that upheld the DACA program and held the Trump administration's decision to rescind DACA as "arbitrary and capricious." The 5–4 ruling by the Supreme Court protects about 700,000 DACA recipients from deportation. The Supreme Court ruling is especially important for families of mixed legal status, who number in the millions and among whom many thousands reside in the borderland region (LeMay 2019, 191).

Lujan, Ben Ray (1972–)

Ben Ray Lujan was the U.S. representative of the Third Congressional District of New Mexico, elected to the House of Representatives in 2008. As of January 2021, Lujan is the U.S. Senator from New Mexico (D-NM). His House of Representatives district contains 15 separate Pueblo tribes. Lujan exemplifies the nonconfrontational political evolution path to incorporation (Geron 2005; LeMay 2009). Lujan grew up in Nambe', a small farming community north of Santa Fe bordered by the Nambe' and Pojoaque pueblos. He was the assistant speaker of the House in the 116th Congress (2019)—the highest-ranking Hispanic in the U.S. Congress. Prior to being elected to the House of Representatives, Lujan was on the New Mexico Regulation Commission (2005–2009), and before that he was the director of administrative services and chief financial officer of the New Mexico Cultural Affairs Department.

Lujan has a BBA degree from the New Mexico Highlands University, which he earned in 2007. He served as the deputy state treasurer during which time he pushed to increase funding for the New Mexico Indian Health Service, which is of much significance to the U.S.-Mexico border region given the many healthcare challenges that it faces.

As U.S. congressman, Lujan introduced five bills regarding water accessibility for the region and pushed for rural broadband connectivity. The latter is highly important for addressing cases of missing and murdered Native American women. In 2020, Lujan ran for and was successfully elected to the U.S. Senate from New Mexico. In the U.S. Senate, Lujan advocates for green jobs, the expansion of healthcare, and the preservation of the region's natural resources. Lujan was a member of the House Energy and Commerce Committee and its Health Subcommittee and served on the Consumer Protection and Commerce Subcommittee and on the Communications and Technology Subcommittee—all of which dealt with legislation important to the borderland region. While in the House, he advocated and voted for the Green New Deal, which called for net zero carbon emissions and expands environmental protection in New Mexico.

Lujan was the House sponsor of the National Monument designation for the Rio Grande del Norte National Conservation area and the Organ Mountains Desert Peaks, and a bill for the Protection of the Greater Chaco Canyon region. Lujan is a long-time advocate for New Mexico's acequias (irrigation systems) and traditional lands. In the U.S. Senate, he continues his work begun in the U.S. House of Representatives to assist rural farming and ranching via grants to the food-providing communities to advance their entrepreneurship.

He was a member of several caucuses that are important to the border region: the Congressional Hispanic Caucus, the Native American Caucus, the National Labs Caucus (which he co-chairs), the Clean Up Caucus, and the Tech Transfer Caucus. In 2013, he was selected to be the chief deputy whip of the Democratic Party in the House of Representatives, and from 2015 to 2019 he was chair of the Democratic Congressional Campaign Committee.

In the Senate, Lujan has sponsored several bills of importance to the borderland region: (1) a grant program to improve the health of residents along the U.S.-Mexico (and the U.S.-Canada) border, including against infectious diseases and emerging biothreats; (2) a bill to enhance the rights of domestic workers, cosponsor of the Zero-Emission Housing Act of 2021; (3) the Native American Child Protection Act of 2021; (4) the Native American Housing Assistance and Self-Determination Reauthorization Act of 2021; and (5) the Native Behavioral Health Access Improvement Act of 2021 (Congress.gov 2021a, 2021b, Members/Ray Lujan).

Obama, Barack (1961–)

Barack Obama was the 44th president of the United States, serving in office from 2009 to 2017. Obama was born in Hawaii and raised by his grandparents in Kansas. He worked his way through college and received some scholarships. He then moved to Chicago, where he worked with a group of churches as a community organizer to help rebuild communities devastated by high unemployment because of the closing of local steel plants. Obama went on to study at Harvard Law School where he became the first African American president of the prestigious *Harvard Law Review.*

He returned to Chicago to lead voter registration drives and taught constitutional law at the University of Chicago. He eventually ran for the Illinois state legislature. In the Illinois State Senate, he authored the first major ethics reform law passed in 25 years. He worked in the state senate to cut taxes for working-class families and expanded healthcare in the state. As U.S. senator from Illinois (D-IL), Obama worked on bipartisan lobbying reform and transparency in government by putting the federal spending data online. Obama burst onto the national political scene when he gave the Democratic National Convention keynote speech in 2004. He ran for president in 2008, and after a tough primary battle with then-Senator Hillary Clinton (D-NY), Obama won the nomination and went on to win the office. He was sworn in as POTUS on January 20, 2009. He was reelected in 2012. His campaign motto was "Yes, we can," paying homage to the United Farm Workers' "Si, se puede" slogan.

During his two terms in office, Obama appointed two secretaries of Homeland Security—Janet Napolitano and Jeh Johnson. He impacted the borderland region substantially by issuing two executive orders on unauthorized immigration—DACA and DAPA. However, his administration also set a record for deporting unauthorized immigrants by focusing on those with criminal convictions. He also affected the region with enactment of his signature legislation, the Affordable Care Act (Act of March 23, 2010, 124 Stat. 119). The ACA, better known as Obamacare, had substantial economic and healthcare impact on working-class families throughout the United States, including the borderland region. Given the extensiveness of poverty in the area, ACA is of particular benefit to the borderland region. ACA added millions of persons to the health insurance rolls across the nation and in the borderland region.

Since leaving office, President Obama had remained silent on the actions of his successor, Donald Trump, until mid-2020. He then began to speak out very critically of the administration's zero-tolerance policy, rescinding of DACA and DAPA, asylum and refugee decisions, and attempts to abolish the ACA. He was highly critical of the failures of the Trump administration to effectively cope with the COVID-19 pandemic, which has hit the borderland region especially hard.

President Obama and his wife, Michelle, are parents to two daughters, Malia and Sasha. President Obama is the recipient of the Nobel Peace Prize, one of only four U.S. presidents so honored. He personifies the nonconfrontational political evolution path to incorporation. Indeed, as president, he exemplified the ultimate level of political incorporation. He is author of three best-selling books: *Dreams from My Father*

(2004), *The Audacity of Hope* (2007), and *Of Thee I Sing* (2010) (LeMay 2009, 158–159; LeMay 2019, 203–204).

Parker, Quanah (1845/1852–1911)

Quanah Parker was a war leader of the Quahadi band of the Comanche Nation, the son of Peta Nocona, a Comanche chief, and Cynthia Ann Parker, an Anglo-American who in 1836 had been kidnapped (when she was nine years old) and assimilated into the Comanche tribe (Carlson and Crum 2011). Quanah Parker emerged as a dominant figure in the Red River War, fought many battles with the U.S. Army, and was never defeated in battle (Exley 2001). He eventually surrendered and led his band to the reservation at Fort Sill, Oklahoma. He helped settle the Comanche on the Kiowa-Comanche-Apache Reservation, in what was then the southwestern Indian Territory (Neeley 2009).

On the reservation Parker was appointed by the federal government as the principal chief of the entire Comanche Nation (the various bands of the Comanche Nation elect chiefs but have no principal chief), and he represented Native Americans from the Southwest in the U.S. Congress. He is also considered one of the founders of the Native American Church and notably fought for the legal use of peyote in their religious practices (Hagan 1993). Following Native American religious practice, he had several wives, up to eight during his lifetime. He has been described as the Last Chief of the Comanche, since after his death the leadership title of "Chief" was replaced by "Chairman" (Neeley 2009; Selden 2006).

On the reservation he proved to be a resourceful leader and became friends with the Burnett family of cattle ranchers. Parker originally opposed opening the reservation lands for grazing by white ranchers, but he later changed his position. He became one of the wealthiest Native Americans of his day,

embracing much of the white culture and adopting the sur-
name of his white mother, Parker. He went on hunting trips
with President Theodore Roosevelt.

Parker died on February 23, 1911. His remains were buried
at the Post Oak Mission Cemetery in Oklahoma, but in 1957,
his remains and those of his wife and mother were moved to
Fort Sill, Oklahoma.

Polk, James K. (1795–1849)

James K. Polk served as president of the United States from
1845 to 1849. Arguably, there would be no U.S.-Mexico
border as we know it today without his one-term presidency.
He was born in North Carolina but moved to the Nashville,
Tennessee area where he became a community leader, county
judge, businessman, and prominent slave owner. He graduated
from the University of North Carolina in 1818 and studied
law in Nashville. His life on the western frontier shaped his
politics, as did his life-long interaction with enslaved people.
He favored westward expansion but advocated the expansion
of slave states as well.

He began his political career in 1823 in the Tennessee House
of Representatives. He befriended and supported General
Andrew Jackson. He was elected to the U.S. House of Representatives in 1835 and became Speaker of the House. He
served in the House until 1839, when he was elected governor
of Tennessee. He supported President Andrew Jackson's Indian
Removal Act (1830) that forced the Choctaw Nation from
southern Mississippi to the west. In 1844 he sought the vice
presidency, expecting Martin Van Buren to become the party's
nominee for president. Instead, he was chosen as the nominee
at the convention, as a "dark horse" candidate, on the strength
of his advocacy of the doctrine of Manifest Destiny. He supported the expansion of territorial holdings. He defeated Whig
candidate Henry Clay, becoming the 11th POTUS in 1845
(Chaffin 2014; Pinheiro 2007).

Polk successfully negotiated with Great Britain the Canadian boundary line to the 49th parallel. Immediately after, he began negotiations with Mexico for the annexation of Texas. In 1846, he sent John Slidell to purchase the territories of New Mexico and California for $30 million. When the Mexican government refused, he ordered American troops under General Zachary Taylor to move into the disputed territory, inciting conflict with Mexico. Mexican troops attacked Taylor's forces but lost the battle. Polk used the conflict to ask Congress to declare war on Mexico. The Mexican American War was successful and the United States acquired one-third of Mexico's holdings through the provisions of the Treaty of Guadalupe Hidalgo, including present-day California, Utah, Nevada, Arizona, and New Mexico. President Polk supported the expansion of slavery into the newly acquired territories. He retired after one term and died just four months later due to a cholera outbreak in Nashville in 1849.

Richardson, Bill (1947–)

Bill Richardson is the former governor of New Mexico (D-NM, 2003–2011). His life and political career best exemplify the nonconfrontational political evolution path to political incorporation (Geron 2005; LeMay 2009). When he was reelected to the governorship in 2006, he won with 69 percent of the vote, the largest margin for any governor in New Mexico's history. For two years he served as chairman of the Democratic Governors' Association. He had previously been chair of the Western Governors' Association, chairman of the Border Governors' Conference, and chairman of the 2004 Democratic National Convention. Richardson's distinguished public service career included terms as a U.S. Representative from New Mexico's Third Congressional District (1982–1996), which is one of the most ethnically diverse congressional districts in the United States, straddling much of the border with Mexico within New Mexico. He also served as U.S. ambassador to the United Nations (1997–1998). At the UN he worked to increase security against international terrorism and promoted cooperation on issues like global warming and public health.

Richardson served as secretary of energy in President Bill Clinton's cabinet (1998–2000). In 2001, he chaired the Freedom House, a nonpartisan organization promoting democracy and human rights worldwide. Richardson also served on several boards, including the National Resource Defense Council and United Way International. In 2008, he briefly sought his party's presidential nomination. He is a distinguished diplomat and special envoy who has been nominated for the Nobel Peace Prize four times. As a special envoy, he won the release of hostages and American servicemen in North Korea, Cuba, Iraq, and the Sudan. He secured the release of Marine Sgt. Andrew Tabmooressi from a prison in Tijuana, Mexico. He was special envoy to the Organization of American States (OAS) and a Special Fellow on Latin America at the James Baker III Institute for Public Policy at Rice University. He was on the boards of the World Institute and Refugees International.

Richardson was born and raised in the barrio of San Francisco in Coyoacan. He earned a BA in French and Political Science from Tufts University in 1970. He taught courses at New Mexico State University, at the University of New Mexico, at Harvard University's Kennedy School of Government, and at the United World College at Montezuma, New Mexico. In 2010, Richardson was named the "best education governor" by the National Education Association. As governor, he expanded healthcare under the ACA, which was particularly helpful in the poverty-ridden border region.

Richardson authored or coauthored the following books: *Between Worlds: The Making of an American Life* (2005), *Leading by Example: How We Can Inspire an Energy and Security Revolution* (2007), *Universal Transparency* (2011), *Sweeping Up*

Dirty Bombs (2011), and *How to Sweet-Talk a Shark* (2013) (LeMay 2009, 149).

Roosevelt, Franklin D. (1882–1945)

As the 32nd president of the United States, Franklin D. Roosevelt had a significant impact on the U.S.-Mexico border region. He is unique among U.S. presidents in being elected to the office four times, serving from 1933 until his death while in office in 1945, in Warm Springs, Georgia, at the age of 63. He impacted the border region through the Great Depression and his New Deal Coalition and what became known as the Fifth Party System (Zentner and LeMay 2020, 162–194). Franklin Roosevelt is consistently ranked among the top three presidents in U.S. history (Daniels 2015, 2016; Pedersen 2011).

Roosevelt was born in Hyde Park, New York, to the prominent Roosevelt family. He earned a BA degree from Harvard University in 1903. During the period 1904–1907 he attended Columbia Law School and dropped out before graduating but passed the bar. He served in the New York state senate (1910–1913) and later as assistant secretary of the Navy (1913–1919); he was nominated for vice president of the Democratic ticket in 1920 but lost the election. He was afflicted with a paralytic illness in 1921 (either polio or Guillain-Barré Syndrome). He went on to be elected governor of New York (1929–1932). He won the presidency in the 1932 election.

During his first term he launched the first New Deal (1933–1935) and the second New Deal (1935–1936). The Second New Deal included the Public Works Administration, established in 1935, that had a profound impact on the border region. Arguably, Roosevelt most significantly affected the border region with the executive order that began the Bracero Program in 1942. He signed into law the congressional enactment of the program in 1944 (Act of February 14, 1944, Supply of Farm Labor; LeMay and Barkan 1999, 197–198). It set patterns of migration from Mexico to the United States that persist to this day (LeMay 2009, 108–109, 355–357; LeMay 2015, 6–8, 66). Roosevelt influenced the region through the Conservation Movement, which created the National Park and National Forest systems. He negotiated the Good Neighbor foreign policy with Latin America that further affected patterns of immigration to the region. He carried the entire region's states in the elections of 1936, 1940, and 1944. He influenced the various tribes in the region with the Indian Reorganization Act of 1934. He influenced the Southern California portion of the region (San Diego area) with his Executive Order 9066 that relocated Japanese and Japanese Americans from the area to the various internment camps (LeMay and Barkan 1999, 192–194). Finally, the region's entire economy (and that of the United States) was greatly boosted out of the Depression by the buildup to the war (1940–1941) that spurred, for example, the San Diego area of the region, influencing the migration of people out of the region to work in the war industries of urban areas and thereby inducing the migration of Mexicans into the region.

Roybal, Eduardo (1916–2005)

Representative Edward Roybal served in the U.S. House of Representatives from 1963 to 1993. He is a prime example of a person using the nonconfrontational political evolution approach to incorporation (Geron 2005; LeMay 2009). He represented the 30th Congressional District from 1963 to 1975. It was redrawn and renumbered as the 25th Congressional District, which he represented from 1975 to 1993.

Ed Roybal was educated at UCLA, where he earned a degree in business, and at Southwestern University, where he earned his law degree. He served in the U.S. Army during World War II. He served on the Los Angeles City Council from 1947 to 1962. In 1960, he formed the CSO and later organized MAPA (LeMay 2009, 299–301).

While in the House of Representatives, Roybal served on two committees that have had considerable impact on the border region—the Interior and Insular Affairs Committee and the House Appropriations Committee. His emphasis on programs aimed at helping veterans, the elderly, and Mexican Americans was important for the border region. In 1967, Roybal wrote the first Bilingual Education bill. He served as chair of the House Select Committee on Aging. In 1976, Roybal was cofounder of the Congressional Hispanic Caucus, which he chaired until 1986. He unsuccessfully opposed enactment of the Immigration Reform and Control Act (IRCA) of 1986 (LeMay 1994). He was cofounder of the National Association of Latino Elected and Appointed Officials (Burt 2007). Roybal retired from Congress in 1993 and was proudly able to assist his daughter Lucille Roybal-Allard's election to the 33rd Congressional District in 1994 (the 33rd CD included much of his former district). In 2001, President Bill Clinton awarded him the Presidential Medal of Freedom. He died in 2005, at age 89.

Sessions, Jeff (1946–)

Jeff Sessions exemplifies the nonconfrontational political evolution strategy regarding incorporation (Geron 2005; LeMay 2009). He impacted, very negatively his critics would point out, the U.S.-Mexico border region in his capacity as U.S. senator from Alabama (1997–2017) and even more so as attorney general of the United States (2017–2018). Throughout his political career, he evidenced a very conservative record on immigration.

Sessions was born in Selma, Alabama, in 1946. In 1969, he received his BA degree from Huntington College. In 1973, he earned his JD degree from the University of Alabama. He served in the U.S. Army and Army Reserve from 1973 to 1977, attaining the rank of Captain and working in the Transportation Terminal Unit. Sessions was U.S. attorney for the southern district of Alabama from 1981 to 1983; the 44th attorney general of Alabama (1995–1997); and U.S. senator from Alabama (1997–2017). He culminated his career as attorney general of the United States (February 2017–November 2018).

While in the U.S. Senate, Sessions served on the Armed Services Committee, the Committee on the Budget, the Committee on Environment and Public Works, and the Committee on the Judiciary. He chaired the Judiciary's Subcommittee on Immigration, Border Security, and Refugees. He was a member of the International Narcotics Control Caucus.

When President Trump nominated him for attorney general, he was barely confirmed—the senators voted 52–47 in what was a strictly partisan vote. As soon as he assumed office as the 84th attorney general, Sessions fired 46 U.S. attorneys and disbanded the National Commission on Forensic Science. He was embroiled in political controversy for his role in the firing of FBI director James Comey. Throughout his time as attorney general, he was highly criticized by the U.S. Commission on Civil Rights. Despite the controversies, in July 2017, Sessions ordered the reviving of a policy of civil assets forfeiture—aimed at drug smuggling operations among other criminal enterprises.

Importantly for the border region, Attorney General Sessions promised prosecution of the infamous MS-13 gang (although he delivered little on the promise), and in March 2017, he threatened to defund sanctuary cities. In July 2018, Sessions announced the administration's "zero tolerance" policy that separated detained children at the U.S.-Mexico border from their parents, which various religious leaders described as "unnecessarily cruel." In July 2018, he reversed a decision by the Board of Immigration Appeals granting asylum to battered women. Critics asserted he singlehandedly dismantled 60–70 percent of asylum jurisprudence from the previous 30 years.

The United Methodist Church, of which he was an active member, brought charges against him for "child abuse, immorality, and racial discrimination contrary to the standards of the United Methodist Church." In 2018, Sessions rescinded the Cole Memorandum regarding bringing charges against state legalized marijuana laws. He was forced to resign as attorney general by a disgruntled President Trump (for his recusing himself from the probe of Russian interference in the 2016 election) in November 2018, the day after the midterm elections. He ran, unsuccessfully for his old U.S. Senate seat in 2020, perhaps in part because President Trump endorsed his Republican Party rival, former Auburn University football coach, Tommy Tuberville, who won the nomination and went on to win the Senate seat in the 2020 general election.

Trump, Donald (1946–)

Donald J. Trump is a billionaire real-estate mogul and a former reality television star who served as the 45th president of the United States. In 2012, he briefly considered running for president and was embroiled in—and largely led—the anti-Obama "birther" movement. He strenuously opposed President Obama's DACA and DAPA executive orders, arguing that they were unconstitutional and required congressional authorization to be legal. On June 15, 2016, he announced his candidacy for the Republican Party nomination for president, running in a field of 17. On July 15, 2016, he clinched the nomination and announced his choice for vice president, Governor Mike Pence of Indiana. Trump accepted the nomination on July 21, 2016 and went on to win the Electoral College vote (although he lost the popular vote by about 3 million votes). In the 2016 election, Trump essentially split in the border region with Clinton.

Clinton carried California by 62 percent to Trump's 32 percent; in Arizona, Trump won the popular vote by 48 percent to Clinton's 44.6 percent; in New Mexico, Clinton won 48 percent to Trump's 40 percent; and in Texas, Trump won 52.5 percent to Clinton's 43.5 percent.

Immediately after taking office, Trump nominated John Kelly as secretary of the DHS and Senator Jeff Sessions as attorney general. They in turn issued departmental regulations turning back President Obama's reforms, particularly as pertaining to immigration. His DOJ, DHS, and HHS policies have been controversial and greatly and negatively impacted the U.S.-Mexico border region with respect to expedited removal, a zero-tolerance policy for undocumented or unauthorized immigrants, and the separation of children from their parents in border-area detention centers run by the CBP and the ORR.

President Trump rescinded DACA and DAPA, although those moves were challenged in federal district, appellate, and ultimately, the U.S. Supreme Court. He issued executive orders that cut the number of refugees who could be admitted from 50,000 to 25,000 and put a ban on asylum-seekers who transited a third country (Mexico) (a ban that essentially ended asylum). President Trump further impacted the U.S.-Mexico border region by approving the building of a border wall (under a pilot project) and by replacing or expanding existing border fences. The zero-tolerance policy resulted in the removal of some 2,500 children before Trump was forced to announce he was ending that policy. His administration ignored a court-ordered ruling about not holding them in custody longer than 20 days. Trump emphasized the immediate deportation of unauthorized immigrants without a judicial hearing on the matter, and in many cases without due process. At least six migrant children died while in ICE, CBP, or ORR custody.

His administration was marked by foreign policy tensions with Mexico. He was highly critical of NAFTA and forced a renegotiation of that treaty resulting in the United States-Mexico-Canada Agreement (USMCA) in 2020. It is too early yet to assess the impact of this move on the border region, but it will likely be extensive and involve some unintended consequences, as did NAFTA.

In the 2020 presidential election, President Trump again split the results in the borderland states with President Biden. Biden carried California by 63.5 percent to Trump's 31.3 percent; Trump also lost Arizona, although narrowly so, Biden's

49.39 percent to Trump's 49.09 percent; Biden carried New Mexico over Trump, 54.2 percent to 43.5 percent; and in Texas, as expected, Trump won by 52 percent to Biden's 46.5 percent.

Donald Trump is author of nine books: *Trump: The Art of the Deal* (1987), *The America We Deserve* (2000), *Trump: How to Get Rich* (2004), *Why We Want You to Be Rich* (1996), *Think Big and Kick Ass in Business* (2007), *Trump 101: The Way to Success* (2007), *Trump: Never Give Up* (2008), *Think Like a Champion* (2009), and *Time to Get Tough* (2011).

Vargas, Juan (1961–)

Representative Juan Vargas serves California's 51st Congressional District (D-CA-51 CD), the district that spans the entire border region in the state. Vargas was raised on a chicken ranch in National City, within the district. Juan is one of ten children born to Tomas and Celina Vargas. His father immigrated to the United States from Mexico in the late 1940s as part of the Bracero Program. Through the Bracero Program, Tomas became a legal resident, and Vargas's mother went on to earn her U.S. citizenship.

Juan attended the University of San Diego on a scholarship, graduating Magna Cum Laude with a BA in political science in 1983. He went on to earn his MA from Fordham University in 1987 and a JD from Harvard Law School, where he was a classmate of Barack Obama.

Juan entered the Jesuit order where he worked with disadvantaged communities, including orphaned children, and internally displaced people in El Salvador. His work while in the Jesuits focused on the health and welfare of children and on issues of social justice.

He left the Jesuits to pursue family life. He married and returned to San Diego to work as an attorney with a prestigious San Diego law firm. He decided to seek public office and was elected to the San Diego City Council in 1993; he rose to a leadership role in planning, funding, and advocating for public safety, municipal infrastructure, and schools. During his tenure (1983–2001), he helped establish community-based policing, which became a national model. He helped create the City of San Diego's 6 to 6 afterschool program and sponsored a graffiti and home rehabilitation program, Operation Restore, that employed homeless persons in an effort to improve and revitalize blighted homes and neighborhoods in San Diego's urban core.

In 1999, after the invasion of Kosovo to end the terrifying regime of "ethnic cleansing," Vargas and his wife took in a refugee Kosovar family for two years. In 2000, he was elected to the California state assembly from the 79th assembly district, representing the southern part of San Diego, the western portion of Chula Vista, and the cities of Coronado, Imperial Beach, and National City. In the assembly, he was appointed assistant majority leader. In 2006, he served as vice president of external affairs of a major corporation and as vice president of corporate legal for the Liberty Mutual Group, which enabled him to help bring jobs to Southern California communities.

In 2010, Vargas was elected to the California State Senate; he served the 40th state senate district, which includes the southern portion of San Diego County, portions of Riverside, all of Imperial County, and California's entire U.S.-Mexico border region. In the U.S. House, Vargas serves on two committees, the Financial Services Committee, and the Foreign Affairs Committee. He went on to chair the Banking and Financial Institutions Committee. He has worked on public safety and to protect the services to the poor and elderly in his borderland district.

References

Adams, Florence. 2018. *Latinos and Local Representation: Changing Realities, Emerging Voices—Political, Social, Cultural, and Legal Issues.* Oxfordshire, UK: Routledge/ Taylor Francis.

Araiza, Lauren. 2014. *To March for Others: the Black Freedom Struggle and the United Farm Workers*. Philadelphia: University of Pennsylvania Press.

Bailey, John, and Roy Godson. 2000. *Organized Crime and Democratic Governability: Mexico and the U.S.-Mexican Borderlands*. Pittsburgh: University of Pittsburgh Press.

Burt, Kenneth. 2007. *The Search for a Civic Voice: California Latino Politics*. Claremont, CA: Regina Books.

Caffey, David. 2014. *Chasing the Santa Fe Ring: Power and Privilege in Territorial New Mexico*. Albuquerque: University of New Mexico Press.

Carlson, Paul, and Tom Crum. 2011. *Myth, Memory and Massacre: The Pease River Capture of Cynthia Ann Parker*. Lubbock: Texas Tech University Press.

Center for Biological Diversity. n.d. "Our Mission: Saving Life on Earth." https://www.biologicaldiversity.org/about/.

Center for Disease Control. 2020. "Disparities in COVID-10 Illness." https://www.cdc.gov/coronavirus/2019-ncov /community/health-equity/racial-ethnic-disparities /increased-risk-illness.html.

Chaffin, Tom. 2014. *Met His Every Goal? James K. Polk and the Legends of Manifest Destiny*. Chattanooga: University of Tennessee Press.

Chicanos Por La Causa. 2020. "About: A History of Advocacy." https://www.cplc.org/about/history.php.

Child Trends. 2020. https://www.childtrends.org/indicators /racial-and-ethnic-composition-of-the-child-population.

Congress.gov. 2021a. https://crsreports.congress.gov/product /pdf/R/R46705.

Congress.gov. 2021b. https://www.congress.gov/members /ben-lujan/L000570.

Crosthwaite, Luis Humberto. 2002. *Puro Border: Dispatches, Snapshots, and Graffiti on La Frontera*. El Paso, TX: Cinco Puentos Press.

Daniels, Roger. 2015. *Franklin D. Roosevelt: Road to the New Deal, 1882–1939*. Champaign: University of Illinois Press.

Daniels, Roger. 2016. *Franklin D. Roosevelt: The War Years, 1939–1945*. Champaign: University of Illinois Press.

De la Garza, Rudolfo, and Louis DeSipio. 2005. *Muted Voices: Latino Politics in the 2000 Elections*. Lanham: Rowman and Littlefield.

DeSipio, Louis. 1996. *Counting on the Latino Vote: Latinos in a New Electorate*. Charlottsville: University of Virginia Press.

Dimas, Pete. 2019. *Here We Stand: Chicanos Por La Causa and Arizona's Chicano/a Resurgence, 1968–1974*. Phoenix: CPLC and Arizona State University Press.

Ebright, Malcolm. 1994. *Land Grant and Law Suites in Northern New Mexico*. Guadalupe: New Mexico Center for Land Grant Studies.

Ellingwood, Ken. 2009. *Hard Line: Life and Death in the U.S.-Mexico Border*. New York: Vintage Books.

Exley, Jo Ann Powell. 2001. *Frontier Blood: The Saga of the Parker Family*. College Station: Texas A & M University Press.

Flores, Lori. 2016. *Grounds for Dreaming: Mexican Americans, Mexican Immigrants, and the California Farmworkers Movement*. New Haven, CT: Yale University Press.

Frey, Juan Carlos. 2019. *Sand and Blood*. E-book: Public Affairs Press.

Ganz, Marshall. 2009. *Why David Sometimes Wins: Leadership, Organization, and Strategy in the California Farm Worker Movement*. New York: Oxford University Press.

Garcia, Ignacio. 1997. *Chicanismo: The Forging of a Militant Ethos among Mexican Americans*. Tucson: University of Arizona Press.

Garcia, Mario. 2015. *The Chicano Generation: Testimonios of the Movement*. Berkeley: University of California Press.

Gardner, Richard M. 1970. *Grito! Reies Tijerina and the New Mexico Land Grant War of 1967*. New York: Random House.

Geron, Kim. 2005. *Latino Political Power*. Boulder, CO: Lynne Rienner Publishers.

Gutierrez, David. 1995. *Walls and Mirrors: Mexican Americans, Mexican Immigrants, and the Politics of Ethnicity*. Berkeley: University of California Press.

Hagan, William. 1993. *Quanah Parker: Comanche Chief*. Norman: University of Oklahoma Press.

Hagedorn, Sara, and Michael LeMay. 2019. *The American Congress: A Research Handbook*. Santa Barbara, CA: ABC-CLIO.

Haugen, Brenda. 2005. *Geronimo: A Biography*. Mankato, MN: Capstone Publishers.

Human Rights First. 2020a. "With Asylum Effectively Blocked at Southern Border, Those Seeking Safety Face Escalating Violence, Punishing Conditions." May 13, 2020. https://www.humanrightsfirst.org/press-release /asylum-effectively-blocked-southern-border-those-seeking -safety-face-escalating.

Human Rights First. 2020b. "Human Rights First Condemns Rule that Seeks to Rewrite Refugee Laws, Eliminate Asylum." June 11, 2020. https://www.humanrightsfirst .org/press-release/human-rights-first-condemns-rule-seeks -re-write-refugee-laws-eliminate-asylum.

Kirkpatrick, Terry. 2012. *60 Miles of Border*. New York: Berkley Books.

LeMay, Michael. 1994. *Anatomy of a Public Policy*. Westport, CT and London: Praeger Press.

LeMay, Michael. 2009. *The Perennial Struggle, 3e*. Upper Saddle River, NJ: Prentice-Hall.

LeMay, Michael. 2015. *Illegal Immigration: A Reference Handbook, 2e*. Santa Barbara, CA: ABC-CLIO.

LeMay, Michael. 2019. *Immigration Reform: A Reference Handbook.* Santa Barbara, CA: ABC-CLIO.

LeMay, Michael, and Elliott Barkan. 1999. *U.S. Immigration and Naturalization Laws and Issues: A Documentary History.* Westport, CT: Greenwood Press.

Marquez, Benjamin. 2003. *Constructing Identities in Mexican-American Political Organizations: Choosing Issues, Taking Sides.* Austin: University of Texas Press.

Martinez, Deirdre. 2008. *Who Speaks for Hispanics? Hispanic Interest Groups in Washington.* Albany: State University of New York Press.

Meier, Matt, and Margo Gutierrez. 2000. *Encyclopedia of Mexican-American Civil Rights Movement.* Westport, CT: Greenwood Press.

Navarro, Amando. 2005. *Mexicano Political Experience in Occupied Aztlan: Struggles and Change.* Lanham, MD: Roman and Littlefield/Altamira.

Neeley, Bill. 2009. *The Last Comanche Chief: The Life and Times of Quahah Parker.* New Zealand: Castle Books.

Oropeza, Lorena. 2019. *The King of Adobe: Reies Lopez Tijerina, Lost Prophet of the Chicano Movement.* Chapel Hill: University of North Carolina Press.

Orozco, Cynthia. 2009. *No Mexicans, Women, or Dogs Allowed: The Rise of the Mexican American Civil Rights Movement.* Austin: University of Texas Press.

Pedersen, William. 2011. *A Companion to Franklin D. Roosevelt.* New York: Wiley Blackwell.

Pinheiro, John. 2007. *Manifest Ambition: James K. Polk and Civil-Military Relations During the Mexican War.* Westport, CT: Greenwood Press.

Schaefer, Richard. 2008. *Encyclopedia of Race, Ethnicity, and Society.* Thousand Oaks, CA: Sage.

Selden, Jack. 2006. *Return: The Parker Story.* Palestine, TX: Clacton Press.

Shondaland.com. 2020. "Latino Voters May Be the Difference in 2020." October 19, 2020. https://www.shondaland.com/act/news/politics/a34399408/latino-voters-may-be-the-difference-in-2020.

Slack, Jeremy, Daniel Martinez, and Scott Whiteford. 2018. *The Shadow of the Wall.* Tucson: University of Arizona Press.

Steiner, Stan. 1969. *La Raza.* New York: Harper and Row.

Strum, Philippa. 2010. *Mendez v. Westminster: School Desegregation and Mexican American Rights.* Lawrence: University Press of Kansas.

Suro, Roberto, Richard Fry, and Jeffrey Passel. 2005. "Hispanics and the 2004 Election." June 27, 2005. https://www.pewresearch.org/hispanic/2005/06/27/hispanics-and-the-2004-election/.

Tijerina, Reies Lopez. 2001. *They Called Me "King Tiger": My Struggle for the Land and Our Rights.* Houston, TX: Arte Publico Press.

Truax, Eileen. 2018. *We Built the Wall.* London and New York: Versa Books.

Utley, Robert. 2012. *Geronimo.* New Haven, CT: Yale University Press.

Vulliamy, Ed. 2010. *Amexica: War Along the Borderline.* New York: Farrar, Straus and Giroux/Macmillan.

Zentner, Scot, and Michael LeMay. 2020. *Party and Nation.* Lanham, MD: Lexington Books.

5 Data and Documents

Introduction

This chapter presents data and documents on the U.S.-Mexico border region that show changes over time. It begins with a data section that presents tables, maps, and figures relating to the border line, twin cities, and congressional districts spanning the border. These are followed by a listing of congressional caucuses affecting the region. Data regarding U.S. border patrol staffing and apprehensions along the Southwest border completes the data section. Finally, the chapter presents excerpts from 15 primary documents relevant to the border region from 1819 to 2020. The documents are from treaties, U.S. laws, executive orders, and a federal court case. Collectively, the documents illustrate the course of public policy around the U.S.-Mexico border and how it changed over time.

Data

Table 5.1. The Pueblos of New Mexico and the Language Spoken

There are more Pueblos located within New Mexico than in any other state along the U.S.-Mexico border. This table lists the Pueblos in New Mexico and the Indigenous language spoken in each.

The international border wall between San Diego, California, and Tijuana, Mexico, as it begins its journey from the Pacific coast over rolling hills. Most of the "wall" is actually a border fence barrier. (Sherry V. Smith/Dreamstime.com)

Table 5.1   The Pueblos of New Mexico and the Language Spoken

Name of Pueblo	Language Speakers
Acoma Pueblo	Keres Speakers
Cochiti Pueblo	Keres Speakers
Isleta Pueblo	Tiwa Speakers
Jemez Pueblo	Towa Speakers
Kewa Pueblo	Keres Speakers
Laguna Pueblo	Keres Speakers
Nambe' Pueblo	Tewa Speakers
Ohkay Owingeh Pueblo	Tewa Speakers
Picuris Pueblo	Tiwa Speakers
Pojoaque Pueblo	Tewa Speakers
Sandia Pueblo	Tiwa Speakers
San Felipe Pueblo	Keres Speakers
San Idelfonso Pueblo	Tewa Speakers
Santa Ana Pueblo	Keres Speakers
Santa Clara Pueblo	Tewa Speakers
Taos Pueblo	Tiwa Speakers
Tesuque Pueblo	Tewa Speakers
Zia Pueblo	Keres Speakers
Zuni Pueblo	Zuni Speakers

Map 5.1. The Adams-Onis Treaty, 1819

The United States negotiated with Spain for a border line between itself and what was then the Viceroyalty of Spain, called New Spain. The Adams-Onis Treaty of 1819 was also known as the Florida acquisition. It demarcated the line that was the border until the Treaty of Guadalupe Hidalgo in 1848.

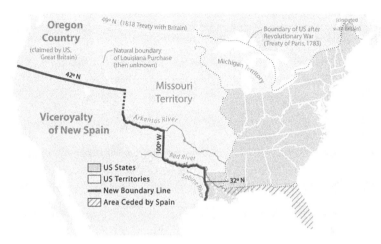

Map 5.1   The Adams-Onis Treaty, 1819
Source: Citynoise, CC BY-SA 2.5.

Table 5.2. Twinning Cities of the U.S.-Mexico Border, West to East

Table 5.2 presents the cities on either side of the SW border that are "twin cities" or sister cities. They are also major border crossing points.

Table 5.2   Twinning Cities of the U.S.-Mexico Border, West to East

United States City, State	Mexican City, State
San Diego, California	Tijuana, Baja California
Cross Border Xpress, Otay, Mesa, California	Tijuana International Airport, Baja California
Otay Mesa, California	Tijuana, Baja California
Tecate, California	Tecate, Baja California
Calexico, California	Mexicali, Baja California
Andrade, California	Los Algodones, Baja California
San Luis, Arizona	San Luis Rio Colorado, Sonora
Lukeville, Arizona	Sonoyta, Sonora
Sasabe, Arizona	Altar, Sonora
Nogales, Arizona	Nogales, Sonora

(continued)

Table 5.2   (*continued*)

United States City, State	Mexican City, State
Naco, Arizona	Naco, Sonora
Douglas, Arizona	Agua Prieta, Sonora
Antelope Wells, New Mexico	El Berrendo, Chihuahua
Columbus, New Mexico	Palomas, Chihuahua
Santa Teresa, New Mexico	San Jeronimo, Chihuahua
El Paso, Texas	Ciudad Juarez, Chihuahua
Fabens, Texas	Praxedi G. Guerrero, Chihuahua
Fort Hancock, Texas	El Porvenir, Chihuahua
Presidio, Texas	Ojinaga, Chihuahua
Heath Canyon, Texas	La Linda, Coahuila
Del Rio, Texas	Ciudad Acuna, Coahuila
Eagle Pass, Texas	Piedras Negras, Coahuila
Laredo, Texas	Nuevo Laredo, Tamaulipas
Laredo, Texas	Colombia, Nuevo Leon
Falcon Heights, Texas	Presa Falcon, Tamaulipas
Roma, Texas	Ciudad Miguel Aleman, Tamaulipas
Rio Grande City, Texas	Ciudad Camargo, Tamaulipas
Los Ebanos, Texas	Gustavo Diaz Ordaz, Tamaulipas
Mission, Texas	Reynosa, Tamaulipas
Hidalgo, Texas	Reynosa, Tamaulipas
Pharr, Texas	Reynosa, Tamaulipas
Donna, Texas	Rio Bravo, Tamaulipas
Progresso, Texas	Nuevo Progresso, Tamaulipas
Los Indios, Texas	Matamoros, Tamaulipas
Brownsville, Texas	Matamoros, Tamaulipas

Map 5.2. The U.S.-Mexico Border Region and Key Twinning Cities

After the Treaty of Guadalupe Hidalgo and the Gadsden Purchase, the current border between the United States and Mexico was finalized. Map 5.2 shows the current border line and border zone, with the major twin cities on each side of the line. It shows the states on the U.S. side as well as the Mexico side of the border.

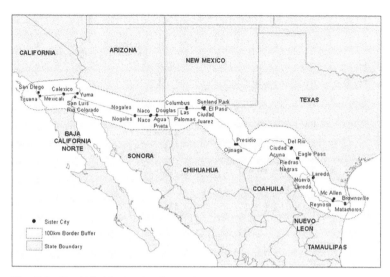

Map 5.2 The U.S.-Mexico Border Region and Key Twinning Cities
Source: Environmental Protection Agency.

Table 5.3. Congressional Districts Spanning the U.S.-Mexico Border and the Member Representing that District (116th Congress, 2019)

Table 5.3 identifies the congressional districts that span the SW border and the member representing each border district in the 116th Congress (2019).

Table 5.3   Congressional Districts Spanning the U.S.-Mexico Border and the Member from Representing that District (116th Congress, 2019)

Name of Member	District Number	State
Vargas, Juan, D	51st, San Diego	California
Grijalva, Raul, D	03rd, Tucson	Arizona
Kirkpatrick, Ann, D	23rd, Tucson	Arizona
Haaland, Debbie, D	1st, Albuquerque	New Mexico
Torres Small, Xochitl, D	2nd, Las Cruces	New Mexico
Lujan, Ben Ray, D	3rd, Santa Fe	New Mexico
Hurd, Will, R	23rd, San Antonio/El Paso	Texas
Gonzalez, Vincente, D	15th, Hidalgo	Texas
Filemon, Vela, D	34th, Brownsville	Texas
Cuella, Henry, D	28th, Laredo	Texas

Table 5.4. Members of the Congressional Border Caucus

Table 5.4 presents the members of the important Border Caucus in the U.S. House of Representatives as of the 2019 session (116th).

Table 5.4   Members of the Congressional Border Caucus

Name of Representative/District	Major City in District
Grijalva, Raul, Co-Chair, D-03-AZ	Tucson, Arizona
Vela, Filemon, Co-Chair, D-34-TX	Brownsville, Texas
Cardenas, Tony, D-29-CA	Sylmar, California
Cuellar, Henry, D-28-TX	Laredo, Texas
Castro, Joaquin, D-20-TX	San Antonio, Texas
Gallego, Ruben, D-7-AZ	Phoenix, Arizona
Green, Gene, D-29-TX	Houston, Texas
Gonzalez, Vincente, D-15-TX	Guadalupe Hidalgo, Texas
Hice, Jody, R-10-GA	Monroe, Georgia
O'Rourke, Beto, D-16-TX	El Paso, Texas
Vargas, Juan, D-51-CA	San Diego, California
Veasey, Marc, D-33-TX	Fort Worth, Texas

Table 5.5. Members of the Congressional Hispanic Caucus

Table 5.5 lists the members of the Congressional Hispanic Caucus, all of whom are Democrats.

Table 5.5   Members of the Congressional Hispanic Caucus

Name of Member, Office
Joaquin Castro, Chair, D-TX-20
Ruben Gallego, First Vice Chair, D-AZ-7
Nanette Diaz Barragan, Second Vice Chair, D-CA-44
Adriano Espaillat, Whip, D-NY-13
Veronica Escobar, Freshman Representative, D-TX-16
Pete Aguilar, D-CA-31
Salud Carbajal, D-CA-24

(continued)

Table 5.5 (*continued*)

Name of Member, Office
Tony Cardenas, D-CA-29
Gil Cisneros, D-CA-39
Luis Correa, D-CA-46
Catherine Cortez Masto, D-NV-Senator
Jim Costa, D-CA-16
Henry Cuellar, D-TX-28
Sylvia Garcia, D-TX-29
Jesus "Chuy" Garcia, D-Ill-4
Jimmy Gomez, D-CA-34
Vincente Gonzales, D-TX-15
Raul Grijalva, D-AZ-3
Mike Levin, D-CA-49
Ben Ray Lujan, D-NM-3
Robert Menendez, D-NJ-Senate
Debbie Mucarsel-Powell, D-FL-26
Grace Napolitano, D-CA-32
Alexandria Ocasio-Cortez, D-NY-14
Xochitl Torres Small, D-NM-2
Lucille Roybal-Allard, D-CA-40
Raul Ruiz, D-CA-36
Gregorio Kilili Camacho Sablan, D-North Mariana Island
Michael San Nicholas, D-Guam
Linda Sanchez, D-CA-38
Jose Serrano, D-NY-15
Albio Sires, D-NJ-8
Darren Soto, D-FL-9
Norma Torres, D-CA-35
Lori Trahan, D-MA, 3
Juan Vargas, D-CA-51
Filemon Vela, D-TX-34
Nydia Valazquez, D-NY-7

Table 5.6. Members of the Congressional Hispanic Conference

Table 5.6 lists the members of the Congressional Hispanic Conference (all of whom are Republican).

Table 5.6   Members of the Congressional Hispanic Conference

Name of Member, District	State
Diaz-Balart, Mario, Chair, CD 25	R-Florida
Rios-Lehtinen, Ileana, Vice Chair, CD 27	R-Florida
Flores, Bill, CD 17	R-Texas
Garcia, Mike, CD 25	R-California
Gonzalez, Anthony, CD 16	R-Ohio
Gonzalez-Colon, Jennifer, Delegate	Puerto Rico
Herrera Beutles, Jaime, CD 3	R-Washington
Nunes, Devin, CD 22	R-California
Radewagan, Amata Coleman, Delegate	R-American Samoat

Map 5.3. Border Patrol Sectors along the Southwest Border

Map 5.3 shows the nine sectors of the U.S. Border Patrol that are located along the border line.

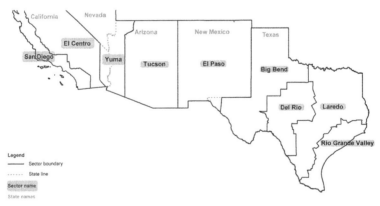

Map 5.3   The Border Patrol Sectors along the Southwest Border
Source: Border Patrol: Actions Needed to Improve Oversight of Post-Apprehension Consequences. Government Accounting Agency. www.gao.gov /products/GAO-17-66.

Table 5.7. Border Agents and Border Apprehensions, 2000–2019

Table 5.7 shows that there is almost an inverse relationship between the number of Border Patrol agents and the number of undocumented migrants apprehended at the border in the period 2000–2019.

Table 5.7   Border Agents and Border Apprehensions, 2000–2019

Year	Total Agents	Apprehensions
2000	9,212	1,643,679
2001	9,821	1,235,718
2002	10,045	919,809
2003	10,717	905,065
2004	10,819	1,139,282
2005	11,264	1,171,396
2006	12,439	1071,972
2007	14,923	858,638
2008	17,499	705,005
2009	20,119	540,085
2010	20,058	447,731
2011	21,444	357,577
2012	21,394	356,873
2013	21,391	414,397
2014	20,863	479,371
2015	20,273	331,333
2016	19,828	408,870
2017	19,437	303,916
2018	19,437	467,000
2019	19,648	851,508

Source: U.S. Border Patrol. Stats and Summaries. https://www.cbp.gov/newsroom/media-resources/stats#.

Figure 5.1. Total Apprehensions at the Southwest Border, FY1960–FY2019

Figure 5.1 is a bar graph showing total apprehensions at the SW border from 1960 to 2019. It shows the marked trend in decreasing apprehensions since 2000.

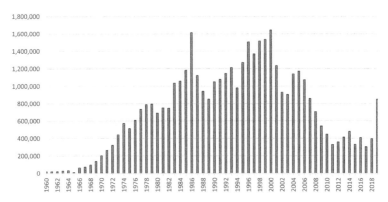

Figure 5.1   Total Apprehensions at the Southwest Border, FY1960–FY2019
Source: U.S. Border Patrol. Fiscal Year Southwest Border Sector Apprehensions
(FY1960–FY2019). https://www.cbp.gov/newsroom/media-resources/stats#.

Figure 5.2. Total Apprehensions at the Southwest Border, by Country of Origin, FY2000–FY2019

Figure 5.2 presents a split bar graph that shows the trend in total apprehensions at the SW border by country of origin of those apprehended, distinguishing between those from Mexico and those from countries other than Mexico (in the latter category, the vast majority are from Central America).

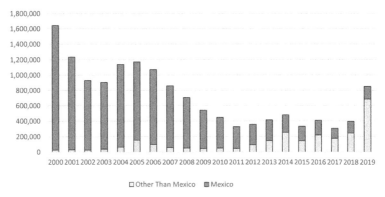

Figure 5.2   Total Apprehensions at the Southwest Border, by Country of Origin,
FY2000–FY2019
Source: U.S. Border Patrol. Apprehensions from Mexico and Other Than Mexico
(FY2000–FY2019). https://www.cbp.gov/newsroom/media-resources/stats#.

Figure 5.3. Percentage of UAC Apprehended by the U.S. Border Patrol at the Southwest Border, by Country of Origin, FY2016

Figure 5.3 presents a pie chart that depicts the percentage of Unaccompanied Alien Children (UAC) apprehended at the SW border by the Border Patrol in FY2016, a typically representative year for those apprehensions. Whereas prior to 2010 the majority of UAC came from Mexico, in subsequent years those from Central America increased and now exceed those from Mexico.

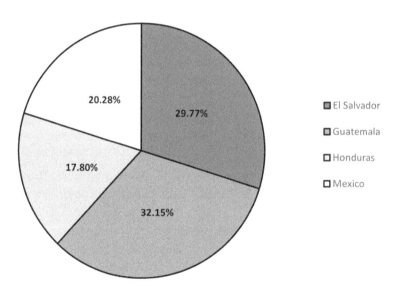

Figure 5.3 Percentage of UAC Apprehended by the U.S. Border Patrol at the Southwest Border, by Country of Origin, FY2016
Source: U.S. Border Patrol. Southwest Border Family Unite and UAC Apprehensions (FY2014–FY2016). https://www.cbp.gov/newsroom/media-resources/stats#.

Documents

Adams-Onis Treaty, 1819

The Adams-Onis agreement of 1819 between the United States and the Viceroyalty of New Spain specified the boundary line between New Spain and the United States. The agreement, also known as the acquisition of the territory of Florida, was ratified on February 22, 1821, and the boundary line thus established was later agreed to by the Republic of Mexico upon achieving independence from Spain a few months afterward. The line defined by the agreement is described in Article 3 of the Adams-Onis agreement.

Article 3: The Boundary Line between the two Countries, West of the Mississippi, shall begin on the Gulf of Mexico, at the mouth of the River Sabine in the Sea (29"40'N 93"50'03'W), continuing along the Western Bank of that River, to the 32nd degree of Latitude (32"00'00'N 94"02'45'W); thence by a Line due North to the degree Latitude, where it strikes the Rio Roxo of Nachitoches, or Red-River (33"33'04N 94"02'45'W), then following the course of the Rio-Roxo Westward to the degree of Latitude, 100 West from London and 23 from Washington (34"33'37'N 100"00'00'W), then crossing the said Red-River, and running thence, following the Course of the Southern bank of the Arkansas to its source in Latitude, 42. North and thence by that parallel of Latitude to the South-Sea (Pacific Ocean). The whole being as laid down in Melishe's Map of the United States, published at Philadelphia, improved to the first of January 1818. But if the Source of the Arkansas River shall be found to fall North or South of Latitude 42, then the Line shall run from the said Source (39"15'30' N 106"20'38'W), due South or North, as the case may be, till it meets the said Parallel of Latitude 42 (42"00'00'N 106"20'38'W), and thence along the said parallel to the South Sea (42"00'00'N 124"12'46'W).

Source: Bevans, Charles I., ed., "Adams-Onís Treaty: 1819." Treaties and Other International Agreements of the United

States of America, 1776–1949. Washington, DC: Department of State, 1968.

Treaty of Guadalupe Hidalgo, 1848

The Treaty of Guadalupe Hidalgo ended the war between the United States and Mexico and ceded to the United States most of Mexico's northern territory. The treaty contained a provision (Article 8) regarding the admission to U.S. citizenship of Mexicans remaining in those territories ceded to the United States and not declaring their wish to remain citizens of Mexico.

Article VIII. Mexicans now established in territories previously belonging to Mexico, and which remain for the future within the limits of the United States as defined by the present treaty, shall be free to continue where they now reside, or to remove at any time to the Mexican republic, retaining the property which they possess in the said territories, or disposing thereof, and removing the proceeds wherever they please, without their being subjected on this account, to any contribution, tax, or charge what-ever.

Those who shall prefer to remain in the said territories, may ether retain the title and rights of Mexican citizens, or acquire those of citizens of the United States. But they shall be under the obligation to make their election within one year from the date of the exchange of ratifications of this treaty, and those who shall remain in the said territories after the expiration of that year, without having declared their intention to retain the character of Mexicans, shall be considered to have elected to become citizens of the United States.

Source: Treaty of Guadalupe-Hidalgo [Exchange copy], February 2, 1848; Perfected Treaties, 1778–1945; Record Group 11; General Records of the United States Government, 1778–1992; National Archives.

Gadsden Purchase Agreement, 1854

The Gadsden Purchase comprised roughly 30,000 square miles of today's southern Arizona and southwestern New Mexico. It was negotiated and signed by James Gadsden, the American ambassador to Mexico, on December 30, 1853. It was ratified by the Senate and signed by President Franklin Pierce on June 8, 1854. It was the last major territorial acquisition in the contiguous United States. The full agreement has nine Articles, several of which slightly amend the language and provisions of the Guadalupe Hidalgo Treaty. The following excerpt is the introductory opening paragraph of the agreement and presents two Articles (III and VII) that detail the obligations of the United States to compensate Mexico and provide for a mechanism to settle possible future disputes.

In the name of Almighty God: The Republic of Mexico and the United States of America desiring to remove every cause of disagreement which might interfere in any manner with the better friendship and intercourse between the two countries, and especially, in respect to the true limit which should be established, when notwithstanding what was covenanted in the Treaty of Guadalupe Hidalgo in the year 1848, opposite interpretations have been urged, which might give occasion to questions of serious moment, to avoid these, and to strengthen and more firmly maintain the peace which happily prevails between the two Republics, the President of the United States has, for this purpose, appointed James Gadsden, Envoy Extraordinary and Minister Plenipotentiary of the same, near the Mexican government, and the President of Mexico has appointed as Plenipotentiary "ad hoc" his excellency Don Manuel Diez de Bonilla, cavalier grand cross of the national and distinguished order of Guadalupe, and Secretary of State, and of the office of Foreign Relations, and Don Jose Salazar Ylarregui and General Mariano Monterde as scientific commissioners, invested with full powers for this negotiation, who having communicated their respective full powers, and finding them in due and proper form, have agree upon the articles following: . . .

Article III. In consideration of the foregoing stipulations, the Government of the United States agrees to pay the government of Mexico, in the city of New York, the sum of ten millions of dollars, of which seven million shall be paid immediately upon the exchange of the ratifications of this treaty, and the remaining three million as soon as the boundary line shall be surveyed, marked, and established.

Article VII. Should there at any future period (which God forbid) occur any disagreement between the two nations which might lead to a rupture of their relations and reciprocal peace, they bind themselves in the manner to procure by every possible method the adjustment of every difference, and should they still in this manner not succeed, never will they proceed to a declaration of war, without having previously paid attention to what has been set forth in article twenty-one of the Treaty of Guadalupe for similar cases; which article, as well as the twenty-second are here reaffirmed.

Source: Statues at Large, Vol 10: 32nd–33rd, 1851–1855. Boston: Little, Brown and Company, 1855, p. 1031.

An Act Granting Citizenship to Certain Indians, November 6, 1919

After World War I, Congress granted citizenship to all Native Americans who had served in the war, in recognition of their outstanding contributions and services during the war. A great many of them resided in the U.S.-Mexico border region that had tribes and reservations in every state along the border.

Be it enacted by the Senate and House of Representatives of the United States of American in Congress assembled, That every American Indian who served in the Military or Naval Establishments of the United States during the war against the Imperial German Government, and who has received or who shall hereafter receive an honorable discharge, if not now a citizen, and if he so desires, shall, on proof of such discharge, and after proper identification before a court or competent jurisdiction, and without other examination except as prescribed by said court, be granted full citizenship with all the privileges pertaining thereto, without in any manner impairing or otherwise affecting the property rights, individual or tribal, of any such Indian or his interest in tribal or other Indian property.

Source: 41 Stat. 350. Available online at https://www.loc.gov /law/help/statutes-at-large/66th-congress/session-1/c66s1 ch95.pdf.

Border Patrol Act of 1925

In order to better enforce immigration laws and to control unauthorized immigrants from entering the United States, most often through the border with Mexico, the U.S. Congress established a Border Patrol in 1925.

Provided. That $1,000,000 of this amount [$5,084,865] shall be available only for coast and land-border patrol, and *Provided further,* Any employee of the Immigration and Naturalization Service authorized to do so by the Commissioner of Immigration and Naturalization, with the approval of the Attorney General, shall have the power without warrant (1) to arrest any alien who in his presence or view is entering or attempting to enter the United States in violation of any law or regulation made in pursuance of law regulating the admission, exclusion, or expulsion of aliens, or any alien who is in the United States in violation of any such law or regulation and is likely to escape before a warrant can be obtained for his arrest, but the person arrested shall be taken without unnecessary delay for examination before an officer of the Immigration and Naturalization Service having authority to examine aliens as to their right to enter or to remain in the United States; (2) within reasonable distance from any external boundary of the United States, to board and search for aliens any vessel within the territorial waters of the United States and any railway car, aircraft, conveyance, or vehicle, and within a distance of twenty-five miles from any such external boundary to have access to private lands, but not dwellings, for the purpose of patrolling the border and to prevent the illegal entry of aliens into the United States; and (3) to make arrests for felonies which have been committed and which are cognizable under any law of the United States regulating the admission, exclusion, or expulsion of aliens, if the person making the arrest has reason to believe the person so arrested is guilty of such felony and if there is likelihood of the person escaping before a warrant can be obtained for his arrest, but the person arrested shall be taken without unnecessary delay before the nearest available commissioner or before any other nearby officer empowered to commit persons charged with such offenses against the laws of the United States; and such employee shall have the power to execute any warrant or other process issued by any law regulating the admission, exclusion, or expulsion of aliens.

Source: 43 Stat. 1049–1050, 8 U.S. C. 110.

Agricultural Act of 1949

In October 1949, Congress codified prior laws and provisions for temporary agricultural workers and established (until 1964) the Bracero Program permitting the legal entry of temporary workers. The Bracero Program established what became a pattern of chain migration from Mexico to the United States and has profoundly affected the border region ever since.

Be it enacted by the Senate and the House of Representatives of the United States of America in Congress assembled, That this act may be cited as the "Agricultural Act of 1949."

Sec. 501. For the purpose of assisting in such production of agricultural commodities and products as the Secretary of Agriculture deems necessary, by supplying agricultural workers from the Republic of Mexico . . . the Secretary of Labor is authorized—

(1) to recruit workers . . .
(2) to establish and operate reception centers at or near places of actual entry of such workers into the continental United States for the purpose of receiving and housing such workers for their employment in, or departure from, the continental United States;
(3) to provide transportation of such workers from recruitment centers . . . to such reception centers and transportation from [them] . . . to such recruitment centers after termination of employment;
(4) to provide workers with such subsistence . . . while . . . at reception centers;
(5) to assist such workers and employers in negotiating contracts for agricultural employment;
(6) to guarantee the performance by employers of provisions of such contracts . . .

Sec. 502. No workers shall be made available under this title to any employer unless such employer enters into an agreement with the United States—

(1) to indemnify the United States against loss . . .
(2) to reimburse the United States for essential expenses . . .
(3) to pay to the United States, in any case in which a worker is not returned [essentially the costs incurred].

Source: 63 Stat. 1051.

Multilateral Protocol and Convention Relating to the Status of Refugees (1954 and 1966)

Refugee movement in numbers as large as tens of thousands across the Southwestern border has been the result of war or natural disaster, and large numbers of refugees, many from Central America who have crossed Mexico to arrive at the Southwest border, have settled in the borderland zone. The United States agreed to the protocols of the United Nations as to the status and treatment of refugees. The following excerpts are from the original 1954 convention and from a follow-up protocol in 1966.

Convention Relating to the Status of Refugees (April 22, 1954)

Article III—Non-Discrimination

The Contracting States shall apply the provisions of this Convention to refugees without discrimination as to race, religion, or country of origin.

Article VII—Exemption from Reciprocity

1. Except where this Convention contains more favorable provisions, a Contracting State shall accord to refugees the same treatment as is accorded to aliens generally.

2. After a period of three years' residence, all refugees shall enjoy exemption from legislative reciprocity in the territory of the Contracting States.

3. Each Contracting State shall continue to accord to refugees the rights and benefits to which they are already entitled, in the absence of reciprocity, at the date of entry into force of this Convention for that States.

Article XVII—Wage Earning Employment

1. The Contracting State shall accord to refugees lawfully staying in their territory the most favorable treatment accorded to national of a foreign country in the same circumstances, as regards to engage in wage earning employment.

Article XXVII—Identity Papers

1. The Contracting States shall issue identity papers to any refugee in their territory who does not possess a valid travel document.

Article XXXII—Expulsion

1. The Contracting State shall not expel a refugee lawfully in their territory save on grounds of national security or public order.

2. The expulsion of such a refugee shall only be in pursuance of a decision in accordance with due process of law.

3. The Contracting States shall allow such a refugee a reasonable period within which to seek legal admission into another country. The Contracting States reserve the right to apply during that period such internal measures as they may deem necessary.

Article XXXIII—Prohibition of Expulsion or Return ["Refoulement"]

1. No Contracting State shall expel or return ("refouler") a refugee in any manner whatsoever to the frontiers of territories where his life or freedom would be threatened on account of his race, religion, nationality, membership in a particular social group or political opinion.

2. The benefit of the present provision may not, however, be claimed by a refugee whom there are reasonable grounds for regarding as a danger to the security of the country in which he is, or who, having been convicted by a final judgment of a particular serious crime, constitutes a danger to the community of that country.

Article XXXIV—Naturalization

The Contracting States shall as far as possible facilitate the assimilation and naturalization of refugees. They shall in particular make every effort to expedite naturalization proceedings and to reduce as far as possible the charges and costs of such proceedings.

Source: United Nations, *Treaty Series*, vol. 189 (1954), No. 2545.

Protocol Relating to the Status of Refugees (December 16, 1966)

Considering that the Convention relating to the Status of Refugees done at Geneva on 28 July 1951 . . . covers only those persons who have become refugees as a result of events occurring before January 1, 1951,

Considering new refugee situations have arisen since the Convention was adopted and that the refugees concerned may therefore not fall with the scope of the Convention,

Considering that it is desirable that equal status should be enjoyed by all refugees covered by the definition in the Convention irrespective of the dateline 1 January 1951. Have agreed as follows:

Article I—General Provisions.

1. The States Parties to the present Protocols undertake to apply articles 2 to 34 inclusive of the Convention to refugees as hereinafter defined.

2. For the purpose of the present Protocol, the term "refugee" shall except as regards to the application of paragraph 3 of this article, mean any person within the definition of Article 1 of the Convention as if the words "As a result of events occurring before 1 January 1951 and " and the words ". . . as a result of such events," in article 1 A (2) were omitted.

3. The present Protocol shall be applied by the States Parties hereto without any geographic limitation, save that existing declarations made by the States already Parties to the Convention in accordance with Article 1 B (1)(a) of the Convention shall, unless extended under article 1 B (2) thereof, apply also under the present Protocol.

Article II—Co-operation of the National Authorities with the United Nations.

1. The States Parties to the present Protocol undertake to co-operate with the Office of the United Nations High Commissioner for Refugees, or any other agency of the United Nations which may have succeeded it, in the exercise of its functions, and shall in particular facilitate its duty of supervising the application of the provisions of the present Protocol . . .

Source: *Official Records of the General Assembly, Twenty-first Session, Supplement No. 11A* (A/6311/Rev.1/Add.1).

Refugee Act of March 17, 1980

In 1980 Congress dealt specifically with the refugee admissions issue. The Refugee Act attempted to systematize refugee policy and increased the number of refugees allowed to enter to 50,000 persons annually. It authorized the president, if events warranted it, to increase the number further but also gave him the responsibility to present to Congress a recommendation for a total annual figure.

Be it enacted by the Senate and the House of Representatives of the United States of America in Congress assembled, That this Act may be cited as the "Refugee Act of 1980."

Sec. 101. (a) The Congress declares that it is the historic policy of the United States to respond to the urgent needs of persons subject to persecution in the homelands, including, where appropriate, humanitarian assistance for their care and maintenance in asylum areas, efforts to promote opportunities for resettlement or voluntary repatriation, aid for necessary transportation and processing, admission to this country of refugees for special humanitarian concern to the United States, and transitional assistance to refugees in the United States. The Congress declares that it is the policy of the United States to encourage all nations to provide assistance and resettlement opportunities to refugees to the fullest extent possible. . . (b) The objectives of this Act are to provide permanent and systematic procedures for the admission to this country of refugees of special humanitarian concern to the United States, and to provide comprehensive and uniform provisions for the effective resettlement and absorption of those refugees who are admitted.

Sec.201(a)(42) The term "refugee" means (A) any person who is outside any country of such person's nationality or, in the case of a person having no nationality, outside any country in which such person last habitually resided, and who is unable or unwilling to return to, and is unable, unwilling to avail himself or herself of the protection of, that country because of persecution, or a well-founded fear of persecution on account of race, religion, nationality, membership in a particular social group, or political opinion, or (B) in such special circumstances as the President, after appropriate consultation . . . may specify. . . . The term "refugee" does not include any person who ordered, incited, assisted, or otherwise participated in the persecution of any person on account of race, religion, nationality, membership in a particular social group, or political opinion. . .

Section 207. (a) (1) Except as provided in subsection (b), the number of refugees who may be admitted under this section in fiscal year 1980, 1981, or 1982, may not exceed fifty thousand unless the President determines, before the beginning of the fiscal year and after appropriate consultation . . . that admission of a specific number of refugees in excess of such number is justified by humanitarian concerns or is otherwise in the national interest . . .

(b) If the President determines, after appropriate consultation, that (1) an unforeseen emergency refugee situation exists, (2) the admission of certain refugees in response to the emergency refugee situation is justified by grave humanitarian concern or is otherwise in the national interest, and (3) the admission to the United States of these refugees cannot be accomplished under subsection (a), the President may fix a number of refugees to be admitted to the United States during the succeeding period (not to exceed twelve months) in response to the emergency refugee situation and such admission shall be allocated among refugees of special humanitarian concern to the United States in accordance with a determination made by the President after the appropriate consultation provided under this subsection . . .

(4) The refugee status of any alien (and of the spouse or child of the alien) may be terminated by the Attorney General pursuant to such regulations as the Attorney General may prescribe if the Attorney General determines that alien was not in fact a refugee within the meaning of subsection 101 (a) (42) at the time of the alien's admission. . .

Sec. 208 (a) The Attorney General shall establish a procedure for an alien physically present in the United States or at a land border or port of entry, irrespective of such alien's status, to apply for asylum, and the alien may be granted asylum at the discretion of the Attorney General if the Attorney General determines that such alien is a refugee within the meaning of subsection 101 (a)(42)(a) . . .

Sec. 209 (b) Not more than five thousand of the refugee admissions authorized under section 207(a) in any fiscal year may be made available by the Attorney General, in the Attorney General's discretion and under such regulations as the Attorney General may prescribe, to adjust to the status of an alien lawfully permitted for permanent residence the status of any alien granted asylum—(1) who applies for such adjustment; (2) has been physically present in the U.S. for at least one year after being granted asylum; (3) contuse to be a refugee in the meaning of section 101 (a)(42)(a) or a spouse or child of such refugee, (4) is not firmly resettled in any foreign country, and (5) is admissible . . .

Sec. 203 (b)(1) The Attorney General shall not deport or return any alien . . . to a country if the Attorney General determines that such alien's life or freedom would be threatened in such country on account of race, religion, nationality, membership in a particular social group, or political opinion.

Sec. 204 (2) The Attorney General shall establish the asylum procedure referred to in section 208 (a) of the Immigration and Nationality Act . . . not later than June 1, 1980 . . .

Source: 94 Stat. 102.

La Paz Agreement of August 14, 1983

In 1983 the United States and Mexico signed what became known as the La Paz Agreement on the Environment in the border area. La Paz is the capital of Baja California Sur, where the agreement was negotiated and signed. The agreement has 23 articles; the more important articles are excerpted here.

Acknowledging the important work of the International Boundary and Water Commission and the contribution of the agreements concluded between the two countries relating to environmental affairs; *Reaffirming* their political will to further strengthen and demonstrate the importance attached by both Governments to cooperation on environmental protection and in furtherance of the principle of good neighborliness. Have agreed as follows:

ARTICLE 1. The United States of America and the United Mexican States, hereinafter referred to as the Parties, agree to cooperate in the field of environmental protection in the border area on the basis of equality, reciprocity and mutual benefit.

The objectives of the present Agreement are to establish the basis for cooperation between the Parties for the protection, improvement and conservation of the environment and the problems which affect it, as well as to agree on necessary measures to prevent and control pollution in the border area, and to provide the framework for development of a system of notification for emergency situation . . .

ARTICLE 2. The Parties undertake, to the fullest extent practical, to adopt the appropriate measures to prevent, reduce and eliminate sources of pollution in their respective territory which affect the border area of the other. Additionally, the Parties shall cooperate in the solution of the environmental problems of mutual concern in the border area, in accordance with the provisions of this Agreement.

ARTICLE 3. Pursuant to this Agreement, the Parties may conclude specific arrangements for the solution of common problems in the border area, which may be annexed thereto . . .

ARTICLE 4. For the purposes of this Agreement, it shall be understood that the "border area" refers to the area situated 100 kilometers on either side of the inland and maritime boundaries between the Parties.

ARTICLE 5. The Parties agree to coordinate their efforts, to conformity with their own national legislation and existing bilateral agreements to Address problems of air, land, and water pollution in the border area.

ARTICLE 6. To implement this Agreement, the Parties shall consider and, as appropriate, pursue in a coordinated manner practical, legal, institutional, and technical measures for protecting the quality of the environment in the border area. Forms of cooperation may include: coordination of national programs; scientific and educational exchanges; environmental monitoring; environmental impact assessment; and periodic exchanges of information and data on likely sources of pollution in their respective territory which may produce environmentally polluting incidents, as defined in an annex to this Agreement . . .

ARTICLE 8. Each Party designates a national coordinator who principal function will be to coordinate and monitor implementation of this Agreement, make recommendations to the Parties, and organize the annual meetings referred to in Article 10, and the meetings of the experts to in Article 11 . . .

ARTICLE 9. Taking into account the subjects to be examined jointly, the national coordinators may invite, as appropriate, representatives of federal, state and municipal governments to participate in the meetings provided for in this Agreement. . .

ARTICLE 10. The Parties shall hold at a minimum an annual high-level meeting to review the manner in which this Agreement is being implemented. These meetings shall take place alternately in the border area of Mexico and the United States of America . . .

ARTICLE 11. The Parties may, as they deem necessary, convoke meetings of experts for the purposes of coordinating their national programs referred to in Article 6, and of preparing the drafts of specific arrangements and technical annexes referred to in Article 3. These meetings of experts may review technical subjects . . .

ARTICLE 12. Each Party shall ensure that its national coordinator is informed of activities of its cooperating agencies carried out under this Agreement. . . The national coordinators of both Parties will present to the annual meeting a report on the environmental aspects of all joint work conducted under this Agreement and on implementation of other relevant agreements between the Parties, both bilateral and multicultural . . .

ARTICLE 13. Each Party shall be responsible for informing its border states and for consulting them in accordance with their respective constitutional systems, in relation to matters covered by this Agreement.

ARTICLE 14. Unless otherwise agreed, each Party shall bear the cost of its participation in the implementation of this Agreement, including the expenses of personnel who participate in any activity undertaken on the basis of it . . .

ARTICLE 15. The Parties shall facilitate the entry of equipment and personnel related to this Agreement, subject to the laws and regulations of the receiving country. In order to undertake the monitoring of polluting activities in the border area, the Parties shall undertake consultations relating to the measurement and analysis of polluting elements in the border area.

ARTICLE 16. All technical information obtained through the implementation of this Agreement will be available to both Parties. Such information may be made available to third parties by the mutual agreement of the Parties to this Agreement.

ARTICLE 17. Nothing in this Agreement shall be construed to prejudice other existing or future agreements concluded between the two Parties, or affect the rights and obligations of the Parties under international agreements to which they are a party. . .

ARTICLE 20. The present Agreement shall remain in force indefinitely unless one of the Parties notifies the other, through diplomatic channels, of its desire to denounce it, in which case the Agreement will terminate six months after the date of such written notification. Unless otherwise agreed, such termination shall not affect the validity of any arrangements made under this Agreement.

Source: 35 UST 2916, TIAS 10827; 1352 UNTS 67.

Immigration Reform and Control Act (IRCA) of November 6, 1986

In reaction to the continued and ever increasing migration into the United States, and especially into the border region across the Southwestern border, Congress enacted the Immigration Reform and Control Act (IRCA) in 1986. It enacted a control device known as employer sanctions—making it illegal to knowingly hire undocumented immigrants. Illegal immigration declined for about a year as a result of IRCA, but it quickly rose back to pre-IRCA levels and soon even exceeded them. IRCA also enacted a legalization program that ultimately allowed more than 3 million previously unauthorized immigrants to legalize their status. A great many of those legalizing (called LAWS or SAWS) worked in agriculture in the border region. IRCA had four impacts that were particularly important to the border region: (1) it induced unauthorized immigrants residing in the region to remain there rather than going back and forth as they had previously so often done, (2) it reinforced the importance of the chain-migration patterns to the region, (3) it increased the importance and value of using human smugglers and had the ancillary effect of greatly spurring the fraudulent documents industry operating on both sides of the border, and (4) it legalized the status of more than 3 million previously unauthorized migrants, the vast majority of them being SAWs (Season Agricultural Workers) who were resident in the border region.

Title I—Control of Illegal Immigration
  Sec. 101 (a) In General
  (1) It is unlawful for a person or other entity to hire, or to recruit or refer for a fee, for employment in the United States (A) an alien knowing the alien is an unauthorized alien (as defined in subsection (h)(3) . . . (B) an individual without complying with the requirements of subsection (b)
  (2) Continuing employment—It is unlawful for a person or other entity, after hiring an alien for employment in accordance with paragraph (1), to continue to employ the alien in the United States knowing the alien is (or has become) an unauthorized alien with respect to such employment.
  (3) Defense—A person or entity that establishes that it has complied in good faith with the requirements of subsection (b) with respect to the hiring, recruiting, or referral for employment of an alien in the United States who has established an affirmative defense that the person or entity has not violated paragraph (1)(A) with respect to such hiring, recruiting, or referral.

(4) Use of Labor through Contract—For the purposes of this section, a person or other entity who uses a contract, subcontract, or exchange, entered into, renegotiated, or extended after the date of the enactment of this section, to obtain the labor of an alien in the United States knowing that the alien is an unauthorized alien . . . with respect to performing such labor, shall be considered to have hired the alien for employment in the United States in violation of paragraph (1)(A).

(5) Use of State Employment Agency Documentation—For the purposes of paragraph (1)(B) and (3) are, in the case of a person or other entity hiring, recruiting, or referring an individual for employment in the United States, the requirements in the following three paragraphs:

(1) Attestation After Examination of Documentation—(A) In General—The person or entity must attest, under penalty of perjury and on a form designated or established by the Attorney General by regulation, that it has verified that the individual in not an unauthorized alien by examining a document described in subparagraph (B), or (ii) a document described in subparagraph (C) and (D) (B) Documents Establishing Both Employment Authorization and Identity—. . . is an individual's (i) United States passport; (ii) certificate of United States Citizenship; (iii) certificate of naturalization; (iv) unexpired foreign passport, if the passport has an appropriate, unexpired endorsement of the Attorney General authorizing the individual's employment in the United States, or (v) resident alien card or other alien registration, if the card—(I) contains a photograph of the individual . . . (II) is evidence of authorization of employment in the United States. © Documents Evidencing Employment Authorization—A document . . . is [a] (1) social security

account number card . . . (ii) certificate of birth in the United States, or establishing United States nationality at birth; (iii) other documents evidencing authorization of employment in the United States which the Attorney General finds, by regulation, to be acceptable for the purposes of this section. . . .

Title II—Legalization
Sec. 201. Legalization of Status
Sec. 245A (a) Temporary Resident Status—The Attorney General shall adjust the status of an alien to that of an alien lawfully admitted for temporary residence if the alien meets the following requirement: (a) Timely Application . . . (2) Continuous Lawful Residence Since 1982 . . . (4) Admissible as Immigrant . . . (D) Basic Citizenship Skills—the alien must demonstrate that he either—(I) meets the requirements of section 312 (relating to minimal understanding of ordinary English and a knowledge and understanding of the history and government of the United States . . . (II) is satisfactorily pursuing a course of study (recognized by the Attorney General) to achieve an understanding of English and such knowledge and understanding of the history and government of the United States . . .

[It then stipulates the temporary disqualification of newly legalized aliens from receiving public welfare assistance . . .

Title III—Reform of Legal Immigration [goes on to provide for new H-2A nonimmigrant classification of Agricultural Workers . . .]

Title IV—specifies various reports to Congress over the next three years dealing with comprehensive reports on immigration, unauthorized alien employment, the H-2A program, the legalization program, evidence of discrimination, and the visa waiver pilot program.

Source: 100 Stat. 3360.

Immigration Act of 1990 (IMMACT) of November 29, 1990

In 1990 Congress enacted reforms aimed at legal immigration law and processes. It redefined the preference system by setting new ceilings for worldwide level of immigration, impacting the border region by setting conditions relating to family reunification and employment, and establishing a new category of "diversity immigrations." It provided for a temporary stay of deportation to certain unauthorized immigrants for family unity and temporary protected status (important for Mexicans and Central Americans resident in the border zone).

Sec. 201 (a) In General—Exclusive of aliens described in subsection (b), aliens born in a foreign country or dependent area of a country may be issued immigrant visas or who may otherwise acquire the status of an alien lawfully admitted to the United States for permanent residence are limited to:

(1) family-sponsored immigrants described in section 203(a) . . .
(2) employment-based immigrants described in subsection 203(b) . . .
(3) for fiscal years beginning with fiscal year 1995, diversity immigrants described in section 203(c)

2 (A) (i) Immediate relatives—for purposes of this subsection, the term "immediate relative" means the children, spouses, and parents of a citizen of the United States, except that, in the case of parents, such citizens be at least 21 years of age. In the case of an alien who was the spouse of a citizen of the United States for at least 2 years at the time of the citizen's death and was not legally separated from the citizen at the time of the citizen's death, the alien shall be considered, for the purposes of this subsection, to remain an immediate relative . . . but only if the spouse files a petition under section 204(a)(1) (A) within 2 years after such date and only until the date the spouse remarries.

(c) Worldwide Level of Family Sponsored Immigrants . . . under this subsection for a fiscal year is (B) equal to (i) 480,000 minus (ii) the number (if any) computed under paragraph (2), plus (iii) the number (if any) computed under paragraph (3). . . . In no case shall the number computed under subparagraph (A) be less than 226,000.

(A) Worldwide Level of Employment-Based Immigrants—
(1) The worldwide level of employment-based immigrants under this subsection for a fiscal year is equal to—140,000 plus, the number computed under paragraph (2) . . .
(C) Worldwide Level of Diversity Immigrants—The worldwide level of diversity immigrants is equal to 55,000 for each fiscal year.

Subtitle B—Preference System . . .

(a) Preference Allocation for Family Sponsored Immigrants . . . shall be allotted visas as follows: (1) unmarried sons and daughters of citizens . . . not to exceed 23,400 . . .
(2) Spouses and unmarried sons and daughters of permanent resident aliens shall be allotted visas in a number not to exceed 226,000 . . .
(3) Married sons and daughters of immigrants—in a number not to exceed 23,4000 . . . (4) Brothers and sisters of citizens—in a number not to exceed 65,000.

Employment-Based Immigrants . . . for employment-based immigrants in a fiscal year shall be allotted visas as follows: (1) priority workers . . . not to exceed 40,000, (A) Aliens with extraordinary ability in sciences, arts, education, business, or athletics which has been demonstrated by sustained national or international acclaim and whose achievements have been recognized in the field through extensive documentation (B) Outstanding Professors and Researchers, (C) Certain

Multinational Executives and Managers, (2) Alien members of Professions holding advanced degrees or aliens of exceptional ability, (3) Skilled workers, professionals and other workers, (4) Certain special immigrants . . . not to exceed 10,000 to qualified special immigrants described in section 101 (a)(27) . . . of which not more than 5,000 may be made available in any fiscal year, (5) Employment Creation—Visas shall be made available, in a number not to exceed 10,000, to qualified immigrants seeking to enter the United States for the purpose of engaging in a new commercial enterprise . . .

Part 3—Diversity Immigrants . . . shall be allotted for visas in each fiscal year as follows: (A) Determination of Preference Immigration—the Attorney General shall determine for the most previous 5-year period for which data are available the total number of aliens who are natives of each foreign state and who (i) were admitted or otherwise provided lawful permanent resident status as an immediate relative or other alien described in section 201 (b) (2) . . .

Subtitle C—Commission and Information

Sec. 141. Commission on Legal Immigration Reform . . .

Source: 104 Stat. 4981.

LULAC et al. v. Wilson et al. (1995)

California passed an initiative titled "Save Our State" initiative (Proposition 187) in 1994. It was designed to "demagnify" the pull of California's economy by denying a host of social services and economic benefits. It was immediately challenged in federal court by the League of United Latin American Citizens (LULAC) on constitutional grounds. In several ways, Proposition 187 was a precursor to initiatives passed by Arizona in 2000 and 2010. They too were directed at immigrants in the Southwest border region of Arizona. Like Proposition 187, they too were challenged and overturned in federal court decisions. Given the high number of undocumented immigrants residing in the U.S.-Mexico border zone, especially in the Southern California area, the decision had direct and significant impact on the border area.

The California voters' overwhelming approval of Proposition 187 reflects their justifiable frustration with the federal government's inability to enforce the immigration laws effectively. No matter how serious the problem may be, however, the authority to regulate immigration belongs exclusively to the federal government and state agencies are not permitted to assume that authority. The State is powerless to enact its own scheme to regulate immigration or to devise immigration regulations which run parallel to or purport to supplement the federal immigration laws.

The classification, notification and cooperation/reporting provisions in sections 4 through 9 of the initiative, taken together, constitute a regulatory scheme (1) to detect persons present in California in violation of state-created categories of lawful immigration status; (2) to notify state and federal officials of their purportedly unlawful status; and (3) to effect their removal from the United States. These provisions create an impermissible state scheme to regulate immigration and are preempted under the first and second *De Canas* tests. Plaintiffs' motions for summary judgment are granted with respect to these provisions.

The benefits denial provisions of the initiative if implemented by state regulations which would require verification of immigration status by reference to federal determinations of status have only an incidental impact on immigration and thus do not violate the first *De Canas* test. Nor do those provisions violate the second *De Canas* test. Plaintiffs have failed to direct the Court to any authority for the proposition that Congress intended to completely oust state authority to legislate in the area of benefits denial. Consequently, the Court must conclude that those provisions are preempted only if their operation conflicts with or impedes the objectives of federal laws.

Section 7's denial of primary and secondary education conflicts with federal law as announced by the Supreme Court in

Plyler v. Doe and is therefore preempted. Section 8's denial of postsecondary education does not appear to conflict with any federal law and thus is not preempted. With respect to the benefits denial provisions in sections 5 and 6, to the extent that they deny *federally funded* benefits and services, those provisions conflict with federal laws authorizing such benefits and services without reference to immigration status. It is unclear from the showing made whether the existence of such conflicts render sections 5 and 6 wholly preempted or preempted only to the extent that they conflict with federal law. Moreover, the Court may not need to reach that issue, for while it appears that the state could permissibly deny wholly *state-funded* benefits and services without impeding the objectives of federal law, it is unclear from the record whether any such purely state-funded programs or health care facilities in fact exist. The showing made on these motions is inadequate to permit the Court to resolve the issue of whether the provisions are wholly preempted or whether they are preempted only to a limited extent. For these reasons, plaintiffs' motions with respect to the denial of benefits provisions in sections 5 and 6 are denied.

Finally, for the reasons set forth above, sections 2 and 3 are not preempted. Plaintiffs motions with respect to those sections are denied.

The preliminary injunction entered by the Court on December 14, 1994, shall remain in effect until further order of the Court.

Source: 908 F. Supp. 755 (C.D. Cal. 1995).

Secure Fence Act of 2006

On September 14, 2006, the House of Representatives passed the Secure Fence Act, Public Law No. 109-367. It authorized the building of a fence along the Southwest border, in certain specified portions, and a variety of other surveillance devices, including the use of drones. It had the effect of shifting the points of illegal crossing of the border to the Arizona desert (Sonoran Desert) and to New Mexico's harsh terrain, resulting in many deaths. The law also had unanticipated negative impact on the border environment. Below is the official summary of the law.

Directs the Secretary of Homeland Security, within 18 months of enactment of this Act, to take appropriate actions to achieve operational control over U.S. international land and maritime borders, including: (1) systematic border surveillance through more effective use of personnel and technology, such as unmanned aerial vehicles, ground-based sensors, satellites, radar coverage, and cameras; and (2) physical infrastructure enhancements to prevent unlawful border entry and facilitate border access by U.S. Customs and Border Protection, such as additional checkpoints, all weather access roads, and vehicle barriers.

Defines "operational control" as the prevention of all unlawful U.S. entries, including entries by terrorists, other unlawful aliens, instruments of terrorism, narcotics, and other contraband.

Directs the Secretary [of Homeland Security] to report annually to Congress on border control progress.

Amends the Illegal Immigration Reform and Immigrant Responsibility Act of 1996 to provide at least two layers of reinforced fencing, installation of additional physical barriers, roads, lighting, and sensors extending: (1) from ten miles west of the Tecate, California, port of entry to ten miles east of Tecate, California, port of entry; (2) from ten miles west of the Calexico, California, port of entry to five miles east of the Douglas, Arizona, port of entry (requiring installation of an interlocking surveillance camera system by May 30, 2007, and fence completion by May 30, 2008); (3) from five miles west of the Columbus, New Mexico, port of entry to ten miles east of El Paso, Texas; (4) from five miles northwest of Laredo, Texas, port of entry to five miles southeast of the Eagle Pass, Texas, port of entry; and (5) 15 miles northwest of the Laredo, Texas, port of entry to the Brownsville, Texas, port of entry (requiring fence completion from 15 miles northwest of the Laredo, Texas, port of entry to 15 southeast of the Laredo, Texas, port of entry by December 31, 2008).

States that if an area has an elevation grade exceeding 10%, the Secretary may use other means to secure such area, including surveillance and barrier tools.

Directs the Secretary to: (1) study and report to the House Committee on Homeland Security and the Senate Committee on Homeland Security and Governmental Affairs on the necessity, feasibility, and economic impact of constructing state-of-the-art infrastructure security system along the U.S. northern international land and maritime border; and (2) evaluate and report to such Committees on U.S. Customs and Border Protection authority (and possible expansion of authority) to stop fleeing vehicles that enter the United States illegally, including related training, technology, and equipment reviews.

Source: H.R. 6061. https://www.congress.gov/bill/109th-congress/house-bill/6061.

Exercising Prosecutorial Discretion with Respect to Individuals Who Came to the United States as Children, 2012

On June 15, 2012, Secretary of Homeland Security Janet Napolitano issued a memorandum to the appropriate immigration agencies (Customs and Border Protection, Citizenship and Immigration Services, and Immigration and Customs Enforcement) to enforce Deferred Action (prosecutorial discretion) with respect to Individuals Who Came to the United States as Children. This policy is known as DACA. DACA has had significant and continuing impact on persons residing in the border region who have DACA-deferred status.

By this memorandum, I am setting forth how, in the exercise of our prosecutorial discretion, the Department of Homeland

Security (DHS) should enforce the Nation's immigration laws against certain young people who were brought to this country as children and know only this country as home. As a general matter, these individuals lacked the intent to violate the law and our ongoing review of pending removal cases is already offering administrative closure to many of them. However, additional measures are necessary to ensure that out enforcement resources are not expended on these low priority cases but are instead appropriately focused on people who meet our enforcement priorities.

The following criteria should be satisfied before an individual is considered for an exercise of prosecutorial discretion pursuant to this memorandum: came to the United States under the age of sixteen; has continuously resided in the United States for at least five years preceding the date of this memorandum and is present in the United States on the date of this memorandum; is currently in school, has graduated from high school, has obtained a general education development certificate, or is an honorably discharged veteran of the Coast Guard or Armed Forces of the United States; has not been convicted of a felony offense, a significant misdemeanor offense, multiple misdemeanor offenses, or otherwise poses a threat to national security or public safety; and is not above the age of thirty.

Our Nation's immigration laws must be enforced in a strong and sensible manner. They are not designed to be blindly enforced without consideration given to the individual circumstances of each case. Nor are they designed to remove productive young people to countries where they have not lived or even speak the language. Indeed, many of these young people have already contributed to our country in significant ways. Prosecutorial discretion, which is used in so many other areas, is especially justified here.

As part of this exercise of prosecutorial discretion, the above criteria are to be considered whether or not an individual is already in removal proceedings or subject to a final order of removal. No individual should receive deferred action under this memorandum unless they first pass a background check and requests for relief pursuant to this memorandum are to be decided on a case-by-case basis. DHS cannot provide any assurance that relief will be granted in all cases.

1. With respect to individuals who are encountered by U.S. Immigration and Customs Enforcement (ICE), U.S. Customs and Border Protection (CBP), or U.S. Citizenship and Immigration Services (USCIS): with respect to individuals who meet the above criteria, ICE and CBP should immediately exercise their discretion, on an individual basis, in order to prevent low priority individuals from being placed into removal proceedings or removed from the United States. USCIS is instructed to implement this memorandum consistent with existing guidance regarding the issuance of notices to appear.

2. With respect to individuals who are in removal proceedings but not yet subject to a final order of removal, and who meet the above criteria: ICE should exercise prosecutorial discretion on an individual basis . . . for a period of two years, subject to renewal, in order to prevent low priority individuals from being removed from the United States; ICE is instructed to use its Office of the Public Advocate to permit individuals who believe they meet the above criteria to identify themselves through a clear and efficient process; ICE is directed to begin implementing this process with 60 days of the date of this memorandum; ICE is also instructed to immediately begin the process of deferring action against individuals who meet the above criteria . . .

3. With respect to individuals who are not currently in removal proceedings and meet the above criteria, and pass a background check: USCIS should establish a clear and efficient process for exercising prosecutorial discretion, on an individual basis, by deferring action against individuals who meet the above criteria and are at least

15 years old, for a period of two years . . .; the USCIS process shall also be available to individuals subject to a final order of removal regardless of their age; USCIS is directed to begin implementing this process within 60 days of the date of this memorandum.

For individuals who are granted deferred action by either ICE or USCIS, USCIS shall accept applications to determine whether those individuals qualify for work authorization during this period of deferred action. This memorandum confers no substantive right, immigration status or pathway to citizenship. Only the Congress, acting through its legislative authority, can confer these rights. It remains for the executive branch, however, to set forth policy for the exercise of discretion within the framework of the existing law. I have done so here.

Signed: Janet Napolitano, Secretary DHS.

Source: Department of Homeland Security. Available at: https://www.dhs.gov/xlibrary/assets/s1-exercising-prosecutorial-discretion-individuals-who-came-to-us-as-children.pdf.

Asylum Eligibility Interim Final Rule, 2019
On July 16, 2019, the Department of Justice issued this interim rule governing asylum claims in the case of unauthorized immigrants who enter or attempt to enter the United States across the southern land border after failing to apply for protection in a third country (Mexico). It is being challenged in court.

The Department of Justice and the Department of Homeland Security ("DOJ" "DHS," or collectively "the Departments") are adopting an interim final rule ("interim rule" or "rule") governing asylum claims in the context of aliens who enter or attempt to enter the United States across the southern land border after failing to apply for protection from prosecution or torture while in a third country which they transited en route to the United States. Pursuant to statutory authority, the Departments are amending their respective regulations to provide that, with limited exceptions, an alien who enters or attempts to enter the United States across the southern border after failing to apply for protection in a third country outside the alien's country of citizenship, nationality, or last lawful habitual residence through which the alien transited en route to the United States is *ineligible* for asylum. This basis for asylum ineligibility applies only prospectively to aliens who enter or arrive in the United States on or after the effective date of this rule. In addition to establishing a new mandatory bar for asylum eligibility for aliens who enter or attempt to enter the United States across the southern border after failing to apply for protection from persecution or torture in at least one third country through which they transited en route to the United States, this rule would also require asylum officers and immigration judges to apply this new bar on asylum eligibility when administering the credible-fear screening process applicable to stowaways and aliens who are subject to expedited removal under section 235(b)(1) of the Immigration and Nationality Act. The new bar established by this regulation does not modify withholding or deferral of removal proceedings. Aliens who fail to apply for protection in a third country of transit may continue to apply for withholding of removal under the Immigration and Nationality Act (INA) and deferral of removal under regulations issued pursuant to the legislation implementing U.S. obligations under Article 3 of the Convention against Torture and Other Cruel Inhuman or Degrading Treatment or Punishment.

Source: 84 FR 33829-33845. https://www.federalregister .gov/documents/2019/07/16/2019-15246/asylum-eligibility -and-procedural-modifications.

6 Resources

Introduction

This chapter presents an annotated list of the major sources of information that the reader is encouraged to consult. It begins with print sources, including brief annotations of books on the subject at hand. The list includes material published since 2000. The chapter also provides a brief annotated list of some of the major scholarly journals that publish original research articles related to immigration reform and the Immigration and Nationality Act of October 3, 1965. For nonprint sources, the chapter provides an annotated list of some feature-length films that depict the issues and people involved in the immigration debate over reform attempts tried or proposed for both laws and policies. The nonprint sources put real "faces" to the numbers and statistics presented in the previous chapter or often used in debates over immigration reform. In doing so, the nonprint sources highlight the human-interest aspects of this controversial topic.

Panoramic view of the skyline and downtown El Paso, Texas, looking toward Juarez, Mexico. El Paso and Juarez are one of more than a dozen such "twin" border towns along each side of the border. (Joe Sohm/Dreamstime.com)

Books

Alienkoff, T. Alexander, and Douglas Klusmeyer, eds. 2000. *From Migrants to Citizens: Membership in a Changing World.* Washington, DC: Brookings Institute.

This edited collection presents a scholarly discussion of the incorporation of immigrants with a multifaceted view of naturalization and immigration law and policy.

Allport, Alan, and John Ferguson, eds. 2009. *Immigration Policy.* 2nd ed. New York: Chelsea House.

This edited volume uses the point/counterpoint approach to present a thorough discussion of the complex topic of U.S. immigration policy and law. Among the wide range of issues it covers, it examines controversies such as the comparative costs/benefits associated with undocumented immigration whose numbers rose exponentially, partly because of the 1965 Act. The editors refrain from taking a position, allowing the reader to decide after reading arguments for both sides of a controversy.

Anderson, Stuart. 2010. *Immigration.* Westport, CT: Praeger.

Anderson presents a penetrating and extensive study of the difficulty involved in enacting and then implementing border control policy to resolve undocumented immigration, focusing on the southern border with Mexico, and by extension, on Central American countries.

Army, Dick, and Matt Kibbe. 2010. *Give Us Liberty: A Tea Party Manifesto.* New York: William Morrow.

A polemic, this manifesto is aimed at tea party activists, but it is useful to anyone seeking to understand what the tea party movement is all about, what it is fighting for, and what is next in terms of its plans and activities. The two authors have been leaders of the movement and of its advocacy organization, Freedom Works. They believe in limited government and individual liberty, and this is their national call to action. The movement's activists are among the strongest voices for strict immigration control and for the crackdown-at-the-border approach to immigration law; they vehemently oppose any "amnesty" programs.

Arnold, Kathleen R., ed. 2011. *Anti-Immigration in the U.S.: A Historical Encyclopedia*. Westport, CT: Greenwood Press.
This two-volume set is one of the first to address recent anti-immigration sentiment. The author organizes the topic alphabetically, using the encyclopedia approach. She puts current anti-immigrant attitudes in context by covering major historical periods as well as relevant concepts, leading figures, and the most important groups within the anti-immigration movement.

Ashcroft, John. 2006. *Never Again: Securing America and Restoring Justice*. Nashville: Center Street Publishing.
This is a provocative book by a former—and quite controversial—attorney general. In it, Ashcroft tells the "behind the scenes, untold story" of the war on terror in post–9/11 America. He shares his perspective on the dangers to and within America from outside forces and explains what he did to repair serious flaws and failures in U.S. security. He has several recommendations pertaining to immigration law and the failure to keep international terrorists out of the country by undocumented crossing at the Southwest border with Mexico.

Bakken, Gordon, and Alexandra Kindell. 2006. *Encyclopedia of Immigration and Migration in the American West*. Los Angeles: Sage.
This two-volume set takes an encyclopedic look at the ethnic groups crossing the plains, landing at the ports, and crossing the northern and southern borders. It contains

focused biographies, community history, and economic enterprises, and uses a variety of demographic data.

Barone, Michael. 2013. *Shaping Our Nation: How Surges in Migration Transformed America and Its Politics*. New York: Crown Forum.
This comprehensive and engaging book examines the long history of immigration and how past surges in immigration influenced American culture, politics, policies, and society.

Bean, Frank D., and Gillian Stevens. 2003. *America's Newcomers: Immigrant Incorporation and the Dynamics of Diversity.* New York: Russell Sage.
In this book, a leading demographer and a language specialist examine the factors influencing the gradual incorporation of immigrants and their children and the variety of aspects that collectively influence their rate of incorporation.

Bean, Frank D., George Vernez, and Stephanie Bell-Rose, eds. 1999. *Immigration and Opportunity: Race, Ethnicity, and Employment in the U.S.* New York: Russell Sage.
This book is composed of an array of essays from leading sociologists and demographers that collectively provide a systematic account of the sundry ways in which immigration impacts the labor-market experiences of the native-born.

Beck, Roy H. 1996. *The Case Against Immigration*. New York: Norton.
This polemic is a thorough articulation of the arguments and data that the author can marshal against high levels of immigration. It well represents the views of many, if not most, of the politicians and the leadership of the anti-immigration—and especially the anti-undocumented immigrant—political and social movements that have

come to be organized in American politics largely in response to the increase in undocumented immigration as an unanticipated consequence of the Immigration and Nationality Act of 1965.

Benton-Cohen, Katherine. 2018. *Inventing the Immigration Problem: The Dillingham Commission and Its Legacy.* Cambridge, MA: Harvard University Press.

In this comprehensive historical work, the author argues that the Dillingham Commission's legacy still influences U.S. immigration policy a century later. Her book is a timely reminder that immigrants shape the present and the future of America. She anchors the development of immigration law in a global context as well as in domestic conflicts over race, ethnicity, and religion. She demonstrates immigration law is a mixture of suspicion and celebration of migrants that remains at the core of current conflicts over these issues and perceived problems.

Brewer, Stuart. 2006. *Borders and Bridges.* Westport, CT: Praeger Security International.

The author examines the complex relationship between the United States and Latin American nations with an introduction to the most important events in the diplomatic, military, social, and economic history of that often-stormy relationship.

Brotherton, David, and Philip Kretsedemas, eds. 2008. *Keeping Out the Other: A Critical Introduction.* New York: Columbia University Press.

The authors provide a historical analysis of recent immigration enforcement in the United States. They show how anti-immigration tendencies have gathered steam for decades. They provide contributions from social scientists, policy analysts, legal experts, community organizers, and journalists. The editors critically examine the discourse that has framed the debate over immigration enforcement. The book explores the politics and practices of deportation and frames the issues in constitutional law and defense of civil liberties. The book draws on theories of structural inequality and institutional discrimination.

Brunet-Jailly, Emmanuel, ed. 2015. *Border Disputes: A Global Encyclopedia.* 3 vols. Westport, CT: Greenwood Press.
This three-volume set covers 80 current international border disputes and conflicts using social science studies, political science, human geography, and related subjects. It analyzes the conflicts as territorial, positional, or functional. It provides key legal rulings and primary documents on the important resolutions of various border disputes. It profiles how key organizations are related to those disputes and to specific border-dispute commissions.

Bryne-Hessick, Carisa, and Gabriel Chin, eds. 2014. *Strange Neighbors: The Role of States in Immigration Policy.* New York: New York University Press.
This book explores the complicated and complicating role of the states in immigration policy and its enforcement. Some contributors explicate the dangers of in-state regulation of immigration policy. Two of the contributors support it, and others offer empirically based examination of state efforts to regulate immigration within their borders. The book demonstrates the wide state-to-state disparities in locally administered immigration policy and laws. It is a timely and spirited discussion on the issue.

Calavita, Kitty. 1992. *Inside the State: The Bracero Program, Immigration, and the INS.* New York: Routledge Press.
In an authoritative narrative history, Calavita presents one of the best examinations of the Bracero Program, offering insights into temporary worker programs and the many problems inherently associated with that approach. The book helps the reader better understand the entrenched

opposition to any proposals that include any large-scale guest-worker program in future comprehensive immigration reform.

Chomsky, Aviva. 2014. *Undocumented: How Immigration Became Illegal.* Boston: Beacon Press.

Using legal, social, economic, and historical context, the author, an immigration rights activist, shows how "illegality" and "undocumented" are concepts created to exclude and exploit. She probes how U.S. policy assigns this status on Mexican and Central American migrants to the United States. The book blends historical narrative with human drama and with what it means to be undocumented in legal, social, economic, and historical contexts. It highlights the complex, contradictory, and ever-shifting natures of status in America.

Cieslik, Thomas, David Felsen, and Akis Kalaitzdis. 2008. *Immigration: A Documentary and Reference Guide.* Westport, CT: Greenwood Press.

Three respected authorities on immigration and international affairs examine the contemporary realities of immigration enmeshed as it is in complex economics, human rights, and national security issues.

Cohen, Steve, Beth Humphries, and Ed Mynott, eds. 2001. *From Immigration Controls to Welfare Controls.* New York: Routledge.

This edited collection examines theoretical, political, and practical aspects of the connection between immigration controls and internal welfare controls. Topics include forced dispersal of asylum-seekers, local authority and voluntary sector regulations, nationalism, racism, class and fairness, strategies of resistance to such controls, and United States of America controls. It includes discussion of the role of welfare workers as immigration control enforcers.

Cornelius, W. A., and Ricardo A. Montoya. 1983. *America's New Immigration Law: Origins, Rationales and Potential Consequences.* San Diego: Center for U.S./Mexican Studies, University of California.

This study of U.S.-Mexico relations examines the social and economic impact of Mexican immigrants on receiving communities, especially in relation to healthcare, education, and labor-market participation.

Craig, Richard. 1971. *The Bracero Program: Interest Groups and Foreign Policy.* Austin: University of Texas Press.

This is one of the early scholarly analyses of the controversial Bracero Program. It focuses on the interest groups for and against the program, and how they shaped the program's implementation and relationship to broader foreign policy concerns. Although it is dated, some of the interest groups discussed are involved in today's immigration reform politics, and the insights relating immigration to foreign policy provide relevant context for current relations and foreign policy arguments.

Daniels, Roger. 1998. *Not Like Us: Immigrants and Minorities in America, 1890–1924.* Chicago: Ivan Dee, Rowman and Littlefield Group.

Roger Daniels examines the conditions of immigrants, Native Americans, and Black Americans during a critical era of American history. He shows how these groups experienced as much repression as "advances" during the Progressive Era. He covers immigration law from the enactment of the Chinese Exclusion laws to the Quota Act of 1924. He details the ethnic strife and race riots of the era.

Daniels, Roger. 2002. *Coming to America: A History of Immigration and Ethnicity in American Life.* 2nd ed. New York: Harper.

In this second edition, the eminent historian offers a brief but insightful history of immigration and ethnicity and their impact on U.S. society, adding a timely new chapter on immigration during the age of globalization. It includes new appendixes with more recent statistics (up to 2000). It is an engrossing study of U.S. immigration from colonial times to the end of the 20th century by a noted historian of Asian Americans and immigration.

Daniels, Roger. 2005. *Guarding the Golden Doors.* New York: Hill and Wang.

Roger Daniels gives a detailed analysis of immigration policy and how and why it changed as it did over time, focusing on the years 1882 to 2000. He provides an enlightening historical context to the current debate over comprehensive immigration reform and the impact on the flow of immigration because of the Immigration and Naturalization Act of 1965.

Daniels, Roger, and Otis Graham. 2001. *Debating American Immigration, 1882 to the Present.* Lanham, MD: Rowman and Littlefield.

Two prominent historians present competing interpretations of past, present, and future immigration policy and American attitudes toward immigrants and immigration. They include supporting primary documents, and each offers recommendations for future policies and legal remedies for immigration law problems.

Eastman, Cari Lee Skogberg. 2016. *Immigration: Examining the Facts.* Santa Barbara, CA: ABC-CLIO.

This book explores the myths and truths regarding U.S. immigration. It provides an impartial understanding of the true state of U.S. immigration policy. It refutes falsehoods, misinformation, and exaggerations on the topic, while confirming the validity of other assertions. It analyzes specific claims about immigration in the media and public discourse. It identifies the origins of the claims and offers empirical data to consider their veracity. It presents a lot of statistical data in an easy-to-read format.

Ferris, Elizabeth G., ed. 1985. *Refugees and World Politics.* New York: Praeger.
The editor provides a thorough collection of essays on the refugee crisis up to the early 1980s. It is an important source of data to that point in time, and many of its issues and problems remain relevant today.

Foner, Nancy. 2005. *In a New Land: A Comparative View of Immigration.* New York: New York University Press.
In this study of comparative immigration, Foner, a leading immigration scholar, draws on the rich history of American immigrants with statistical and ethnographic data. She compares new immigrants with past influxes of Europeans to the United States across cities and regions in the United States and over different periods of time. She offers a comprehensive assessment and analysis that focuses on race, ethnicity, gender, and transnational connections.

French, Laurence A. 2010. *Running the Border Gauntlet.* Westport, CT: Praeger.
French traces the long history of racial, political, religious, and class conflicts that have resulted from America's contentious immigration policies. It is a lucid narrative account accessible to college students and the general-public and, as such, provides a historical context to the current debates over immigration reform.

Gans, Judith, Elaine M. Replogie, and Daniel J. Tichenor. 2012. *Debates on Immigration.* Los Angeles: Sage.
This is an issue-based and solid reference guide that examines immigration policy in the United States and the impassioned debates about the scope and nature of restriction policy. After an introductory essay, it uses a collection of original essays in the point/counterpoint style exploring the multiple sides of this complex topic.

Gomez, Laure. 2007. *Manifest Destinies.* New York: New York University Press.

Gomez, a law professor, and American studies scholar at the University of New Mexico, presents this narrative history of Mexican Americans in the context of race relations and racism in the United States and discusses the racial identity, legal status, and colonization patterns of Mexican Americans.

Hampshire, David. 2010. *U.S. Immigration Handbook.* Bath, UK: Survival Books.

This handbook is aimed at persons planning to live and work in the United States. It has details on how to get a visa, how to get a green card (work-authorization card), a survey of all 50 states, immigration history and pertinent demographics, and both immigrant and nonimmigrant visas. It also contains a discussion of the process for naturalization apart from miscellaneous but useful information for the potential immigrant. It also includes a reference section of relevant resources.

Haugen, David. 2009. *Immigration.* Boston: Greenhaven/Cengage.

Using an opposing viewpoints approach, Haugen explores immigration through a wide range of views by respected experts in the pro-con format. His book is presented in an accessible style aimed at general readers and undergraduate level students.

Hayes, Patrick. 2012. *The Making of Modern Immigration: An Encyclopedia of People and Ideas.* 2 vols. Santa Barbara, CA: ABC-CLIO.

This library reference volume is a comprehensive examination of the legal immigration system of the United States using the encyclopedia format of alphabetical entries covering the major government actors and interest group stakeholders as well as the key concepts of immigration law.

Hernandez, Kelly. 2010. *Migra! A History of the U.S. Border Patrol.* Berkeley: University of California Press.

> Hernandez presents a narrative history of the U.S. Border Patrol from its beginnings in 1924 as a small, peripheral law enforcement outfit to its emergence as a large, professional police force. She mines lost and largely unseen primary documents and records stored in garages, closets, and an abandoned factory as well as those in U.S. and Mexican archives. She details how the U.S. Border Patrol translated the mandate for comprehensive migrant control into a project of policing Mexicans in the U.S.-Mexico borderland.

Hutchinson, E. P. 1981. *Legislative History of Immigration Policy, 1798–1965.* Philadelphia: University of Pennsylvania Press.

> The most comprehensive and authoritative examination of immigration laws from the early republic to the reforms established by the Immigration and Nationality Act of 1965.

Information Plus. 2006. *Immigration and Illegal Aliens: Blessing or Burden?* Farmington Hills, MI: Thomson/Gale.

> This is one of a series of brief but thorough monographs that focuses on the undocumented immigrants issue viewed from a variety of perspectives. It presents many graphs, figures, and tables of data that touch upon every aspect of the illegal immigration issue. It presents the pros and cons on all sides of the issue and offers a solid historical perspective as does every volume in the series.

Information Plus. 2014. *American Immigration: An Encyclopedia of Political, Social, and Cultural Change.* Farmington Hills, MI: Thomson/Gale.

> This library reference volume presents a narrative history of American immigration, with tables, figures, and analyses of immigration to the United States based on current immigration issues, laws, and policies.

Kellas, James. 1998. *The Politics of Nationalism and Ethnicity*. 2nd ed. London: Palgrave Macmillan Press.

> Kellas reviews the key theoretical approaches to the study of nationalism within a wide range of disciplines. He presents multinational case studies to illuminate the power of nationalism and ethnicity in politics. He evaluates the strategies of accommodation that have developed in various attempts to cope with ethnic conflict, all of which are relevant to the borderlands region.

Keller, Morton. 2016. *America's Three Regimes: A New Political History.* New York: Oxford University Press.

> This narrative history is a sweeping view of American political history. The author divides that history into what he terms "three regimes," each of which lasted decades. He portrays the steady evolution of American politics, government, and law. The regimes are: Deferential and Republican, colonial to 1820s; Party and Democratic, 1830s to 1930s; and Populist and Bureaucratic, 1930s to present.

Kennedy, John F. 2008. *A Nation of Immigrants.* New York: Harper Perennial (Re-issued on its 50th anniversary).

> This new release of the former president's book details Kennedy's passion for immigration reform when he was a senator. He notes the many contributions to American culture made by immigrants. He describes the discrimination that they faced, which resonates with the current anti-immigration movement. The rhetoric and reasoning of the current anti-immigrant movement reads the same as that of the 1950s and 1960s; only the targets of their xenophobic fears have changed. With an introduction to the new edition written by Edward Kennedy, this book details what became President John F. Kennedy's immigration reform—the 1965 Act. The law was passed in no small measure as a memorial to the assassinated president.

Kivisto, Peter, and Thomas Faist. 2010. *Beyond a Border: Causes and Consequences of Contemporary Immigration.* Los Angeles: Sage.

> This is a comprehensive look at both legal and illegal immigration to America. It focuses on both push factors and pull factors driving the immigration process. It covers both undocumented and visa overstayers and shows the relationship between problems in the legal immigration system and the unauthorized immigration flow.

Krauss, Erick, and Alex Pacheco. 2004. *On the Line: Inside the Border Patrol.* New York: Citadel Press.

> This book offers an insider's look at the Border Patrol, presented in journalistic style. It portrays the difficult tasks, numerous resource problems, successes, and short-comings of the controversial agency.

Lamm, R. D., and G. Imhoff. 1985. *The Immigration Time Bomb.* New York: Truman Talley Books.

> Published prior to the enactment of Immigration Reform and Control Act of 1986 (IRCA), this book marshals every argument and all the data it can muster to show the costs or detrimental effects of large-scale immigration, in particular, those used to promote policy reforms to "control" the illegal immigration flow. The arguments presented here continue to be used by anti-immigration and especially anti–illegal immigration entities today and give a historical perspective to the Republican Party's intransigent position on any immigration reform that in their view constitutes "amnesty."

Lee, Erika. 2003. *At America's Gates: Chinese Immigration During the Exclusion Era, 1882–1943.* Chapel Hill: University of North Carolina Press.

> In this award-winning book, Professor Lee examines the Chinese Exclusion Acts and how those laws changed the course of American history. She details stories of both

the immigrants and the immigrant officials devoted to keeping them out. She shows how the laws transformed the lives of Chinese Americans, their patterns of immigration, identities, and families. She shows how those laws recast America from being an immigrant-welcoming nation into a gatekeeping nation using immigrant identification, border enforcement, surveillance, and deportation policies that are reflected powerfully in current immigration policy and law and impact the U.S.-Mexico border in myriad ways.

Lee, Erika. 2016. *The Making of Asian America: A History*. New York: Simon and Schuster.

Lee's volume is a sweeping and comprehensive examination of the history of Asian Americans and of their role in American life. She is one of the preeminent scholars of the subject, and her expertise shows throughout this engaging historical narrative. Lee shows how Asian immigrants and their descendants have remade Asian American life. Published 50 years after passage of the Immigration and Nationality Act of 1965, Lee's inspiring stories are epic and eye-opening, illuminating the complicated history of race and immigration and of their place in today's world.

LeMay, Michael, ed. 1989. *The Gatekeepers: Comparative Immigration Policy*. Westport, CT: Praeger.

This monograph provides a historical overview of U.S. immigration policymaking since 1820. It discusses the waves of immigration and distinguishes four phases of immigration policymaking that dominated historical eras in reaction to preceding waves, employing a door analogy to characterize each era of immigration policy.

LeMay, Michael. 2004. *U.S. Immigration: A Reference Handbook*. Santa Barbara, CA: ABC-CLIO.

This library reference volume examines legal immigration from 1965 to 2004, using the standard format of the

Contemporary World Issues series of the publisher. It is an objective presentation of the topic, allowing the reader to reach his or her own conclusions. It has a chapter offering tables of data and figures as well as excerpts from primary documents, including synopses of court cases and laws on the issue.

LeMay, Michael. 2006. *Guarding the Gates: Immigration and National Security.* Westport, CT and London: Praeger Security International.

This monograph is a historical narrative analysis of the inherent linkage between immigration policy and national security policy, from the founding era of American politics to the period after the 9/11 attacks and enactment of laws rushed through the Congress in response to the threat of international terrorism and fears that terrorists would enter the nation through the undocumented immigrant flow.

LeMay, Michael. 2007. *Illegal Immigration: A Reference Handbook.* 1st ed. Santa Barbara, CA: ABC-CLIO.

This library reference volume in the Contemporary World Issues series examines both undocumented and visa overstayer forms of unauthorized immigration to the United States, concentrating on the post–1965 exponential rise in such immigration. It covers the history of the issue and discusses the main problems and controversies related to the subject. It profiles the major stakeholders, both governmental and nongovernmental, on all sides of the issue. It presents tables of data and excerpts of key laws and court cases on the issue. It presents an extensive annotated list of key resources, both print and nonprint, to alert the readers to the basic literature necessary for further examination of the subject.

LeMay, Michael. 2009. *The Perennial Struggle: Race, Ethnicity, and Minority Group Relations in the United States*. 3rd ed. Upper Saddle River, NJ: Prentice-Hall.

> This basic textbook on ethnic and minority group politics in the United States has extensive coverage of the major immigrant groups that came to the United States. It details the effects of immigration laws and policies on them, their struggle to cope with their minority status, and the discrimination they faced. It presents a conceptual framework to better understand the process of political incorporation of ethnic, religious, and racial minority groups into American culture, politics, and society.

LeMay, Michael, ed. 2013. *Transforming America: Perspectives on Immigration*. 3 vols. Santa Barbara, CA: ABC-CLIO.

> This three-volume set presents original essays by 30 leading authorities on the subject written from various disciplinary perspectives. It covers immigration from 1820 to 2012. It offers a thorough view of immigration to the United States in all its complexity.

LeMay, Michael. 2015. *Doctors at the Borders: Immigration and the Rise of Public Health*. Westport, CT: Praeger Press.

> This monograph is a detailed historical narrative that examines the rise of U.S. public health from the early 1800s to 2014. It uses primary documents and copious data to trace the efforts of the U.S. Marine Hospital Service, the precursor to the U.S. Public Health Service, to effectively and efficiently screen the millions of immigrants entering the nation to prevent the spread of pandemic contagious diseases. It is especially relevant to the threat that the coronavirus pandemic poses to the border region where large numbers of immigrants cross without any screening for diseases that they may be carrying.

LeMay, Michael. 2015. *Illegal Immigration: A Reference Handbook.* 2nd ed. Santa Barbara, CA: ABC-CLIO.

> This second edition of a library reference volume of the Contemporary World Issues series updates the examination of the unauthorized immigration issue to 2015. It details the historical background to the issue, including major controversies and problems. It also profiles the key actors and organizations involved in the issue, surveys the scholarly literature on the subject, and offers a useful chronology of the issue from 1965 to 2015.

LeMay, Michael. 2017. *The American Political Party System: A Reference Handbook.* Santa Barbara, CA: ABC-CLIO.

> This Contemporary World Issues volume examines the rise and development of political parties in the United States from the founding era to 2016. It links the various political parties that took positions (pro and con) on immigration and demonstrates how their positions on the issue influenced their development; it also shows how the parties and their policy positions in turn influenced the flow of immigration over some two hundred years of American history. It is helpful in understanding the position of the two major parties with respect to control of the Southwest border.

LeMay, Michael, and Elliott Barkan, eds. 1999. *U.S. Immigration and Naturalization Laws and Issues: A Documentary History.* Westport, CT: Greenwood Press.

> This unique volume by two leading authorities on the subject summarizes and presents excerpts from primary sources, containing 150 documents covering the major laws and court cases concerning U.S. immigration and naturalization law from colonial times to 1990.

Lew-Williams, Beth. 2018. *The Chinese Must Go: Violence, Exclusion, and the Making of the Asian American.* Cambridge, MA: Harvard University Press.

>   Princeton University historian Beth Lew-Williams examines the social consensus that gave rise to the Chinese Exclusion laws of the 1880s and 1890s. She details how the expansion of citizenship came to a halt, denying entire classes of people the right to naturalize—based solely on racism. She shows how immigration laws created the idea that the Chinese were inassimilable. She argues persuasively as to how that concept hurts America to this day.

Louky, James, Jeanne M. Armstrong, and Larry J. Estrada, eds. 2006. *Immigration in America Today: An Encyclopedia.* Westport, CT: Praeger Press.

>   This book offers an interdisciplinary overview of complex immigration-related issues using alphabetically arranged entries that define key terms and concepts, provide a historical background, and suggest future trends in immigration and in the proposals to reform immigration policy.

Lutton, Wayne, and John Tanton. 1994. *The Immigration Invasion.* Petoskey, MI: The Social Contract Press.

>   A largely polemic book, it marshals virtually all the arguments the authors can think to bring to the immigration discourse from the perspective that immigration is too open and needs to be dramatically restricted.

Marshall, Ray. 2007. *Immigration for Shared Prosperity: A Framework for Comprehensive Reform.* Washington, DC: Economic Policy Institute.

>   This insightful book by a prominent economist and former U.S. secretary of labor explains the provisions he maintains are essential in any comprehensive immigration reform package, emphasizing immigration's importance

to the vibrancy of the economy of the United States. Although written a decade ago, its insights are relevant for the current debate over comprehensive immigration reform.

Massey, Douglas, Rafael Alarcon, Jorge Durand, and Humberto Gonzalez. 1987. *Return to Aztlan: The Social Process of Immigration from Western Mexico*. Berkeley: University of California Press.

The authors provide a thorough and many-viewed examination of Mexican immigration to the United States, both legal and unauthorized, focusing on the southwestern United States (the mythical Aztlan of the book's title).

Massey, Douglas, Jorge Durand, and Nolan Malone. 2003. *Beyond Smoke and Mirrors: Immigration in an Era of Economic Integration*. New York: Russell Sage.

The authors provide a fresh perspective on Mexican migration history by systematically tracing the predictable consequences of highly unsystematic policy regimes. They focus on post-9/11 immigration policy actions by marshaling new and compelling evidence to expose the flagrant contradiction of allowing the free flow of goods and capital but not of people, and they argue persuasively for much needed policy reforms.

Meier, Matt S., and Margo Gutierrez. 2000. *Encyclopedia of the Mexican American Civil Rights Movement*. Westport, CT: Greenwood Press.

Using an encyclopedia format, the authors present a reliable, accessible, and broad coverage of the persons, events, movements, and concepts that have informed the Mexican American civil rights movement. It is a thorough review of this ethnic group's experiences of the American way of life.

Merino, Noel. 2012. *Illegal Immigration*. Boston: Greenhaven/ Cengage.

> The author presents a comprehensive discussion of unauthorized immigration using a reference volume format to organize discussion of the issues involved. The book demonstrates why enacting comprehensive immigration reform is politically so difficult and why policy designed to cope with the unauthorized flow is so fraught with unanticipated consequences that impact the border region.

Miller, Debra. 2014. *Immigration*. Boston: Greenhaven/ Cengage.

> Miller uses the library reference volume format to present to the readers an exhaustive examination of legal immigration and its complexities that contribute to the public policy stalemate over border control of the U.S.-Mexico border.

Motomura, Hiroshi. 2006. *Americans in Waiting: The Lost Story of Immigration and Citizenship in the United States*. New York: Oxford University Press.

> Motomura provides an in-depth look at Chinese Americans and Japanese Americans and their struggles to secure citizenship rights from a nation that had institutional racism infusing its immigration and naturalization policy and law. In doing so, the book provides lessons relevant to later policy positions targeting Muslim immigrants in efforts to control the Southwest border.

Motomura, Hiroshi. 2014. *Immigration Outside the Law*. New York: Oxford University Press.

> An immigration history scholar examines the complex issue of unauthorized immigration and why it reflects gaps and problems in legal immigration law and policy. He demonstrates that fixing the illegal immigration

problem requires reform of legal immigration, providing an argument for comprehensive immigration reform.

Muller, Thomas, and Thomas Espanshade. 1985. *The Fourth Wave*. Washington, DC: Urban Institute Press.

This was a groundbreaking book, among the first and most thoroughly analytical examinations of the post–1965 wave of immigrants to the United States. It contributed significantly to renewing the scholarly debate over large-scale immigration and its costs and benefits to the United States. As such, it provides insights to better understand the impact of large-scale immigration on the border region.

Navarro, Armando. 2005. *Mexican Political Experience in Occupied Aztlan*. Lanham, MD: Altamura Press.

Navarro provides a critical look at the Hispanic/Latino, and especially the Mexican immigrants' struggle with American politics and their minority status that is largely the result of racial attitudes. He demonstrates that the attitudes of the 1990–2000 decade predict the policy attitudes and prescriptions of the Republican Party in the era of Trumpism.

Nelson, Michael. 2014. *Resilient America: Reelecting Nixon in 1968, Channeling Dissent, and Dividing Government*. Lawrence: University Press of Kansas.

Nelson's insightful book on the 1968 presidential election explains why it was a reordering of party coalitions, groups, and regions that helped set a hardening and widening partisan and ideological divide. It shows how the election was a watershed event that provides insights regarding our political environment of hyper-partisanship that is so evident in the states of the border region.

Ngai, Mae, ed. 2011. *Major Problems in American Immigration History: Documents and Essays*. Boston: Wadsworth/Cengage.

This excellent collection of essays and documents explores the political and economic forces that cause immigration. It details the alienation and uprootedness caused by relocation. It treats difficult questions of citizenship and assimilation using primary sources and the interpretations of distinguished historians while allowing readers to draw their own conclusions.

Ngai, Mae. 2014. *Impossible Subjects: Illegal Aliens and the Making of Modern America.* Princeton, NJ: Princeton University Press.

In this beautifully written historical narrative, Ngai traces the origins of "illegal alien" in American law and society, explaining its how and why. She details how it profoundly affected ideas and practices relating to U.S. citizenship, race, and state authority. She shows how the national origins system remapped America by creating new categories of racial differences and by emphasizing America's contiguous land borders and the efforts to control them.

O'Leary, Anna Ochea, ed. 2014. *Undocumented Immigrants in the United States: An Encyclopedia of Their Experiences.* Santa Barbara, CA: Greenwood.

This two-volume reference work uses the encyclopedia format to address the dynamic lives of undocumented immigrants. It shows how their experiences are a key part of the nation's demographic and sociological evolution. It supplies extensive and comprehensive coverage of a complex topic by consolidating the insights of scholars who have examined the subject over many years.

Orreniris, Pia, and Madelaine Zavodny. 2010. *Beyond the Gold Door: U.S. Immigration in a New Era of Globalization.* Washington, DC: American Enterprise Institute Press.

The authors document how immigration reforms have resulted in an inefficient patchwork system that short-changes high-skilled immigrants and poorly serves the

American public. They propose a radical overhaul of immigration policy stressing economic competitiveness and long-term growth and favoring employment-based immigration over the family reunification preference system established by the basic immigration law of the United States as established by the Immigration and Nationality Act of 1965.

Papademetrious, Demetrios, and Mark J. Miller, eds. 1984. *The Unavoidable Issue.* Philadelphia: Institute for the Study of Human Issues.

This volume is an impressive array of essays discussing the major issues of U.S. immigration policy and the need for reforms in law and policy. It is a particularly good review of the topic for the 1965–1980 period but provides a historical perspective useful to understanding the complexity of the issue for today's immigration policy debate. It provides insights to better understand the complex politics of the border states and their differing approaches to immigration.

Payan, Tony. 2006. *The Three U.S.-Mexico Border Wars: Drugs, Immigration, and Homeland Security.* Westport, CT: Praeger Press.

The book examines the responses to the 9/11 attacks as felt in the most affected area—the U.S.-Mexico border—and the effects produced by the war against drugs, the war against immigration, and the war against terror. The author shows how these three areas of law are linked inexorably in the border region, affecting the lives of all who live there.

Perea, Juan, ed. 1997. *Immigrants Out! The New Nativism and the Anti-Immigrant Impulse in the United States.* New York: New York University Press.

Perea provides a collection of 18 original essays by leading immigration scholars. The volume approaches the complex subject using interdisciplinary perspectives to examine current nativism compared to past waves. It examines the relationships between the races and the perception of a national immigration crisis resulting largely from race-based attitudes toward immigration. It gives a historical perspective as to why national populism contains racial undertones that make comprehensive immigration reform so difficult to achieve.

Pfaelzer, Jean. 2008. *Driven Out: The Forgotten War Against Chinese Americans*. Berkeley: University of California Press.
Pfaelzer tells the story of thousands of Chinese immigrants who were violently herded into railroad cars, steamers, or logging rafts to be marched out of towns or killed, from the Pacific Coast to the Rocky Mountains. Using primary documents including local and national laws and several court cases, she chronicles the Chinese immigrants' campaign against what they called "Dog Tag Law" and the launching of what she calls "the largest organized act of civil disobedience in the United States," against "ethnic cleansing." She offers a new understanding—in terms of geography, chronology, and cast of characters—of the civil rights movement. Her groundbreaking book records over 100 roundups, pogroms, expulsions, and ethnic cleansings used by white Westerners to drive the Chinese out of their communities from 1850 to 1906. She details how they used warnings, arson, boycotts, and outright violence to achieve their political goals.

Portes, Alejandro, and Reuben G. Rumbaut, eds. 2001. *Ethnicities: Children of Immigrants in America*. 2 vols. New York: Russell Sage.
These two volumes present the findings of an extensive examination of the "political incorporation" of second-generation immigrants. This collection of essays explains

how while assimilation was a relatively homogeneous linear process in the past, it is now a segmented one.

Powell, John. 2005. *Encyclopedia of North American Immigration.* New York: Facts on File.
This narrative history shows how, for good or bad, immigration has shaped and transformed America. It covers the magnitude and diversity of migration to North America. It is a solid, one-volume encyclopedia with more than 300 A–Z entries, and an extensive bibliography of resources for further research.

President's Commission on Immigration and Naturalization. 1953. *Whom Shall We Welcome?* Washington, DC: U.S. Government Printing Office.
This report of the President's Commission examines in detail emigration and U.S. immigration law. The commission was established by President Harry Truman. It recommended that the National Origins quota system be abolished because the system discriminated against potential southern and eastern European immigrants as well as Asia and the Pacific/Oceanic regions whose immigrants were limited to 100 persons a year. The report set in motion a long public debate over immigration law that culminated in the Immigration and Nationality Act of 1965 that finally abolished the restrictive national origins quota system.

Salomone, Rosemary. 2010. *True American: Language, Identity, and the Education of Immigrant Children.* Cambridge, MA: Harvard University Press.
The author uses the heated debate over how best to educate immigrant children as an approach to explore what national identity means in an age of globalization, transnationalism, and dual citizenship. She addresses the myths that bilingualism impedes success, that English is under threat, and that immigrants in the 2000–2010 decade are

more reluctant to learn English than were immigrants of the past. She provides a vivid narrative of the history of bilingual education.

Salyer, Lucy E. 1995. *Laws Harsh as Tigers: Chinese Immigrants and the Shaping of Modern Immigration Law.* Chapel Hill: University of North Carolina Press.

In her award-winning book, Salyer analyzes the popular and legal debates about immigration law and its enforcement policies during the height of the nativist movement of the early 20th century. She links Asian immigrants on the West Coast with European immigrants on the East Coast. She discusses their sophisticated and often successful legal challenges to exclusionary immigration laws. Salyer shows, however, that by 1924 immigration law diverged from constitutional norms and that the Bureau of Immigration emerged as an exceptionally powerful organization, largely free from the constraints imposed on other government agencies. Her book offers a powerful lesson for the "control of the border" approach to immigration law and its enforcement policies.

Samito, Christian. 2009. *Becoming American Under Fire.* Ithaca, NY: Cornell University Press.

Samito provides a rich account of how African American and Irish American soldiers in the Civil War influenced the modern vision of citizenship that developed during the war. They helped define the legal meaning and political practices of American citizenship as embodied in the Constitution and U.S. laws. Citizenship determines official membership in the country and helps define the duties and rights that members/citizens enjoy; it defines inclusion and exclusion in a community as well as personal identities and collective patriotism. The definition and understanding of citizenship is basic to an understanding of the politics of the border region.

Schrug, Peter. 2010. *Not Fit for Our Society: Nativism and Immigration.* Berkeley: University of California Press.

This historical narrative covering 300 years of U.S. history is a timely, thoughtful, and extensive look at anti-immigration attitudes in the United States from its founding to the present, emphasizing periodic spasms and the long history of ambivalence and inconsistency with strands of welcome and rejection that are especially relevant to the border region and its partisan politics.

Select Commission on Immigration and Refugee Policy. 1981. *Final Report.* Washington, DC: U.S. Government Printing Office.

The Select Commission on Immigration and Refugee Policy (SCIRP) was a joint presidential/congressional commission established in 1979 by President Jimmy Carter, Senator Edward Kennedy (then chair of the Senate Judiciary Committee), and Representative Joshua Eilberg (then chair of the House Judiciary's Subcommittee on Immigration). The massive (400 page plus) report's recommendations shaped the debate from 1982 to 1986 and the enactment of IRCA. Many of its recommendations influenced subsequent immigration debates (such as the Immigration Act of 1990) as well.

Stolarik, M. Mark, ed. 1988. *Forgotten Doors: The Other Ports of Entry to the United States.* Philadelphia: Balch Institute Press.

A comparative study of seven ports of entry other than New York from the early 19th century to the 1980s.

Strobel, Christopher. 2010. *Daily Life of the New Americans: Immigration Since 1965.* Westport, CT: Praeger.

This is a detailed historical narrative that is an engaging look at the daily life of the new immigrants (defined as those coming after 1965). It provides an extensive chronology of the main events in immigration history since

1970. It provides a helpful historical perspective to better understand the politics of today's debates over immigration policy reforms that are so impactful for the politics of the border region.

U.S. Commission on Immigration Policy. 1997. *Becoming American: Immigration and Immigration Policy.* Washington, DC: U.S. Government Printing Office.

After 40 hearings and both domestic and foreign on-site visits, the Commission released this report in June 1997. It focuses on the goals of Americanization, setting out recommendations to help orient immigrants to their new communities, to help them learn English and civics, and to reinforce the integrity of the naturalization process. It includes a chapter titled "A Credible Framework for Immigration Policy."

U.S. Commission on Immigration Policy. 1997. *U.S. Refugee Policy: Taking Leadership.* Washington, DC: U.S. Government Printing Office.

The commission held more than 40 hearings. This report presents the Jordan Commission's recommendations for a comprehensive and coherent U.S. refugee policy. It features data on Russian Jews, Iraqis, Kurds, Hmong, Somalis, and Yugoslavians. It suggests changes to the refugee resettlement program.

Waters, Mary C., Reed Ueda, and Helen B. Marrow, eds. 2007. *The New Americans: A Guide to Immigration Since 1965.* New York: Russell Sage/Harvard University Press.

This volume focuses on the wave of immigrants to the United States that began with and is influenced by laws and policies since 1965. It is written by an interdisciplinary group of scholars who discuss immigration law and policy, refugees, unauthorized immigrants, naturalization, and the economic impact of immigration on religion, education, and family relations, which shape the border region.

Wolbrecht, Christina, and Rodney E. Hero. 2005. *The Politics of Democratic Inclusion*. Philadelphia: Temple University Press.
    This book is an innovative examination of the complexity of the incorporation process for immigrants, explaining the "inclusion" or "incorporation" approach to the issue instead of the linear "assimilation" approach. It provides useful insights to better understand the process as it affects Muslims and Hispanics in post–9/11 America. It also provides the reader with a useful counterpoint to view the arguments of the nativist and populist strain in U.S. politics that essentially views immigrants coming after 2001 as unable to assimilate in the way past immigrant groups did.

Wood, Andrew G., ed. 2008. *The Borderlands: An Encyclopedia of Culture and Politics in the U.S. Mexico Divide*. Westport, CT: Greenwood Press.
    This volume presents a broad collection of essays from multidisciplinary backgrounds. It uses the encyclopedia format to examine complex issues around migration flows, legal and unauthorized, across the U.S.-Mexico border.

Zolberg, Aristide. 2008. *A Nation by Design: Immigration Policy in the Fashioning of America*. Cambridge, MA: Russell Sage Foundation at Harvard University Press.
    The late Harvard professor explores American immigration policy from the colonial period to the present, discussing how it has been used as a tool of nation building. It covers policy at the local and state levels and profiles the vacillating currents of opinions on immigration throughout American history. It examines legal, unauthorized, and asylum-seeking immigration and how opinion varies so greatly among them. Those issues are central to the politics of the border region.

Zucker, Norman, and Naomi Flink Zucker. 1987. *The Guarded Gate: The Reality of American Refugee Policy.* New York: Harcourt Brace Jovanovich.

> The authors examine U.S. policy toward refugees as it emerged and was amended over a 40-year period. They show how refugee policy was and is shaped by foreign relations with both allies and adversaries abroad. They link refugee and asylum policy to domestic immigration history. They trace the history of restrictive policy of the national origins system and America's failure to respond to the Holocaust during the interwar and World War II years. They show how refugee policy continued to discriminate during the post–World War II years in favor of refugees fleeing communist countries and against those fleeing authoritarian regimes.

Zuniga, Victor, and Ruben Hernandez-Leon, eds. 2005. *New Destinations: Mexican Immigration in the United States.* New York: Russell Sage.

> This book is an eclectic array of essays on the new Mexican immigration to the United States. It includes a discussion of both legal and unauthorized immigration matters. It examines census data to discern the historical evolution of Mexican immigration to the United States, discussing the demographic, economic, and legal factors that led to moves of immigrants to areas since 2000 to areas in the United States beyond where their predecessors had settled. They conclude that undocumented immigrants did a better job than did their documented peers of the past in incorporating into the local culture. The book examines paternalism and xenophobic attitudes held by local residents toward the new immigrants. It details the strong work ethic of the new migrants and provides hopeful examples of their progress toward incorporation. It is one of the first scholarly assessments of the new settlements and related experiences in the Midwest, Northeast, and

The U.S.-Mexico Border

the deep South, and of America's largest immigrant group from the perspective of demographers, sociologists, folklorists, anthropologists, and political scientists.

Scholarly Journals

American Demographics

Published 10 times per year, this peer-reviewed journal is an outlet for multidisciplinary articles of original research dealing with all aspects related to demography as well as occasional articles and reflective essays on migration, legal and unauthorized immigration, and an annually published useful resource guide.

American Journal of Sociology

This is a peer-reviewed quarterly journal of sociology that frequently publishes articles concerning assimilation, incorporation, integration, and social trends as well as policies regarding migration (both legal and unauthorized immigration). It also reviews books on immigration-related topics.

Annual Review of Sociology

This quarterly peer-reviewed academic journal has been published since 1975. It covers significant developments in the field of sociology including theoretical and methodological developments as well as current research in the major subfields. Review chapters typically cover social processes, institutions and culture, organizations, political and economic sociology, stratification, demography, social policy, historical sociology, and major developments in other regions of the world.

Citizenship Studies

This peer-reviewed journal, published by Taylor and Francis in print and online, puts out internationally recognized scholarly work on contemporary issues of citizenship, human rights, and democratic processes. It is an interdisciplinary journal covering politics, sociology, history, anthropology, and cultural studies. It features aspects of citizenship such as gender, equality, migration, and borders.

Columbia Law Review
Published eight times per year, the law review frequently has case reviews and analytical articles and original essays dealing with immigration law matters.

Demographics
This peer-reviewed journal of the Population Association of America publishes scholarly research of interest to demography from a multidisciplinary perspective, with an emphasis on social sciences, geography, history, biology, statistics, business, epidemiology, and public health.

Ethnohistory
This is a peer-reviewed quarterly publication and the official journal of the American Society for Ethnohistory. It contains articles of original research, commentaries, review essays, and useful book reviews.

Geographical Review
The quarterly, official journal of the American Geographical Society, it publishes research on all topics related to geography, including those dealing with legal and unauthorized immigration, immigration reforms, and the incorporation of immigrants. It also publishes book reviews in each issue.

Georgetown Immigration Law Journal
This quarterly law review is the law journal most specifically dealing with U.S. immigration law, current developments in law, and reform-related matters concerning all

three branches of the U.S. government. It frequently focuses on unauthorized immigration. It contains case reviews, articles, notes and commentaries, and workshop reports devoted to the topic.

Harvard Law Review

Arguably the most influential law journal, this law review is published eight times per year. It contains original articles, case reviews, essays, commentaries, and book reviews that occasionally are on topics related to U.S. immigration law and its reform.

International Migration

This quarterly is an intergovernmental publication featuring documents, conference reports, and articles dealing with international migration topics. It regularly features articles dealing with revisions in laws affecting emigration and immigration matters. It provides a useful international context to American immigration law reform issues.

International Migration Review

This is the leading quarterly journal in the field of migration. It contains current research articles, book reviews, documents, and bibliographies. It is a publication of the Center for Migration Studies in New York.

International Social Sciences Journal

This quarterly journal is published by Blackwell Publishers for UNESCO. It regularly contains articles concerning international migration, refugee and asylum issues and their impact on societies and social systems, and other topics related to UNESCO.

Journal of American Ethnic History

This peer-reviewed scholarly journal has been published since 1981 for the Immigration and Ethnic History

Society. It addresses various aspects of North American immigration, including emigration, race and ethnic relations, immigration policies and the processes of incorporation, integration, and acculturation. Each issue contains articles, review essays, and book reviews. It features occasional scholarly forums and "research comments." It occasionally publishes special issues on a specific theme.

Journal of American Studies
Published three times per year, this multidisciplinary, scholarly refereed journal is multinational with articles on politics, economics, and geography; and in each issue it contains book reviews that often relate to immigration matters.

Journal of Economic Issues
This peer-reviewed scholarly economics journal covers all aspects of economic issues, including original research on immigration and migration, with a focus on the economic impact of migration, especially on labor-market issues. Each issue has book reviews of related matters as well.

Journal of Economic Perspectives
This official journal of the American Economic Association publishes occasional symposium issues apart from regularly publishing original scholarly articles, features, and economic analysis on a variety of public policy issues, including both legal and unauthorized immigration, and book reviews on related matters.

Journal of Ethnic and Migration Studies
This peer-reviewed academic journal has been in existence since 1998 and publishes 16 issues per year. It features original research on all forms of migration and its consequences with articles about ethnic conflict, discrimination, racism, nationalism, citizenship, and policies of

integration. An international journal, it publishes comparative research in Europe, North America, and the Asia-Pacific region.

Journal of Intercultural Studies

This journal presents international research related to intercultural studies across national and disciplinary boundaries. One issue per year is thematic. It examines common issues across a range of disciplinary perspectives. Peer-reviewed research, theoretical papers, and book reviews are included in each issue.

Journal of International Refugee Law

This quarterly publishes articles on refugee law and policy matters, including legislation, documentation, and abstracts of recent publications in the field.

Journal of Migration and Human Security

A publication of the Center for Migration Studies of New York, this is an online, peer-reviewed public policy academic journal focusing on the social, political, and economic dimensions of human security. It publishes an annual bound volume of its articles.

Journal of Social Policy

This journal publishes original research articles about all aspects of social policy. It has been published since 1972 by Cambridge University Press. It is a British journal that is international and interdisciplinary. It contains relevant book reviews in each issue.

Migration News

This monthly newsletter is published by the University of California, Davis. It concerns all manner of topics related to migration, with particular emphasis on how unauthorized immigration impacts U.S. society both positively and negatively.

Migration World

This journal publishes articles and information about migration and refugee problems worldwide. It is a readable and accessible publication that is a good source for school and college reports.

Patterns of Prejudice

This is a journal providing a forum for exploring the historical roots and contemporary varieties of demonization of "the other." It probes the language and social construction of race, nation, color, and ethnicity as well as the linkages between these categories. The journal discusses topics and policy agendas that impact asylum issues, unauthorized immigration, hate crimes, Holocaust denial, and citizenship.

Perspectives on Politics

Published since 2003, this journal is an official publication of the American Political Science Association. It is a peer-reviewed scholarly quarterly aimed at nurturing political science within the public sphere. It is released both in print and online. It occasionally has featured articles on inclusion and exclusion and on public policy debates about immigration, both legal and unauthorized.

Political Research Quarterly

This peer-reviewed quarterly scholarly journal publishes original research on all aspects of politics. It is published on behalf of the Western Political Science Association by the University of Utah. Published since 1948, it was renamed in 1992. It features articles on public policy, race, and ethnicity.

Political Science Quarterly

This scholarly, peer-reviewed quarterly discusses public and international affairs. It is nonpartisan, with scholarly articles devoted to the study and analysis of government, politics, and international affairs, with original articles, essays, thematic review essays, and book reviews.

Public Opinion Quarterly

This peer-reviewed academic journal is published by Oxford University Press for the American Association for Public Opinion Research. Published since 1937, it is a social science interdisciplinary journal and is also one of the most often cited journals of its kind. Its original research studies concern analyses of public opinion on all sorts of political topics.

Refugee Reports

This is a monthly report of information and documents concerning refugees and the legislation, policies, and programs that affect them. A year-end statistical issue is published every December and is considered an authoritative source on data on refugees, their treatment, the problems they face in refugee camps, and their migration to asylum locations.

Refugee Survey Quarterly

This quarterly lists abstracts of the many publications concerning refugees, including a selection of "country reports" and one on human rights–related legal documents.

Review of Politics

This peer-reviewed academic journal publishes articles on political theory, public law, comparative politics, and international relations. Founded in 1939, it is published by the University of Notre Dame. Each issue has book reviews of recent academic books on politics. It has occasional symposium issues organized around a specific theme.

Social Science Quarterly

Published for the Southwestern Social Science Association by Blackwell, this interdisciplinary quarterly has articles of original research, review essays, book reviews, and occasional symposium issues. It contains articles dealing with U.S. immigration and illegal immigration policy and issues related to the incorporation of immigrants and their children into U.S. society.

Sociological Forum

This peer-reviewed quarterly is published by Wiley-Blackwell for the Eastern Sociological Society. It has been published since 1986. It publishes original research on comparisons in the study of immigrant integration, on belonging and "othering," and on critical ethnographies on immigrants and refugees to the United States.

Sociological Perspectives

Published by Sage since 1957, it is the official journal of the Pacific Sociological Association. It regularly features original research articles on social processes related to economic, political, and historical issues. Published six times per year, it has "up-to-the-minute" articles within the field of sociology.

Films

America 101. 2005. 86 minutes, color. Fabia Films.

This documentary film traces the trials and tribulations of two Mexican brothers who get smuggled over the border to find their American dream.

Backyard (El Traspatio). 2009. 122 minutes, color. Tarazod films, Tardon/Berman Productions.

This feature-length film stars Jimmy Smits. It tells the true story of the border town of Juarez, Mexico where, since the mid-1990s, thousands of women have either gone missing or turned up as sun-burnt corpses in the Sonora Desert.

Beyond Borders: The Debate Over Human Migration. 2007. 51 minutes, color.

Brian Ging Films.

The debate covered in this documentary is between Noam Chomsky and Jim Gilchrist, and it presents both sides of the controversy over illegal immigration to the United States and what can or should be done to address the problem.

Coyote. 2007. 94 minutes, color. Side Street Productions.

Filmed in Los Angeles, this documentary feature-length film is directed by Brian Petersen. It tells the tale of two young Americans who decide to begin smuggling immigrants into the United States for profit. It is in Spanish and English.

Crossing Over. 2009. 113 minutes, color. MGM/The Weinstein Company.

This is an independent crime film drama starring Harrison Ford, Ashley Judd, Ray Liotta, and Jim Sturgess. It presents a multicharacter canvas showing how immigrants of different nationalities struggle to achieve legal status in Los Angeles.

Dying to Get In: Undocumented Immigration at the U.S.-Mexico Border. 2005. 40 minutes, color. Films for the Humanities and Sciences.

This documentary film by Christopher Deufert, directed by Brett Tolley, traces the experiences and insights of Tolley who imbedded himself with a group of Mexicans crossing the U.S.-Mexico border. It presents their story as they make their way in a harrowing journey across the border.

Facing Up to Illegal Immigration. 2004. 23 minutes, color.
Films Media Group.

This compelling video presents a discussion of the issue of
whether there is a realistic way to stop unauthorized immigrants at America's borders. It grapples with the fact that
the world's only superpower cannot seem to control its
borders and cannot seem to function without unauthorized, undocumented immigrants. An ABC News special,
it offers a balanced look at the illegal immigration issue
and related topics such as the liability of porous borders
in a time of terrorism, the apparent need for unauthorized
workers in the U.S. workforce, and whether they really
take jobs away from U.S. citizens or whether they are
doing work that American citizens themselves are unwilling to do.

From the Other Side. 2002. 99 minutes, color. Icarus Films.

This multiple-award-winning documentary film drama-
tizes how technology developed by the U.S. military is
being used to stem the flow of unauthorized immigrants
in the San Diego area, and how the success there is forcing desperate, unauthorized immigrants to hazard crossing the dangerous deserts of Arizona. It is directed by
renowned documentary filmmaker Channel Ackerman.

The Golden Cage: A Story of California's Farmworkers. 1990. 29
minutes, color. Filmmakers Library.

Sort of a modern version of the "Grapes of Wrath," this
documentary video presents a moving and vivid portrait
of contemporary farmworkers using historical footage,
newspaper clippings, and black-and-white stills. It traces
the history of the United Farm Workers Union from the
1960s to 1990. It shows the tactics used by many companies to evade using union labor. It offers candid interviews

with legal and unauthorized migrant workers, growers, doctors, and others.

Human Contraband: Selling the American Dream. 2002. 22 minutes, color. Films for the Humanities and Sciences.

This ABC News program investigates the lucrative trade in smuggling into Mexico desperate human beings from all over the world, but mostly from Central America, who view Mexico as the back door to the United States. INS officials discuss multilateral efforts to combat such smuggling and unauthorized, undocumented entry into the United States.

Illegal Americans. 2002. 45 minutes, color. Films for the Humanities and Sciences.

This CBS news documentary examines the hazardous enterprise of immigrants coming to the United States illegally, focusing on their desperate plight. It examines their living conditions in detention centers and the growing strains they place on U.S. cities. It also looks at the people who assist these unauthorized immigrants. It shows how immigrants manage to evade capture, the sweatshops that employ and exploit them, and the efforts of some who attempt to beat the system using false IDs and marriages of convenience.

Immigrant Nation: The Battle for the Dream. 2010. 96 minutes, color. An IMDbPro by Josh Flander, Juan Carlos Hernandez, and Particia Lofthouse.

This documentary film won an award at the Oaxaca Film Fest. It portrays the story of the modern immigrant rights movement and its struggle as seen through the eyes of a single mother, Elvira Arellano, who fought against her forced deportation and separation from her American-born child.

Laredoans Speak: Voices on Immigration. 2011. 75 minutes, color. Border Town Pictures.

Featuring veteran actor Pepe Serana, this documentary is directed by Victor Martinez. It takes the viewers through the issues involved in the debate over undocumented immigration as seen through the eyes of the citizens of Laredo, Texas.

Legacy of Shame: Migrant Labor; an American Institution. 2002. 52 minutes, color.

Films for the Humanities and Sciences.

This CBS news documentary is a follow-up to the 1960 award-winning film, *Harvest of Shame.* It documents the ongoing exploitation of America's migrant labor by highlighting efforts made to protect them. It investigates pesticide risks, uneven enforcement of employment and immigration regulations, and virtual peonage conditions. It covers the efforts of rural legal services as advocates for this truly "silent-minority."

The Line in the Sand. 2005. 100 minutes, color. Sun Films, Inc.

This documentary film deals with illegal immigration and the issue of security along the southern border of the United States. It has a segment on the Minutemen Project whose members practice vigilantism along the border to enforce border control when and where they feel the U.S. government is failing in its duty to secure the border.

Precious Knowledge. 2011. 75 minutes, color. Dos Vatos Productions, ITVS.

In this documentary, filmed in Tucson, Arizona, disenfranchised high school seniors become academic warriors and community leaders trying to save their embattled ethnic studies classes when state lawmakers seek to eliminate the program.

Sin Nombre (Without a Name). 2009. 96 minutes, color. Creando Film, Focus Films.

> This feature-length film won several awards at the 2009 Sundance Film Festival. It features the life and experiences of a Honduran teenager, Sayra, who reunites with her father and tries to realize her dream of a life in the United States. It is directed by Cary Toji Fukunaga and is in Spanish with English subtitles.

The State of Arizona. 2014. 90 minutes, color. PBS/ITVS, Latino Public Broadcasting Production.

> This riveting documentary covers the turbulent battle over unauthorized immigration in Arizona that came to a head with the passage of the Arizona Senate Bill 1070. It tracks multiple perspectives as America eyes the results of the law's passage.

They Come to America: The Cost of Amnesty. 2012. 99 minutes, color. Corinth films.

> This polemical film by Dennis Lynch of FAIR depicts the human and financial costs of undocumented immigration.

Those Who Remain. 2008. 96 minutes, color. Sombre del Guyabo Productions.

> This documentary film is directed by Carlos Hagerman. It tells an intimate and discerning tale depicting the impact of migration on the families and communities left behind by loved ones who have traveled north to find work in the United States.

Under the Same Moon. 2007. 106 minutes, color. Creando Films.

> This documentary won a Sundance Film Festival award. It is directed by Patricia Riggin, in Spanish and English, and follows a young Mexican boy who travels to the United

States to find his mother after his grandmother, who was caring for him in Mexico, passes away.

The Undocumented. 2004. 90 minutes, color. ITVS/Two Tone Production.

This documentary film depicts the tragic tale shared by approximately 2,000 immigrants who died while trying to cross the Sonora Desert in search of a better life in the United States. It gives faces to some of the dead and follows their long journey home.

Wetback: The Undocumented Documentary. 2005. 96 minutes, color. IMDb Productions.

This is a Canadian documentary film that chronicles the struggles and hardships of a handful of Mexicans trying to relocate to the United States.

Videos

The Dream Is Now. 2013. 31 minutes, color. At http://www.thedreamisnow.org/.

This video is a moving and thought-provoking look at the undocumented youth in America commonly known as "the Dreamers." It is directed by an award-winning documentary film director and the short video brings the pressing issue to the nation's attention for the viewers to debate and decide for themselves.

Facing Up to Illegal Immigration. 2004. 23 minutes, color. Films Media Group.

This video discusses whether there is a realistic way to stop unauthorized immigrants at the border. An ABC News special, it presents a balanced look at addressing issues such as the liability of porous borders in a time of terrorism, the seeming need for unauthorized workers, and whether they really take work away from citizens or are doing work that Americans themselves are unwilling to do.

The Immigration History of the United States. 2014. 21:22 minutes. The Daily Conversation.

This is the Documentary Channel (TDC) original documentary explaining the history of immigration to America from the "natives" who first populated the land to Mexican migrants coming in huge numbers today.

Immigration: Who Has Access to the American Dream? 2002. 28 minutes, color. Film for the Humanities and Sciences.

The program reviews how post–9/11 policy affects the survival of new immigrants to the United States. It covers a variety of questions such as how many should be let in, who should receive preferential treatment, and how unauthorized immigrants should be handled when apprehended. It examines the issue from several perspectives.

7 Chronology

1790 Congress establishes uniform rule of naturalization imposing a two-year residency for unauthorized immigrants who are "free white persons of good moral character."

1802 Congress revises 1790 Act to require a five-year residency and that naturalizing citizens renounce allegiance and fidelity to foreign powers.

1819 Congress requires shipmasters to deliver a manifest enumerating all unauthorized immigrants transported for immigration and requiring the secretary of state to inform Congress of the numbers. For the first time, an official count of legal immigrants is kept.

1848 Treaty of Guadalupe Hidalgo guarantees citizenship to Mexicans remaining in the territory ceded by Mexico to the United States. Treaty sets the basis for the flow of Mexicans to the United States and provides the basis for future legal and undocumented immigration forging the first link in "chain migration" from Mexico.

1855 Castle Garden becomes New York's port of entry for legal immigration. The volume of immigration sets the stage

---

Several buildings and adjacent walls are covered by graffiti art in Tijuana Beach, close to the U.S. border. Such art often make a political point about the crossing points and exemplify the "border culture." (Leszek Wrona/ Dreamstime.com)

for later development of "visa overstayers" who remain because such extensive numbers overwhelm the ability of immigration authorities to keep track of them.

1862 Congress passes Homestead Act granting acres of free land to settlers who develop land in frontier regions and remain on it for five years, spurring high levels of immigration.

1868 The Fourteenth Amendment is ratified guaranteeing that all persons born within the jurisdiction of the United States or naturalized are citizens and that no state may abridge their rights without due process or deny them equal protection under the law, ensuring citizenship rights to former slaves and ending "free white persons" phrase of citizenship. It establishes supremacy of federal law over acts by state governments in matters pertaining to citizenship, naturalization, and immigration.

1870 Congress enacts law granting citizenship to persons of African descent.

1882 Congress passes Chinese Exclusion Act barring immigration of Chinese laborers for 10 years and denying them eligibility for naturalization. Its harsh provisions induced many Chinese immigrants to get around the law by using false documents—such as paper sons and daughters—setting the precedent for "illegal aliens" using fraudulent documents to the present day.

1885 Congress enacts law banning laborers from immigrating under a contract with a U.S. employer who in any manner prepays passage of the laborer.

1886 *Yick Wo v. Hopkins* overturns a San Francisco ordinance against Chinese laundry workers as discriminatory and unconstitutional under the Fourteenth Amendment on grounds of depriving any person, even a noncitizen, of life, liberty, or property without due process.

1888 Congress passes the Scott Act that expands the Chinese Exclusion Act by rescinding reentry permits for Chinese laborers and prohibiting their return.

1889 In *Chae Chan Ping v. United States,* the Supreme Court upholds the right of Congress to repeal the certificate of reentry as in the 1888 Scott Act, thereby excluding ex post facto certain Chinese immigrants who previously entered legally.

1891 Congress expands the classes of individuals excluded from admission, forbids soliciting immigrants, and creates the office of superintendent of immigration.

1892 Ellis Island is opened and immediately becomes the leading port of entry.

1894 Congress extends the Chinese Exclusion Act and establishes the Bureau of Immigration within the Treasury Department.

1897 A federal district court decides the case *In re Rodriquez,* affirming the citizenship rights of Mexicans based on the 1848 Treaty of Guadalupe Hidalgo notwithstanding that such persons may not be considered "white."

1898 In the case of *Wong Kim Ark v. United States* the Supreme Court rules a native-born son of Asian descent is indeed a citizen of the United States despite the fact that his parents may have been ineligible for citizenship.

1903 Congress moves immigration responsibility to the Department of Commerce and Labor.

1906 The Basic Law of Naturalization codifies a uniform law for naturalization that, with some amendments and supplements, forms the basic naturalization law thereafter.

1907 Congress adds regulations about issuing passports and about the expatriation and marriage of U.S. women to foreigners that is not repealed until 1922. President Theodore Roosevelt issues the executive order known as the Gentleman's Agreement by which Japan agrees to restrict emigration of laborers from Japan and Korea, then under Japanese jurisdiction. Picture brides are permitted emigration. Congress passes the White-Slave Traffic Act forbidding importation of any woman or girl for the purpose of prostitution or similar immoral purposes.

1911   The Dillingham Commission issues its report whose recommendations form the basis for the quota acts of the 1920s.

1915   The Americanization/100 Percent campaign begins supported by government and businesses. These social movements are the first attempt at "forced assimilation" and the adoption of the English language and social customs. After World War I, its perceived failures set the stage for the quota acts of the 1920s.

1917   The United States enters World War I in April. Congress enacts a literacy test and bars all immigration from a specified area known as the Asian barred zone. The Departments of State and Labor issue a joint order requiring issuance of visas by U.S. consular officers in the country of origin rather than seeking permission to enter the United States when arriving at the port of entry.
Puerto Ricans are granted U.S. citizenship.

1918   Congress grants the president sweeping power to disallow entrance or departure of unauthorized immigrants during time of war, similarly used in virtually all periods of war thereafter.

1919   Congress grants honorably discharged Native Americans citizenship for their service in World War I. In the summer, the Red Scare following the Bolshevik Revolution in Russia leads to summary deportation of certain specified "radical" unauthorized immigrants deemed a threat to national security, serving as a precursor to the USA Patriot Act in that respect.

1921   Congress passes the first Quota Act basing immigration from a particular country at 3 percent of the foreign-born population from that country as enumerated in the 1910 census.

1922   Congress enacts the Cable Act stating that the right of any woman to become a naturalized citizen shall not be abridged because of her sex or because she is wed to an unauthorized immigrant ineligible for citizenship.

1923   In *United States v. Bhagat Singh Thind,* the Supreme Court rules that "white person" means those persons who appear and would be commonly viewed as white. East Asian Indians, although Caucasians, are not "white" and are therefore ineligible for citizenship through naturalization.

1924   Congress passes the Johnson-Reed Act setting the national-origin quota for a particular country at 2 percent of the foreign-born population from that country as of the 1890 census, drastically shifting immigration from south, central, and eastern Europe to northern and western Europe. It bars the admission of most Asians, classified as "aliens ineligible for citizenship." Congress passes an act granting citizenship to those Native Americans who had not previously received it by the 1887 Dawes Act or by military service during World War I.

1925   Congress establishes the Border Patrol to police the U.S. borders against undocumented entrants. The Border Patrol is charged with finding and deporting unauthorized immigrants from the interior who had eluded apprehension at the border.

1929   President Herbert Hoover proclaims new and permanent quotas in which national-origin quotas for European immigrants are based on the proportion of those nationalities in the total population using the 1920 census and fixing the total number to be admitted annually at just over 150,000.

1929 to 1939   U.S. immigration levels slow dramatically in response to the worldwide Great Depression.

1940   Congress passes the Registration Law requiring noncitizens to register their addresses every year. The process remains in effect until 1980. Millions of those forms are backlogged and "lost" in Immigration and Naturalization Service warehouses. The failure of this program contributes to the push in the 1980s to crack down on unauthorized immigrants and visa overstayers through enhanced capability of the INS, which is never achieved.

1941   President Franklin D. Roosevelt issues a proclamation to control persons entering or leaving the United States based on the first War Powers Act.

1942   The United States and Mexico allow migrant farmworkers to enter the former as temporary labor to satisfy wartime labor shortages in agriculture in what becomes known as the Bracero Program.

1943   The Supreme Court rules, in *Hirabayashi v. United States,* that the executive orders for curfews and evacuation programs are constitutional, based on "military necessity."

1944   On December 18, in *Korematsu v. United States,* the Supreme Court again affirms the constitutionality of the executive orders excluding Japanese Americans from remaining in certain "excluded zones." The Court rules in *Ex Parte Mitsuye Endo* that the internment program is an unconstitutional violation of the habeas corpus rights of U.S. citizens—namely the Nisei.

1945   Congress passes the War Brides Act to admit unauthorized spouses and unauthorized children of citizen members of the U.S. Armed Forces.

1949   Congress passes the Agriculture Act with provisions to recruit temporary farmworkers from Mexico establishing by law the Bracero Program.

1956   President Dwight Eisenhower establishes a "parole" system for Hungarian Freedom Fighters. Two years later Congress endorses the procedures by an Act to admit Hungarian refugees.

1959   Congress amends the Immigration and Nationality Act of 1952 to provide for unmarried sons and daughters of U.S. citizens to enter as "nonquota" immigrants.

1960   On July 14, Congress enacts a program to assist resettlement of refugees from communist countries who are paroled by the attorney general, mostly Cubans.

On November 8, John F. Kennedy is elected president of the United States.

1963   On November 22, John F. Kennedy is assassinated in Dallas, Texas.

1964   The Bracero Program ends. On November 3, Lyndon B. Johnson is elected president of the United States.

1965   On October 3, Congress passes the Immigration and Nationality Act amending the 1954 Act, ending the quota system, and establishing a preference system emphasizing family reunification and meeting certain skill goals, standardizing admission procedures, and setting per country limits of 20,000 for Eastern Hemisphere nations, with a total of 170,000, and setting the first ceiling on Western Hemisphere immigration at 120,000.

1966   Congress amends the 1965 Act to adjust the status of Cuban refugees setting the distinction between refugees based on anti-communist U.S. foreign policy goals and on economic refugee status.

1967   The UN Convention and Protocol on Refugees is established; 130 nations sign the protocol accords. Refugees entering under its provisions, such as Cuban refugees, are given resettlement assistance whereas those entering as economic refugees, such as the Haitians, are excluded.

1968   The Bilingual Education Act is passed.

President Johnson issues a proclamation on the UN Protocols on the Status of Refugees endorsing the U.S. commitment to the multinational protocols.

1972   The U.S. House of Representatives passes, but the Senate kills, a bill that would have made it illegal to knowingly hire an unauthorized immigrant, becoming the first attempt prior to 1986 to impose what became known as "employer sanctions" for hiring them.

1975   The fall of Saigon and Vietnam, along with Cambodia and Laos, precipitates a massive flight of refugees to the United

States from the Indochina region. As refugees from communist countries, Vietnamese, Cambodians, and Laotians are assisted in resettlement and aided by assimilation-assistance programs, many conducted by church-based organizations assisting immigrants.

Congress passes the Indochina Migration and Refugee Assistance Act on May 23, 1975.

Soviet Jews flee in large numbers and a civil war in El Salvador causes refugees from there to arrive in large numbers, as do economic refugees from Haiti.

1976 Congress amends the 1965 Act extending the per country limits of visa applications on a first-come first-served basis to Western Hemisphere nations as regulated by the preference system.

The Supreme Court rules, in *Matthews v. Diaz*, that an unauthorized immigrant has no right to Social Security or Medicare benefits, notwithstanding that while working in the United States they contributed to the Social Security System.

1978 President Jimmy Carter and Congress establish the Select Commission on Immigration and Refugee Policy (SCIRP).

1979 SCIRP begins its work. An influx of refugees, known as "boat people," from Vietnam and Southeast Asia arrive.

1980 Congress passes the Refugee Act to systematize refugee policy, incorporating the UN definition of refugee into U.S. law and accepting 50,000 persons annually who have a "well-founded fear" of persecution based on race, religion, nationality, or membership in a social or political movement, and providing for the admission of 5,000 "asylum-seekers."

1981 An economic recession begins. On March 1, SCIRP issues its final report recommending changes in policy that form the basis for the Immigration Reform and Control Act of 1986 and subsequent reform acts underlying proposed reforms even after 2001. President Ronald Reagan creates a Task Force on Immigration and Refugee Policy.

1982   A federal district judge rules the incarceration of Haitians unconstitutional; orders the release of 1,900 detainees. A major bill to amend the Immigration and Nationality Act of 1965 is introduced into Congress.

1983   Another immigration reform bill is introduced into Congress.

The Supreme Court rules, in *Chadha et al.*, that the use of the legislative veto to overturn certain INS deportation proceedings, rules, and regulations by the House of Representatives is unconstitutional.

1984   Immigration reform bills pass in different versions in both chambers of Congress but then died by stalemate in the conference committee.

1985   Senator Alan Simpson (R-WY) reintroduces what is known as the Simpson/Mazzoli/Rodino bill to reform U.S. immigration law with a focus on unauthorized immigration.

1986   The Supreme Court rules, in *Jean v. Nelson,* that the INS denial of parole to certain undocumented immigrants (Haitians) is unconstitutional.

Congress enacts the Immigration Reform and Control Act (IRCA) that imposes employer sanctions and establishes a legalization program granting amnesty to about 1.5 million unauthorized immigrants and more than 1 million special agricultural workers.

1987   In *INS v. Cardoza-Fonseca,* the Supreme Court decides that the government must relax its standards for deciding whether unauthorized immigrants who insist they would be persecuted if they returned to their homelands are eligible for asylum.

1988   The Senate passes, but the House kills, the Kennedy-Simpson bill in what becomes the 1990 Act. The U.S.-Canada Free Trade Implementation Act is signed into law.

Congress amends the 1965 Immigration Act regarding H-1 category use by nurses.

1989   The International Conference for Central American Refugees is held.

1990   Congress passes IMMACT, a major reform of legal immigration that sets new ceilings for worldwide immigration, redefines the preference system for family reunification and employment-based preference, and establishes a category called "the diversity immigrants." It enacts special provisions regarding Central American refugees, Filipino veterans, and persons fleeing Hong Kong and provides for revisions to the naturalization process.

1993   Congress ratifies the North American Free Trade Agreement (NAFTA).
Donald Huddle issues his report, "The Cost of Immigration," beginning a decades-long debate over the relative costs and benefits of legal and illegal immigration.

1994   California passes Proposition 187, the "Save our State" initiative.
Congress passes the Violence Against Women Act granting special status through cancellation of removal and self-petitioning provisions.

1995   A federal district court rules, in *LULAC et al. v. Wilson et al.*, many of the provisions of Proposition 187 unconstitutional. The Government Accountability Office issues its first major report on the costs of unauthorized immigrants to governments and to the overall economy.
A Human Rights Watch report is highly critical of the INS and alleged abuses.

1996   In June, the Board of Immigration Appeals grants for the first time asylum to a woman on the basis of gender persecution (female genital mutilation).
Congress passes the Personal Responsibility and Work Opportunity Act with numerous immigration-related provisions that essentially enact aspects of Proposition 187 regarding welfare and other public benefits that had been overturned by the

LULAC v. Wilson decision. Congress passes the Illegal Immigration Reform and Immigrant Responsibility Act (IIRIRA) with more than 60 provisions of the Omnibus Spending Bill removing welfare and economic benefits to unauthorized immigrants and to some legal resident immigrants.

The Anti-Terrorism and Effective Death Penalty Act passes giving INS inspectors the power to make "on-the-spot credible fear" determinations involving asylum.

The Central American Regional Conference on Migration is held in Puebla, Mexico.

The Border Patrol records 1.6 million apprehensions at U.S. borders, and Congress authorizes the addition of 1,000 new Border Patrol agents annually.

1997 The Jordan Commission on Immigration Reform recommends restructuring the INS. Expedited Enforcement Rules of the IIRIRA take effect at U.S. land borders, international airports, and seaports to issue and enforce expulsion orders, and 4,500 INS officers are added at 300 ports of entry. The Government Accountability Office issues its Report on the Fiscal Impact of Newest Americans.

1998 President Clinton sends a bill to Congress to restructure the INS, but it dies in committee when the Judiciary Committee begins impeachment hearings.

The Agriculture Job Opportunity Benefits and Security Act creates a pilot program for 20,000 to 25,000 farmworkers.

The Social Security Board documents the effects of immigration on the Fund and on the long-term Social Security Fund crisis as the U.S. population ages and fewer active workers support ever-growing numbers of retirees.

Congress passes the American Competitiveness and Workforce Improvement Act expanding the H-1B category to include the computer industry.

California voters approve Proposition 227 ending bilingual education in state schools. The Children of Immigrants Longitudinal Study is issued.

1999   The Carnegie Endowment for International Peace presents its International Migration Policy Program.

21 nongovernmental organizations involved in immigration policy call for INS restructuring, the separation of enforcement from visa and naturalization functions, and sending some of its functions to the Department of Labor and to Health and Human Services. INS provides Border Patrol adjudication.

In *INS v. Aguirre-Aguirre,* a unanimous Supreme Court rules that unauthorized immigrants who have committed serious nonpolitical crimes are ineligible to seek asylum regardless of the risk of persecution when returned to their country of origin.

The Trafficking Victims Protection Act is passed. With a restored economy, President Clinton restores some of the benefits stripped away from legal immigrants by the 1996 IIRIRA act.

On November 22, Elian Gonzales is rescued off the Florida coast.

UNHCR issues guidelines related to detention of asylum-seekers in Geneva, Italy.

The Trafficking Victims Protection Act is passed.

2000   Negotiations on the Elian Gonzalez case begin.

Attorney General Reno approves a U.S. Department of Justice (DOJ) raid on the Miami home to return Gonzales to his father in Cuba.

On June 1, in *Gonzales v. Reno,* a circuit court rules that only the father of Elian Gonzalez can speak for the boy.

2001   September 11, terrorists attack the World Trade Center's towers in New York City and the Pentagon in Washington, D.C. Immediate calls for a crackdown on terrorists begin.

On October 24, Congress passes the USA Patriot Act granting the attorney general (AG), the FBI, and the DOJ sweeping authority to detain "enemy combatants" involved in or suspected of terrorism.

The "Dream Act" is introduced for the first time.

2002 The INS issues notice to several of the (by then dead) hijackers permission to enroll in U.S. flight training programs. This results in immediate calls to restructure the INS and to remove its Border Patrol functions.

In November, Congress creates a cabinet-level Department of Homeland Security (DHS), giving the AG sweeping new powers for expedited removal. The INS is abolished and immigration policy is moved to the DHS.

The UN issues its Protocols on Human Trafficking and Immigrant Smuggling, signed by 141 countries.

2003 In January, the Terrorist Threat Integration Center is created.

2004 The 9/11 Commission issues its report. Congress passes the Intelligence Reform and Terrorism Prevention Act with a director of National Intelligence. A National Counterterrorism Center is created, largely housed and staffed in the CIA.

Unauthorized immigrants in the United States reach an estimated record 11 million. Immigration and Customs Enforcement reports 1.1 million apprehensions at U.S. borders.

2005 The Real ID Act is passed. Nine states pass anti–human trafficking laws.

2006 Congress extends the USA Patriot Act and passes the Secure Fence Act authorizing construction of a 700-mile bollard-type fence on the southwestern border.

2008 President Obama's administration begins a surge in use of expedited removals to deport unauthorized immigrants under the Trafficking Victims Protection Reauthorization Act.

2009 President Barack Obama uses executive action to mitigate certain aspects of IIRIRA.

Arizona enacts law mandating state and local police demand anyone suspected of being unauthorized to show documents to prove their legal status.

2010 In *Arizona v. U.S.*, the Supreme Court rules the Arizona measure unconstitutional.

2012   President Obama issues the Deferred Action for Childhood Arrivals (DACA) executive order granting temporary, legal status to "Dreamer" children.

2013   Senate passes S.744, a comprehensive immigration reform measure that is blocked in the House of Representatives and dies.
Senator David Vitter (R-LA) and Rep. Steve King (R-Iowa) introduce a bill to end birthright citizenship to persons born in the United States to parents in unauthorized status.
President Obama issues Deferred Action for Parental Accountability (DAPA) order.

2014   A surge in arrivals of children unaccompanied by adults from El Salvador, Guatemala, and Honduras arrives; President Obama grants temporary protected status to 5,000 such children deemed unsafe to return to their country of origin.

2015   House Republicans introduce the Secure Our Borders First Act of 2015.
President Obama issues DAPA order.

2016   U.S. District Judge Andrew Hanen places injunction on the Obama administration's implementation of the DAPA order.
In November, Donald Trump is elected president of the United States.

2017   President Trump appoints John Kelly secretary of DHS. President Trump issues an executive order to start a pilot program to build a wall at the U.S.-Mexican border, issues an executive order against sanctuary cities, and issues a travel ban against people coming from predominantly Muslim countries. He fires Acting AG Sally Yates for refusing to defend the travel ban. Former Senator Jeff Sessions is sworn in as AG. The DOJ issues a crackdown on the sanctuary cities order. President Trump orders DHS to establish a Victims of Immigration Crime Enforcement program.

2018   In February, the Trump administration announces a "zero tolerance" policy. Policy results in separation of about 3,000 children from their parents.

In April, United States Citizenship and Immigration Services changes rules regarding H-4 visas that stop spouses of H1-B visa holders from applying for work permits.

In May, the Trump administration rescinds the International Entrepreneur Rule.

In June, the DOJ announces policy of separating children from their parents being held in detention for unauthorized crossing of U.S. borders. Judge Dana Sabraw orders that some 3,000 children separated from their parents must be reunited within 30 days. President Trump issues an executive order instructing the DHS to maintain custody of parents and children "jointly." The U.S. Supreme Court, in a 5–4 decision along ideological lines, upholds the third iteration of the travel ban as constitutional. DOJ implements policy to deny protection for gender-based or gang violence as basis for claiming asylum.

In July, DHS issues new guidance to USCIS regarding asylum-seekers.

In September, the Trump administration changes the definition of "public charge" policy to make it harder for immigrants to qualify for green card visas.

In November, President Trump issues a proclamation suspending the right to asylum to any immigrant crossing the U.S.-Mexico border outside of a lawful port of entry.

In December, the Trump administration publishes new rules changing H-1B visas. The federal government partially shuts down over a funding dispute for the border wall. Secretary of State Pompeo announces new caps on the number of refugees allowed to enter the United States as 45,000 for 2018 and 30,000 for 2019.

2019   In January, DHS announces Migrant Protection Protocols—soon called the "remain in Mexico" policy—that asylum-seekers had to remain in Mexico while awaiting an asylum hearing.

Between February and June, media reports that the Trump administration continues to separate families even after the court order of June 2018 that put a stop to that practice.

In April, President Trump orders new restrictions on asylum-seekers at the Mexican border, including an application fee and imposing restraints on work permits.

In May, DHS steps up the collection of biometric data from migrant families including a DNA pilot program and the fingerprinting of children under the age of 14.

In June, DHS's inspector general issues a scathing report on the conditions found at five South Texas detention centers managed by U.S. Customs and Border Protection (CBP), citing "squalor," overcrowding, lack of adequate food and clothing, and numerous violations of the Flores Settlement prohibiting prolonged detention of children at such centers.

In July, DHS and DOJ announce a final rule making foreigners who cross the U.S.-Mexico border ineligible for asylum if they had not previously applied for asylum in countries through which they had traveled. Judge Jon Tigar of the Northern California District Court issues a preliminary injunction against the new DHS/DOJ-announced asylum rule.

In September, the U.S. Supreme Court upholds President Trump's authority to require Central Americans to seek asylum in Mexico.

President Trump issues executive order 9844 declaring national emergency at the U.S. southwestern border.

2020   In January, COVID-19 pandemic reaches the United States, with outbreaks on both West Coast and East Coast. President Trump orders end of "birth-tourism" and partially closes U.S. southwestern border to travelers from China.

In January, President Trump diverts $7.2 billion in military funds to build the border wall. In February, Trump diverts another $3.8 billion in Department of Defense funds to build the border wall. The total devoted to border wall equals $18.4 billion—to complete 101 miles of border barrier (all but 14 miles in replacement fencing, no real wall).

In *DHS v. Regents of UCLA* decision, the Supreme Court rules the DHS's decision to rescind DACA is arbitrary and capricious.

In October, a federal appellate court rules that the Trump administration's transfer of $2.8 billion for the border wall was unauthorized. President Trump appeals the appellate court decision in the U.S. Supreme Court.

In mid-October 2020, court-appointed lawyers overseeing the attempt to reunite separated children with their parents announce that there were 545 children whose parents could not be found.

2021   The Biden administration reduced the number of unaccompanied children in U.S. CBP facilities from 5,676 in March 2021 to 570 on June 14, 2021, reduced the time children spent in CBP facilities from 131 hours on April 1, 2021, to 26 hours in June 2021, and reduced the number of unaccompanied children in the care of the Department of Health and Human Services (HHS) from 22,000 in April 2021 to 16,000 in June 2021.

The DHS and HHS rescinded an agreement from the Trump administration that subjected undocumented parents to immigration enforcement when they came forward to claim their child.

The DHS processed over 11,900 eligible people who had been returned to Mexico under the Migrant Protection Protocols, announced 6,000 new temporary, non–agricultural worker (H-2B) visas for nationals of Honduras, El Salvador, and Guatemala for FY 2021, and reopened the Central American Minors Program to reunited children from Honduras, El Salvador, and Guatemala who had been separated from their parents on June 15, 2021.

President Biden issued a new FY 2021 Presidential Determination on refugees creating 4,000 additional slots for refugees from Latin America and the Caribbean.

On June 10, 2021, the administration announced $57 million in funds for urgent humanitarian needs of refugees and migrants from Central America, adding to the $310 million declared in April 2021.

The DHS implemented "Operation Sentinel" to crack down on international migrant smuggling, and on her trips to Guatemala and Mexico, Vice President Harris announced a new Human Smuggling and Trafficking Task Force. She also announced the creation of an anticorruption task force and that the United States Agency for International Development (USAID) will provide $48 million to advance economic opportunities in Guatemala. Further, the vice president proclaimed a USAID three-year regional initiative to partners in the Northern Triangle to increase economic resilience and a three-year program funded at $40 million to create the Young Women's Empowerment Initiative. While in Mexico, she signed an MoU between the United States and Mexico to establish a partnership to address the lack of economic opportunities in El Salvador and Honduras and to foster agricultural development and youth empowerment programs.

Mexico increased border checkpoints and deployed more than 12,000 security personnel to southern Mexico, and it received 31,800 asylum requests from January to April 2021, compared to 18,500 for the same period in 2018.

Glossary

absconders people who had been ordered deported but failed to leave.

adjustment to immigrant status a procedure whereby a nonimmigrant must apply for a change of status to lawful permanent resident if an immigrant visa is available for his or her country. The alien is an immigrant as of the date of the adjustment.

advocacy the support given by the sanctuary movement to unauthorized immigrants; involving attendance at immigration court hearings and accompanying individuals to mandatory check-ins with the Department of Homeland Security.

alien is a person who is not a citizen or national of a given nation-state.

amnesty is a legal pardoning of a person who entered the United States illegally or is otherwise in nonlegal status, thereby changing his or her legal status to legal resident alien. It was used extensively by IRCA to cover more than 3 million persons.

apprehensions refers to the physical control or temporary detainment of a person who is not lawfully in the United States, which may or may not result in an arrest.

Aztlan is the Chicano word or name for the southwestern United States region that used to be part of Mexico prior to the Treaty of Guadalupe Hidalgo.

Barrio is the section of a major American city, such as the border cities of San Diego, California, Tuscon, Arizona, Las

Cruces, New Mexico, or El Paso, Brownsville, and Laredo, Texas that is almost entirely comprised of a Hispanic population.

biometric identification   is the use of DNA, fingerprints, iris scans, facial recognition technology, and voice imprints at places of entry to the United States to identify someone; it is used as an anti-terrorist screening procedure and to attempt to identify unauthorized immigrants.

border card   is a card allowing a person living within a certain zone of the U.S. border to legally cross back and forth for employment purposes without a passport or visa.

Border Patrol   is the law enforcement arm of the Department of Homeland Security.

brain drain   refers to the flow of talented migrants from less developed to developed countries.

caucus   is an informal structural device of the U.S. Congress in which members who share a common interest or goal meet to discuss and reach some degree of consensus on how best to pursue that interest, to vote on a proposed bill, and sometimes to draft provisions to be incorporated into a bill.

chain migration   occurs when one family member first enters the United States as a legal, permanent resident and then brings in many family members (extended, not just nuclear family members). It can also refer to the arrival of immigrant groups who are not related but come from the same place of origin and settle in the same place in the United States, probably due to their ethnic or religious association with each other in the home country.

conundrum   is a confusing or difficult problem or question.

DACA   is an acronym for Deferred Action for Childhood Arrivals—a program of the Obama administration's Department of Homeland Security (DHS) that protected Dreamer children from deportation as unauthorized immigrants.

DAPA   is an acronym for Deferred Action for Parental Accountability.

de facto   is a Latin phrase meaning "by action."

de jure   is a Latin phrase meaning something being done "by law."

deportation   is a legal process by which a nation sends individuals back to their countries of origin after refusing them legal residence.

devolution   is the transfer or delegation of power to a lower level, especially by a central government to local or regional administration.

Dream Act   is an acronym for Development, Relief, and Education for Alien Minors—a proposed law that would provide a path to citizenship for unauthorized immigrants brought to the United States as minor children.

due process of law   is the constitutional limitation on government behavior to deal with an individual according to prescribed rules and procedures.

earned legalization   is a proposal to allow unauthorized immigrants to change their status to that of legal permanent resident by paying fines and satisfying stipulated conditions akin to those who came as authorized permanent resident aliens.

earned residency   is a path to get a green card and the right to stay in the United States but not a path to citizenship. It involves paying taxes, learning English, and committing no substantial crime.

emigrant   is a person who voluntarily leaves his or her country of birth for permanent resettlement elsewhere.

employer sanctions   are a provision of the 1986 Immigration Reform and Control Act that provided legal penalties (fines and/or prison) for knowingly hiring an illegal alien.

equal protection of the law   is the constitutionally guaranteed right that all persons be treated the same before the law.

executive orders   are actions issued by a president that are assigned numbers and published in the federal register, akin to laws passed by Congress, that direct members of the executive branch to follow a new policy or directive.

exempt   is an individual or class or category of individuals to whom a certain provision of the law does not apply.

expedited removal   is a stipulation in law changing the procedures by which persons in the United States without legal status may be deported with fewer judicial protections to do so.

expulsion   is the decision of a sovereign nation to legally compel an individual to permanently leave its territory.

Gang of Eight   is the name or term used to refer to eight U.S. senators in the Senate and eight representatives in the House of Representatives who collectively drafted and sponsored the Comprehensive Immigration Reform bill in the Senate and the House respectively; in 2013 the bill passed in the Senate but died in the House.

globalization   is a tide of economic, technological, and intellectual forces that is integrating a global community.

green card   is a document issued by the DHS that certifies an individual as a legal immigrant entitled to work in the United States.

Guest-Worker Program   is a program enabling the legal importation of workers for temporary labor in specified occupations.

H-1B Visa   is a category of temporary visa issued to a nonimmigrant allowing employers to employ guest-workers temporarily in a specialty occupation or field for a stipulated time.

illegal aliens   are individuals who are in a territory without documentation permitting permanent residence.

immediate relatives   are spouses, minor children, parents, grandparents, and brothers and sisters of a U.S. citizen or permanent resident alien.

immigrant   is an alien admitted to the United States as a lawful permanent resident.

inadmissibles are persons encountered at ports of entry who are seeking lawful admission into the United States but are determined to be inadmissible, individuals presenting themselves to seek humanitarian protection under U.S. laws, and individuals who withdraw their application for admission and return to their countries of origin within a short timeframe.

inclusion is an individual's or group's engagement with a process or organization that recognizes the individual or group by conferring membership or by providing resources such as social welfare entitlements and protections of those benefits; it provides a sense of security, stability, and predictability understood primarily as an ability to plan for the future.

investor immigrant is an individual permitted to immigrate based upon the promise to invest $1 million in an urban area or $500,000 in a rural area to create at least 10 jobs.

La Huelga is the movement of or strike by Chicano workers led by the UFW in the 1960s.

La Raza means "the people," and refers to Hispanics or Chicanos who led the more radical movement in the 1970s.

lone-wolf terrorist is a person perpetrating a terrorist act or plot who is inspired by but not associated with an international terrorist group or organization such as al Qaeda or the Islamic State of Iraq and Syria (ISIS).

machos is the Spanish term for "manly" or "strong"; a man who is aggressively proud of his maleness.

maquiladoras refers to the complex of sweat shop factories located on the Mexican side of the U.S.-Mexico border where Mexican laborers, especially women, often work under difficult, even exploitive, conditions.

naturalization is the legal act of making an individual who is not born a citizen of a particular country into a citizen of that country.

nonimmigrant is an alien seeking temporary entry into the United States for a specific purpose other than permanent settlement—such as a foreign government official, tourist, student, temporary worker, or cultural exchange visitor.

overstayers   are persons who enter the United States on a temporary visa but stay beyond the time specified in their visa (the time at which they are to voluntarily depart the United States); and because they overstay, their status becomes unauthorized/ illegal.

passport   is a legal identification document issued by a sovereign nation-state attesting to the nationality of an individual for the purpose of international travel.

patriotic assimilation   is the adoption, by a newcomer, of American civic values and the American heritage as one's own.

permanent resident   is a noncitizen who is allowed to live permanently in the United States, who can travel in and out of the country without a visa, and who can work without restriction; such a person is allowed to accumulate time toward becoming a naturalized citizen, legally after five years but usually taking about seven years.

political incorporation   is a model that holds that for a minority community to witness an effective response to its needs, minority leaders must come to occupy positions of government authority.

prosecutorial discretion   is a privilege given to the prosecuting attorney in deciding whether to prosecute or to plea bargain, recommend parole, and so on.

protocol   is an international agreement governing the understanding and procedures that member states who are parties to a treaty agreed upon for a given purpose; for example, the UN protocols regarding the status and treatment of refugees.

pull factor   is an aspect of the receiving nation that draws immigrants for resettlement.

push factor   is an event that compels large numbers of persons to emigrate—that is, leave their country of origin for permanent resettlement elsewhere.

racial profiling is a pattern of behavior of police officers based on racial appearance.

refugee is a qualified applicant for conditional entry into the United States whose application could not be approved because of an inadequate number of preference visas.

requests for detention are requests by the DHS that a local or state law enforcement agency hold an individual beyond the point at which they would otherwise be released.

requests for notification are requests that state or local law enforcement notify ICE of a pending release during the time that a person is otherwise in custody under state or local authority.

robber baron was the term commonly used during the Gilded Age to refer to powerful industrialists who use questionable practices to amass their great fortunes. In California, it referred to the "Big Four," comprising Collis Huntington, Leland Stanford, Mark Hopkins, and Charles Crocker. In New Mexico, it alluded to those who amassed fortunes using legal land grant machinations, such as the Santa Fe Ring.

sanctuary city is a city in the United States that follows certain procedures that shelter illegal immigrants by "de jure" or "de facto" action. The designation has no legal meaning and is used for cities that do not permit municipal funds or resources to be applied in furtherance of enforcement of federal immigration laws; that is, they do not allow police or municipal employees to inquire about one's immigrant status.

Santa Fe Ring was a loose collection of white Anglo politicians and business associates who combined their power in the latter half of the 19th century, mostly from 1872 to 1884, to use land grant laws and law suits of ethically and legally questionable means to amass a fortune and to acquire thousands of acres of land from Mexicans and Native Americans.

stakeholder is a person or organization with an interest or concern in something, especially a business, or one who is involved in or affected by a policy or course of action.

unauthorized immigrants are those who come undocumented or break or overstay the conditions of their visas and become illegal immigrants without the status of permanent resident alien.

undocumented immigrants are individuals who enter the United States without inspection or paper documentation that allows them to enter and to reside in the United States and to legally work while doing so.

unfunded mandates are requirements by the federal government upon state and local governments without offsetting funding for their implementation.

Visa is a legal document issued by a consular or similar state department official allowing a person to travel to the United States for either permanent or temporary reasons—for example, to travel as an immigrant, a student, a tourist, or a government representative, or for business or cultural exchange.

xenophobia is an unfounded fear of foreigners.

Index

Note: Page numbers followed by *t* indicate tables and *f* indicate figures.

About the Author

Michael C. LeMay, PhD, is professor emeritus of political science at California State University, San Bernardino, with 35 years of experience teaching at the university level. He is author of more than two dozen academic books and has authored many books with ABC-CLIO, including *Global Pandemic Threats*; *Illegal Immigration*, First Edition and Second Edition; *Doctors at the Borders*; and *Transforming America: Perspectives on U.S. Immigration*, 3 Vols. His book *The American Political Party System* was selected by Choice as a 2017 Outstanding Academic Title.